2002 [2004]

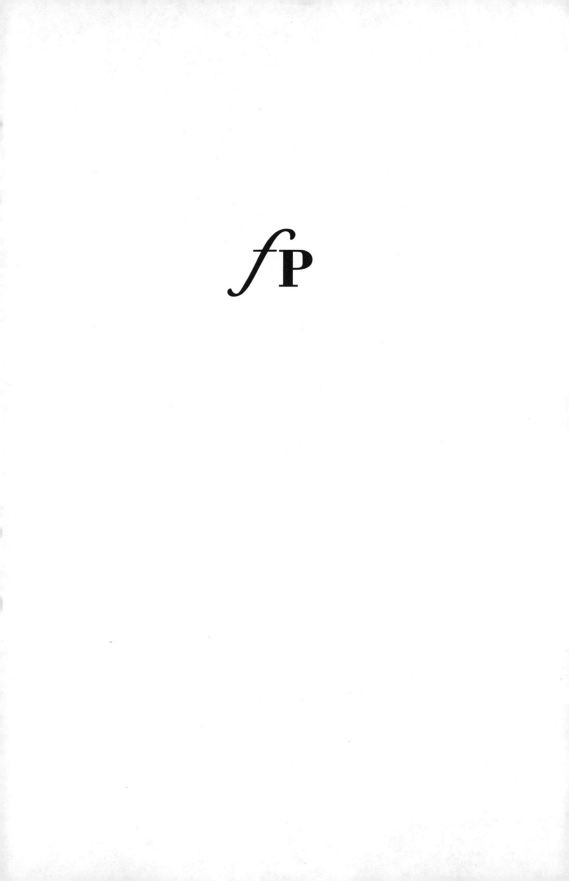

Other Books by Daniel G. Amen, M.D.

Healing ADD
Change Your Brain, Change Your Life
Two Minutes a Day for a Lifetime of Love
Coaching Yourself to Success
New Skills for Frazzled Parents
Images of Human Behavior

The Free Press

New York   London

Toronto   Sydney   Singapore

Healing the Hardware of the Soul

How Making the Brain-Soul Connection Can Optimize Your Life, Love, and Spiritual Growth

Daniel G. Amen, M.D.

ƒP

THE FREE PRESS
A Division of Simon & Schuster, Inc.
1230 Avenue of the Americas
New York, NY 10020

For information regarding special discounts for bulk purchases,
please contact Simon & Schuster Special Sales:
1-800-456-6798 or business@simonandschuster.com
Designed by Karolina Harris
Manufactured in the United States of America

10   9   8   7   6   5   4   3   2   1

Library of Congress Cataloging-in-Publication Data
Amen, Daniel G.
    Healing the hardware of the soul : how making the brain-soul
connection can optimize your life, love, and spiritual growth /
Daniel G. Amen.
        p.   cm.
    Includes bibliographical references and index.
    1. Brain—Religious aspects—Christianity.   2. Soul.
3. Spiritual life—Christianity.   I. Title.
BT741.3 .A48   2002
616.8'52—dc21   2001050142

ISBN 0-7432-0475-1

Medical Disclaimer

The information in this book is for general informational purposes only. It is not a substitute for a medical evaluation. If you feel that medical intervention is necessary, please consult a physician.

For Mom

The brain is the soul's fragile dwelling place.

—WILLIAM SHAKESPEARE

Acknowledgments

THIS book is the product of many years, many friendships and collaborations, and many battles. I am grateful to the best teachers a physician could have—my patients. I wish to acknowledge and thank the staff at the Amen Clinics in Fairfield and Newport Beach, California, especially through all of the growing pains over the past twelve years. In particular, I wish to thank Shelley Bernhard, Sandy Streeter, and the professional staff of our clinics. I am most grateful to Dr. Earl Henslin, Father Charles Ara, and Thomas Muzzio, who reviewed the manuscript and offered many valuable suggestions.

My literary agent, Faith Hamlin, is an amazing woman who continually pushes me to be the best writer I can be and is a constant source of wisdom and support. My editor at The Free Press, Philip Rappaport, believed in this book and saw it could help millions of people. I also appreciate the efforts of my wonderful publicist, Tammy Richards, who has believed in and supported my work through the last three books.

In addition, I am grateful to Jack Griffin for providing nutritional sustenance during the writing of this book.

Contents

2 Optimizing the Brain-Soul Connection

1
Understanding the Brain-Soul Connection

The Brain Is the Soul's Fragile Dwelling Place

The Feedback Loop Between the Brain and the Soul Offers New Answers

The brain is the violin and the soul is the violinist. They both need to work together in order to make beautiful music.

—FATHER CHARLES ARA, CATHOLIC PRIEST

JOSEY experienced a living hell. Not as a far-off place where people burn for unforgiven sins, but in her everyday life. Josey suffered from panic disorder, the most common psychiatric disorder in the United States. It began in her early twenties. She worried constantly, saw the future as negative and frightening, and endured many anxiety attacks. The attacks, which came on suddenly, were associated with crushing chest pain, her heart pounding hard against her chest wall; she also had trouble catching her breath, and she felt that something terrible was about to happen. The attacks made her hide from the world. They came in waves, eight to ten in a month, and then months with none at all. They were unpredictable. Her life started to revolve around the fear of attacks. She dropped out of college after her sophomore year, stopped driving, stopped seeing her boyfriend, and worked at home doing transcription so that she would not have to go out unaccompanied. She did not seek help for years for fear of being labeled crazy.

Josey prayed to God for deliverance from the anxiety attacks. As a child she had felt close to God and prayed every night before bed. Like many young adults, she had drifted away from her prayers but had still believed in a loving, present God, as her parents had taught her. When the attacks first occurred, she prayed many times a day that God would take this curse from her. Over time, as the anxiety attacks persisted, she prayed less and finally stopped. She became angry at God, and wondered why He was punishing her with the attacks. On several occasions the attacks were so bad that she contemplated suicide. When her parents heard about her suicidal ideas, they forced her to see me because I had helped her cousin with similar problems.

The day I met Josey I thought this young woman was in hell—years of torture and torment from her anxiety disorder and disconnection from her friends, her work, her future, and even her God. Many theologians believe that hell is disconnection from God. The illness had caused Josey to lose herself, her relationship with God, and nearly her life.

As part of Josey's evaluation, I ordered a brain SPECT study—an amazing test that examines how the brain works. Josey's scan showed a number of "hot spots," overactive areas, in the part of the brain that generates fear and anxiety. Seeing the physiological problem in her brain for herself was the first step in the healing process that would unfold over the next several months. Rather than thinking that she had a moral, character, or personality problem, she now accepted the fact that she had a medical illness needing treatment. The treatment involved medication, prayer and meditation, and targeted mental exercises. Over time, she successfully rebuilt her life. She was able to travel unaccompanied to work; she fell in love, married, had children, and made peace with God. Josey's brain, the hardware of her soul, all that she was inside, had been ill, a fact that caused everything else in her life to suffer. Helping her brain allowed her to once again have access to her soul, her real self, and even her God.

JOSEY'S SPECT STUDY

The white color indicates the areas of greatest brain activity. A healthy scan shows white in the back of the brain only (cerebellum). Josey's brain shows white or hot areas in the emotional and anxiety centers of her brain.

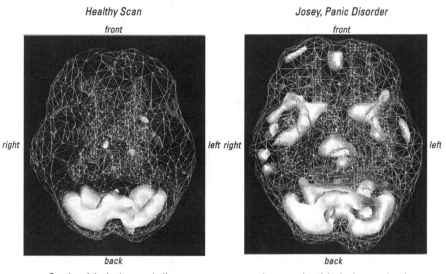

Healthy Scan
front

right — left

back

Good activity in the cerebellum
(back of her brain),
cool everywhere else

Josey, Panic Disorder
front

right — left

back

Increased activity in the emotional
and anxiety centers of her brain

The word "soul" as translated from Old Testament Hebrew means "all of your thoughts, feelings, personality characteristics, self, desires, and passions." The soul is who we are inside, from the top of our head to the bottom of our feet. The soul is felt and translated into action through the day-to-day function of the brain. William Shakespeare said, "The brain is the soul's fragile dwelling place." We can now see actual evidence of this brain-soul connection through the latest brain-imaging techniques. These studies have so clearly taught me that *when the brain is healthy we are compassionate, thoughtful, loving, re-laxed, and goal directed, and when the brain is sick or damaged we are unfeeling, impulsive, angry, tense, and unfocused, and it is very hard for our souls and our relationship with God to be at peace.*

In my previous books *Change Your Brain, Change Your Life* and *Healing ADD,* I use my work with the latest brain-imaging science to teach readers about brain-behavioral problems like anxiety, depression, impulsiveness, obsession, anger, and attention deficit disorder. Through images of the brain the books show that behavioral problems are often related to brain dysfunction and are not the result of a weak will or a character defect. *Healing the Hardware of the Soul* builds upon these books by helping you understand and enhance the connection between brain function and your innermost being, your soul.

Brain-Soul Feedback Loop

This book will teach you how to harness the positive energy at work in the powerful feedback loop between brain function and the condition of your soul. A healthy soul actually enhances brain function, and a healthy brain is essential to a healthy soul.

Like the hardware of a computer, the brain must function at an optimal level in order to run the software programs of life (daily activities like child rearing, teaching and learning, going through adolescence, training for a career, intimate relationships, navigating midlife crises). When a computer does not have enough RAM (random-access memory), speed, or storage space, it cannot run its software programs efficiently. Similarly, a brain that isn't running at optimal efficiency will have trouble keeping a life and soul on track.

As with computers, you need more than hardware to live a full and authentic life. The hardware of a computer is powerless without an efficient operating system or proper software. So too in our lives, we need effective programming—good parenting, optimal nutrition, positive relationships, freedom from chronic stress, clear goals, positive thoughts, and an attitude of gratefulness—in order for the brain to work right. *A dynamic feedback loop exists between the brain and the events of our lives. The brain impacts our behavior, and how we behave impacts actual brain function.* Our latest research has shown that thoughts, feelings, and social interactions all impact brain function in potentially positive and negative ways.

The brain-soul connection is involved in everything we do. Understanding it will lead to a deeper knowledge of our most intimate selves and help us to explain human triumphs and failures. This connection will help us understand:

- good (it is likely that Mother Teresa and Mahatma Gandhi had optimal brain function),
- evil (it is also likely that Adolf Hitler and other brutal dictators had faulty brain wiring, despite being able to rise to power),
- sin (in the New Testament the Greek word for sin is *hermatia,* or quite simply, "missing the mark," which is quite easy to do with poor brain function),
- love (couples who thrive likely have more optimal brain patterns than those who struggle),
- hate (in my clinical experience, many racists have abnormal brain patterns), and
- child abuse (often at the hands of people with brain problems).

I have seen firsthand at the Amen Clinics how many people are searching desperately for a more fulfilling, meaningful, peaceful, hopeful, positive life, who want to live, love, and feel connected to something. Instead, many feel depressed, angry, lonely, unhappy, and disconnected. The clinically based brain-soul healing techniques included in this book will help you optimize your brain and improve your relationships, work, and spiritual connections in the deepest ways possible.

But what do I know about the soul? Isn't soul work off target for a brain scientist? Let me put these ideas into the context of my own life. I grew up in a very religious Roman Catholic Lebanese home, with five sisters and a brother. I attended Catholic school until the end of ninth grade, and was an altar boy for many years. I was taught very clear ideas of right and wrong, good and evil, heaven and hell, and the judgment day. These beliefs followed me into my adult life.

During the Vietnam War, I had a very low draft number and went into the U.S. Army, where I was trained to be a combat medic. I was fortunate enough to be sent to Germany rather than Vietnam. In Germany, as a lonely soldier, I met Christine, a pretty, petite company clerk. She asked me to go to a church service with her. It turned out to be an Assembly of God Pentecostal Church service, with shouting, praying in tongues, and long, intense healing sessions. At first I felt strange, especially with all of the noise in church. As a Roman Catholic, I was used to church being a quiet place. Not this church! There was a lot of intense emotional expression, but also a lot of fellowship and worship. I met some wonderful people and became actively involved with Teen Challenge, a Christian group that worked with drug addicts, which was one of the factors leading to my interest in psychiatry. Many of the addicts had failed traditional drug-treatment programs but were able to rid themselves of their addictions when they developed a deep faith and a connection with God. It was a fascinating process to watch.

After three years in Germany, I was discharged from the military and attended Orange Coast College for a year and then Vanguard University, an Assembly of God Bible college in Southern California. I studied biology and the Bible. I wanted to be a doctor, but I also wanted a solid spiritual foundation for my life. Nothing in the Bible dissuaded me from medicine, and nothing in my biological studies challenged my faith. In 1978, I had the good fortune to be accepted into the charter class of Oral Roberts University (ORU) School of Medicine. Minister and faith healer Oral Roberts had worked hard to bring together spiritual healing and medical healing, a concept that I felt could be extremely powerful. I was suspicious that they accepted me because of my last name: The first graduate from their medical school would be Dr. "Amen."

ORU was an amazing place to attend medical school. We were taught solid medical science in an atmosphere of love, compassion, and prayer. It was different from every other medical school in the country. We were taught how to pray with patients, take spiritual histories, and consider the "mind, body, and spirit" in treating the whole person. In a number of classes we struggled with the issue of sin and sickness. Many fundamentalist Christians believe that physical or emotional sickness comes from a sick soul, and that you are more likely to be physically or emotionally sick if you have sin in your life. Others feel that we all get sick and die—it is part of the human condition. It only causes people to struggle with unnecessary guilt when you blame their illnesses on sin. It was a sticky and complex issue.

After medical school, I did my psychiatric internship and residency at Walter Reed Army Medical Center in Washington, D.C., the military's largest hospital. As a resident, I taught a class to physicians and chaplains on the connection between medicine and spirituality. I taught that 70 percent of the people in the United States have strong fundamental religious beliefs, and that health-care professionals, ministers, and rabbis needed to work together for the best interests of their patients. With each year of medical training and experience it became obvious to me that there were many missing pieces to the puzzle of spirituality and healing. During my residency I found that the more patients were connected to their religious faith, whether Catholic, Protestant, Jewish, Buddhist, or Muslim, the healthier they seemed to be as a whole. They tended to need fewer psychiatric visits than those who were not connected to a body of believers. Researchers at Harvard, Duke, and Johns Hopkins have found that people with deep religious faith show greater physical and emotional health. Of course, one could argue that healthier people are more likely better equipped to make and keep connections to others and subsequently are more likely to thrive in groups of people.

The second piece of the puzzle became clear to me while I was doing a fellowship in child and adolescent psychiatry at Tripler Army Medical Center in Honolulu, Hawaii. During this time I worked extensively with children, teenagers, and families. I consulted with schools, worked with medically ill kids, treated teens whose problems were so severe that they could not live at home, and ran therapy groups for kids and parents. I learned how important early development was to brain function. I saw how positive environments can enhance intellect and emotions, and more often, how negative environments can impair brain function and contribute to both psychiatric and learning disabilities. Any child psychiatrist knows that genetic vulnerability predisposes a person to problems, but the environment plays a large role in the expression of those problems.

The third major piece of the puzzle dropped into place in 1990. After military service, I set up a private psychiatric clinic in Fairfield, California, forty miles northeast of San Francisco. I saw patients in both outpatient and hospital settings, and directed a hospital unit that treated drug and alcohol abusers who also were diagnosed with psychiatric conditions. During one of the hospital's physician lectures I learned about brain SPECT imaging, a nuclear medicine study that uses very small amounts of a radioactive compound to view the inner workings of the living brain. Unlike standard magnetic resonance imaging (MRI) and computerized axial tomography (CAT) scanners, which show brain anatomy, SPECT—which stands for single photon emission computed tomography—evaluates brain physiology. I learned that SPECT was used to look at strokes, head trauma, and dementia. It was also being used by researchers to study depression, attention deficit disorder, schizophrenia, and obsessive-compulsive disorder. We could actually see brain patterns associated with "psychiatric" illness, meaning that many mental illnesses were actually visible brain illnesses. This idea would have made Sigmund Freud salivate—to see the inner workings of the brain as it related to behavior. As I learned more about SPECT and similar technologies, I believed they would change the face of psychiatry in my lifetime, although at the time I had no idea I would become a controversial part of it.

Controversy: To Look or Not to Look

Brain SPECT imaging gives us a visual picture of brain function, a window into the hardware of the soul, as we will see throughout this book. Seeing the initial SPECT studies of my own patients dramatically changed my perception of mental illness and the soul. I had only to look at the brains of people who did bad things to begin to understand that they had poorer access to their own brains, the organ that made them human. I was dumbfounded to find that many physicians strongly resisted the use of brain-imaging tools in clinical psychiatric practice to evaluate serious behavioral or emotional problems. These physicians claimed that you could not see tendencies toward specific psychiatric illness in brain scans, that the scans were overinterpreted, that it was too soon to use brain-imaging tools on patients, and that we needed much more research before it could become a clinical tool.

Over the past decade I have argued with many of my colleagues about the need to look at and evaluate the brain in psychiatry. Psychiatrists are the only medical specialists who rarely look at the organ they treat. In my opinion, the lack of brain imaging has kept psychiatry behind medicine's other specialties, decreasing our effectiveness with patients and helping to maintain stigma and noncompliance with needed treatment. Odds are if you are having serious problems with your feelings (depression or anxiety), thoughts (schizophrenia or bipolar disorder), or behavior (violence, pedophilia, or substance abuse), the psychiatrist treating you will never order a brain scan. He will prescribe psychotherapy or powerful medications without ever looking at how your specific brain works. He will not know which areas of your brain work well, which work too hard, or which do not work hard enough. Can you imagine the outcry if other medical specialists acted without looking? If orthopedists set broken bones without X rays? If cardiologists diagnosed coronary-artery blockages without angiograms or fast CAT scans? If internists diagnosed pneumonia without ordering chest X rays or sputum cultures? Or surgeons performed mastectomies without looking at breast tumors under the microscope to see if they were cancerous or not? Yet, the state of the art in psychiatry is not to look at the organ it treats.

Psychiatrists diagnose and treat patients based on symptom clusters, not underling brain dysfunction. Imagine taking your car to the mechanic because it is smoking, using too much gasoline, or stalling in the middle of intersections. The mechanic listens to the symptoms and decides to change the car's fuel pump, without ever looking under the hood. How would you feel? Probably like going somewhere else. It's silly. We must look at the brain if we are to really understand the problems we face.

One of the criticisms of using brain imaging in clinical practice is that there is not enough published literature to verify that it will be helpful. Yet, there is a very large body of literature on brain imaging for behavioral problems. On my web site, *www.brainplace.com,* you can see over four hundred abstracts on brain imaging for neuropsychiatric reasons. We should image the brain in people who struggle with thoughts, feelings, or behaviors because the brain is complex and needs to be better understood. We need better diagnostic tools. We need more targeted treatments, based on the areas of the brain involved in illness.

Being ahead of your time can be painful. Many people have told me that my brain research and clinical work have been on the cutting edge of brain science. I often respond that I have been "bleeding on the cutting edge" for many years. Applying brain-imaging science to everyday practice seemed natural to me, and most important, it seemed like the right thing to do. When the brain works right, you can work right. When the brain doesn't work right, it is very hard for you to be your best. Yet, when you go up against established psychiatric practice and try to change the ways things are done, bad things can happen.

In October 1996, I was asked to give the State-of-the-Art Lecture in Medicine to the Society of Developmental Pediatrics. I shared my work with brain SPECT imaging with hundreds of physicians. One physician in attendance complained to the California Medical Board about my use of SPECT technology in medical practice. Psychiatrists are not supposed to do brain scans, he said; that is not the standard of care in the medical community. In California, if you do anything outside of the standard of care, you can lose your license. For over a year I attended meetings with investigators and medical board physicians, hired an attorney, worried, and didn't sleep much. My life's love and work were threatened. It was perhaps the most painful time in my life. In the end, my work was labeled by one of the physicians who reviewed it as exciting and good medicine. One is often labeled a heretic for trying to change religious beliefs. I was (am) trying to change the mind-set of a profession steeped in religion. The religion of psychoanalysis and psychodynamic psychotherapy, interestingly enough, was started by a neurologist, Freud.

One of the sustaining factors in my work has been my own personal faith. From the first month that I started to order these scans, I felt that they had a special place in science and that I was led by God to pursue this work. Some of my critics would scoff, saying that religion and science do not mix. Yet, patient after patient benefited from what we were learning, including many of my own family members. My nine-year-old nephew Andrew had an episode of violent behavior accompanied by suicidal and homicidal thoughts. When we uncovered and removed a temporal-lobe cyst, his behavior normalized. Without our work he would have likely died. One of my own children was diagnosed with a learning problem based on the imaging work, and the treatment gave her dramatic benefit in school. There are literally hundreds of stories that have filled my own soul with joy and determination about this work. Despite the trials, I feel incredibly blessed to be able to do this work and to help others. Now, twelve years after we began the imaging work, my clinics have been credited by many as pioneering the use of functional brain imaging in day-to-day psychiatric practice. The Amen Clinics, in Newport Beach and Fairfield, are the most active brain-imaging centers in the world, and we have the world's largest database of brain scans related to behavioral and learning problems.

The imaging work affected every part of my life. I started to dream in brain pictures. When I watched the news, I thought of the brains of people who did bad things and the brains of people who were victimized. I thought of the brains of people who were compassionate and thoughtful and the brains of people who were mean or evil. There has not been a day over the past twelve years when I have not thought about the brain and its relationship to everyday life and to our souls. Some people, like my children, might say I am obsessed with the brain. I think of it as a wonderful personal journey that I love to share.

The Brain Is Involved in Everything You Do

Despite advances in medical science, many people don't seem to realize how important the brain is to everyday life. It is the organ that guides and directs nearly everything we do. How we think, how we feel, how we act, how well we get along with others, and even our faith are influenced by the physical functioning of the brain. When I meet a person whose brain works right, I am likely to see someone with a prosperous, fulfilled, loving, and connected life. When I treat someone whose brain does not work right, more often than not the history I take reveals a life that is associated with struggle, pain, isolation, and failure. The soul's health and the physical functioning of the brain work together to help us be happy, giving, and loving or they are discordant and cause serious emotional or behavioral problems. Here's a very sad example of a sick soul, stemming from an injured brain.

On Wednesday, May 20, 1998, in Springfield, Oregon, Kip Kinkel, fifteen, was caught with a stolen gun on campus and suspended from school, pending possible expulsion. Police booked him on criminal charges and sent him home with his parents. Authorities said that Kip shot his father and mother to death sometime between Wednesday afternoon and Wednesday evening. Dressed in a trench coat, he drove a family car the next morning to a spot near Thurston High School and parked it. Carrying a rifle and two handguns, Kip walked into the school, where he fired fifty-one rounds. Two students died and twenty-five others were injured.

A New Look at Difficult Behavior

By all outward evidence Kip Kinkel is an evil boy who destroyed the lives of many people. Because I had the opportunity to read a scan of Kip's brain, I have another perspective. I do not think that Kip is evil. I know that he is sick. He has one of the most damaged brains that I have ever seen. He has serious decreased activity in his left temporal lobe (an area commonly associated with violence), prefrontal cortex (the part of his brain that supervises behavior and is responsible for conscience, or lack of it, decision making, impulse control, and the ability to focus), and occipital cortex (the visual area of the brain indicating the possibility of past brain trauma). Without proper medical help his damaged brain could only produce an ineffective, broken, and tragic life. The right medication to stabilize and enhance his left temporal lobe and prefrontal cortex likely would have prevented this terrible tragedy.

Challenging Our Basic Beliefs

After many clinical experiences with patients who had serious behavioral problems not unlike Kip's, it became clear to me that the people who struggled with difficult behavior almost always had abnormal brain SPECT studies. Shortly after I started ordering these scans, I felt that my beliefs about good and evil, heaven and hell, and judgment needed to be challenged. How could we judge someone like Kip as bad when the organ that controls his behavior doesn't work right? The judgmental waters seemed murky to me. I trusted that God knew everything that I was discovering and that He had the judgment issue figured out. But what about man? We had been operating under erroneous assumptions. We assumed that *we are all equal and we have an equal ability to choose right or wrong, good or evil, and heaven or hell.* The brain-imaging work taught me that *we are not all equal, and not everyone has the same power to choose.*

In my clinics, where staff psychiatrists and neurologists see over twelve hundred patients a month, we have been able to get an intimate look at the inner workings of the brains of people with depression, obsessive-compulsive disorder, schizophrenia, alcohol and drug problems, attention deficit disorders, premenstrual syndrome, spousal abuse, and suicidal behavior. We have seen how the brain works (or doesn't work) in murderers, rapists, armed robbers, arsonists, stalkers, and pedophiles. In addition, we have been able to look at the brains of people who were healthy, motivated, loving, and organized. Living with a healthy brain gives people the opportunity to be and act healthy; living with a damaged brain often causes great struggle.

New Thinking and Hope

The exciting news is that you are not stuck with the brain that you have; brain problems can be improved and even healed. The brain itself, like a computer, can be optimized to produce better results.

Healing the Hardware of the Soul is a book about hope and healing. It departs radically from traditional thinking and gives you a completely new look at yourself and those you love (or hate). Specifically, it looks at how we need an effectively working supervisor (the brain's prefrontal cortex) to have a healthy conscience. It looks at how religious experience often stems from temporal-lobe and limbic system function, and how obsessions (religious and others) stem from too much activity in the anterior cingulate gyrus and basal ganglia (which allows us to shift gears). In addition, the book looks at the concepts of good and evil, thoughtfulness, and caring as brain functions. For the first time, it discusses our relationship to faith, sin, evil, hatred, love, compassion, judgment, healing, and forgiveness through the lens of brain science. This is not a collection of high-technology excuses for bad behavior. Ultimately, we as individuals have to be responsible for our own behavior. It is, however, a book about understanding behavior that offers new solutions to help us be more effective as a society in dealing with ourselves, our neighbors, and extreme people like Kip, based on and informed by the relatively new science of brain imaging.

This is not a book about a specific religion, although the fact that I grew up in a Roman Catholic family will not be lost on the reader. The principles for healing discussed in it are universal. These healing-soul principles (forgiveness, connection, giving to others, focused thoughts, and leaving judgment to the Almighty) are similar across most world religions. *Healing the Hardware of the Soul* highlights studies that demonstrate how faith and religious connection have a healing impact on brain function. The purpose is to help you understand how important the brain is in everyday life and how through physical, emotional, and spiritual strategies you can optimize the brain and heal the hardware of your soul.

Two

Seeing into the Soul's Hardware

New Insights from Brain Imaging and Neuroscience

If we recognize the brain does all the things that we (traditionally)
attributed to the soul, then God must have some way of interacting with
human brains.

—NANCY MURPHY, A PHILOSOPHER OF SCIENCE AND
RELIGION AT THE FULLER SEMINARY IN PASADENA

THE brain is the complex and powerful organ that makes you who you are. It senses and integrates the world around you. It produces your thoughts, feelings, memories, forethoughts, and actions. Like so many wonderful things in nature, the brain shows organization, learning, growth, complexity, symmetry, seasons, storms, and incredible beauty. It shows God's imprint. I don't think you can see and understand the brain without a sense of awe, wonder, and creation.

In this chapter I will give you a brief introduction to the brain and brain-imaging work, laying the foundation for the rest of the book, and discuss some new research that suggests that the brain influences and may, in fact, be wired to experience God or deep spirituality.

Brain Primer

The brain contains billions of fragile nerve cells, or neurons, which if put end to end would form a line several thousand miles long. Each neuron communicates with other neurons through tens, hundreds, or even thousands of individual synapses, where chemicals or neurotransmitters are released across very tiny (0.02–0.05 micron) gaps. It is estimated that the brain has over a quadrillion synaptic connections within it, more connections than there are stars in the universe. The adult human brain weighs about three pounds, or about 2 percent of the body's weight, yet it is the body's major energy consumer, using 20 to 30 percent of the body's energy.

Even though the brain is extremely complex and interconnected, neuroscientists have learned that specific parts or systems of the brain are involved with certain functions. It is estimated that the brain has over two thousand individual structures. To make things manageable and easier to understand, neuroscientists divide the brain into lobes, or larger systems. The brain is typically divided into cortical (outside surface of the brain) and subcortical (deep brain) areas. The cortex is divided into four lobes: frontal, temporal, parietal, and occipital. A useful, broad generalization is that the back half of the brain (parietal, occipital, and back half of the temporal lobes) perceives the world, whereas the front half of the brain integrates incoming information with past experience, plans future actions, and executes behavior. In general, the frontal lobes are involved with thinking and planning physical movement. The temporal lobes help with memory and processing what you see and hear. The parietal lobes, known as the sensory cortex, help us process incoming sensations, such as touch, temperature, and position. And the occipital lobes process many aspects of vision.

BACK VERSUS FRONT OF THE BRAIN

The back half of the brain (parietal, occipital, and back half of the temporal lobes) is involved in taking in and perceiving the world. The front half of the brain is involved in integrating incoming information with past experience and planning and executing behavior.

Left Side Surface View

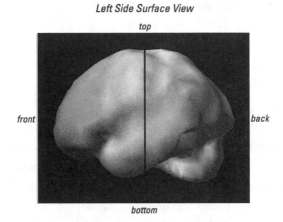

top

front

back

bottom

Seeing into the Soul's Hardware: Imaging the Brain

Scientists have a number of different ways of looking at the brain. Anatomical studies, such as MRI and CAT scans, are rarely helpful in behavior problems, which tend to be functional in nature rather than anatomical. Using the analogy of a car engine, the problem is usually with how the engine works, not how it looks. A car engine might look just fine, but you might not be able to turn it on. Currently, there are five ways to look at brain function:

> *Electroencephalogram (EEG),* a seventy-year-old technology that uses electrodes to record electrical activity from the scalp and infer information about brain function. It has poor resolution and is rarely helpful for psychiatric purposes.
> *Quantitative EEG studies (QEEG),* a more sophisticated version of the EEG, use computers to enhance electrical sig-

nals but still rely on inferring data about the brain through the scalp, skull, and coverings of the brain.

Positron-emission tomography (PET) studies are nuclear medicine studies that use minute doses of radioisotopes to examine brain blood flow and metabolism. PET studies provide elegant views of brain function, but the equipment tends to be located mostly in research centers and cannot be accessed by large numbers of patients.

Single photon emission computed tomography (SPECT) studies are also nuclear medicine studies that evaluate cerebral blood flow. SPECT is the study we perform at the Amen Clinics. These studies are more widely available to individuals seeking diagnosis and treatment, and less expensive, but still provide sophisticated pictures of brain function.

Functional MRI or fMRI, a newer study, is taking over much of the research in psychiatry. fMRI's advantages include no radiation, as opposed to PET and SPECT, but they are in the early stages of use, with little clinical application at this point.

SPECT: A Window into the Soul

Before we go further, it is important to introduce you to the wonderful world of SPECT technology, for it is through this technology that I gained many of the insights described in this book. SPECT stands for *single photon emission computerized tomography.* It is a sophisticated nuclear medicine study that looks at brain blood flow and metabolism. In this study, an isotope (which is akin to a beacon of energy or light) is attached to a substance that is readily taken up by the cells in the brain. A small amount of this compound is injected into a vein in the patient's arm, where it runs through the bloodstream to lock into certain cells in the brain. The isotope produces gamma rays that signal where the compound is located in the brain. The patient then lies on a table for about fifteen minutes while a SPECT "gamma" camera rotates slowly around his head. The camera has special crystals that detect where the compound (signaled by the isotope acting like a beacon of light) has gone. A typical scan is made up of nine million counts, or times the gamma rays hit the crystals. A supercomputer then reconstructs the scan into 3-D images, giving a sophisticated blood flow/metabolism brain map. With these maps, physicians have been able to identify certain patterns of brain activity that correlate with a healthy brain, along with those that are associated with psychiatric and neurological illness.

SPECT studies belong to a branch of medicine called nuclear medicine. Nuclear medicine studies measure the physiological functioning of the body. They are used to diagnose a multitude of medical conditions: heart disease, certain forms of infection, the spread of cancer, and bone and thyroid disease. Brain SPECT studies help in the diagnosis of brain trauma, dementia, atypical or unresponsive mood disorders, strokes, seizures, the impact of drug abuse on brain function, complex forms of attention deficit disorder, and atypical or aggressive behavior.

Brain SPECT studies were initially used in the late 1960s and early to mid-1970s. During the late 1970s and 1980s, SPECT studies were replaced by the sophisticated anatomical CAT and later MRI studies. At the time, the resolution of those studies was superior to SPECT for seeing tumors, cysts, and blood clots. Yet despite their clarity, CAT scans and MRIs could offer only images of a static brain and its anatomy; they gave no information on the activity of a working brain. It was analogous to looking at the parts of a car's engine without being able to turn it on. In the last decade it has become increasingly recognized that many neurological and psychiatric disorders are not disorders of the brain's anatomy but rather problems in how the brain functions.

Two technological advancements have encouraged the use, once again, of SPECT studies. Initially, the SPECT cameras used only one imaging device (and thus were called single-headed cameras), and they took as long as one hour to rotate around a person's brain. People had trouble holding still that long; the images were fuzzy and hard to read (earning nuclear medicine the nickname "unclear medicine"), and they did not give much information about how active or inactive the deep brain structures were. Then multiheaded cameras with special filters were developed: they imaged the brain faster, with enhanced resolution. Advancements in computer technology allowed for improved data acquisition. The brain SPECT studies of today, with their higher resolution, can see deeper into the inner workings of the brain with far greater clarity.

SPECT studies are displayed in a variety of different ways. Traditionally, the brain is examined from three different planes: horizontally (cut from top to bottom), coronally (cut from front to back), and sagittally (cut from side to side). I look for three things when I evaluate a SPECT study:

- areas of the brain that work well,
- areas of the brain that work too hard, and
- areas of the brain that do not work hard enough.

The images that accompany this book will be two kinds of three-dimensional (3-D) images of the brain. The first is a *3-D surface image*, which captures the top 45 percent of brain activity. It shows the blood flow of the brain's cortical surface. These images are helpful for seeing areas of healthy blood flow and activity, as well as seeing areas with diminished perfusion and activity. They are helpful in looking at strokes, brain trauma, and the effects of drug abuse. A healthy 3-D surface scan shows good, full, symmetrical activity across the brain's cortical surface. The second type of SPECT images we will look at are *3-D active brain images*, which compare average brain activity to the hottest 15 percent of activity. These images are helpful in seeing overactive brain areas, as shown in active seizures, obsessive-compulsive disorder, anxiety problems, and certain forms of depression, among other irregularities. A healthy 3-D active scan shows increased activity (seen by the light color in the active scans on page 25) in the back of the brain (the cerebellum and visual or occipital cortex) and average activity everywhere else (shown by the background grid).

3-D SURFACE VIEWS OF A HEALTHY BRAIN

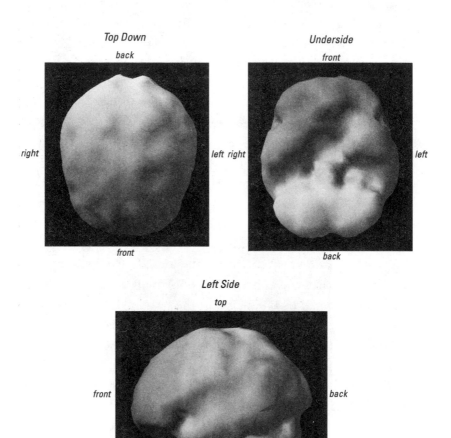

It is important to note that all brains do not look the same. Brains are like faces, and there are variations among them. From

3-D ACTIVE VIEWS OF A HEALTHY BRAIN

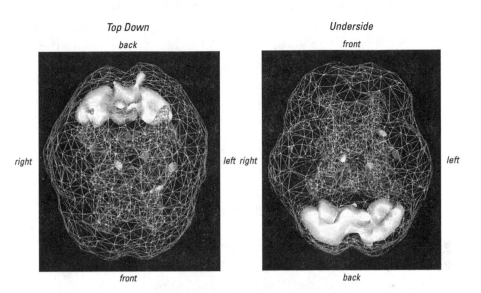

Top Down

back

right   left

front

Underside

front

right   left

back

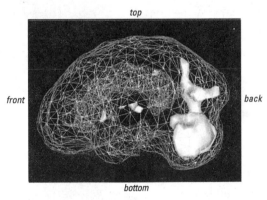

Left Side

top

front   back

bottom

an aesthetic standpoint, on scans some brains are beautiful, whereas others are a bit misshapen and funny-looking. But, beautiful or not, from looking at over twelve thousand brain SPECT studies, it is clear to me that a healthy brain shows good, full, even, symmetrical activity. A healthy brain has all of its major parts intact, and they work together in a relatively harmonious fashion. There are also normal age variations. The brain scans of children and teenagers reveal more activity than the brain scans of adults, although even an elderly brain, if properly cared for during life, looks full, symmetrical, and healthy.

A healthy brain at any age shows a life filled with positive human behavior—love, compassion, thoughtfulness, fun, and goal-directed behavior. A brain that works right helps us to be the most "human" we can be.

Brain-Influenced Spirituality

Our spirituality is influenced by how the brain functions. It has been my experience that when the brain is healthy for people with religious beliefs, God is experienced as loving, compassionate, forgiving, and present. When these people struggle with brain problems, God is often perceived as angry, vengeful, controlling, rigid, judgmental, and distant. Brain physiology impacts our perception of the world, including our perception of God. Let's look at two examples of how brain problems can influence spiritual faith—depression and obsessive-compulsive disorder.

Brain-imaging studies have clearly shown that depression is associated with abnormalities in the emotional and cognitive centers of the brain. These brain abnormalities can lead to negativity, hopelessness, social isolation, distractibility, and despair. These feelings lead to estrangement from God and often to suicidal tendencies. People with depression often feel disconnected from God and, in my experience, they perceive Him as distant, negative, and punishing.

Until Ben experienced his first bout of depression at the age of twenty-eight, he was a devout Jew. He attended religious services twice a week and was an active member of his congregation. He prayed on a regular basis and felt close to God. After his depression began, triggered by the unexpected death of his father in a car accident, Ben stopped attending synagogue. He felt sad most of the time and entertained suicidal thoughts. He had little energy and perceived God as angry, hostile, and punishing. Six months into his depression, when he lost his job and many of his friends, his family brought him to our clinic for treatment. Through treatment Ben began to heal. He returned to religious services, once again became an active member of his synagogue, and felt close to God.

3-D UNDERSIDE ACTIVE VIEW OF THE BRAIN

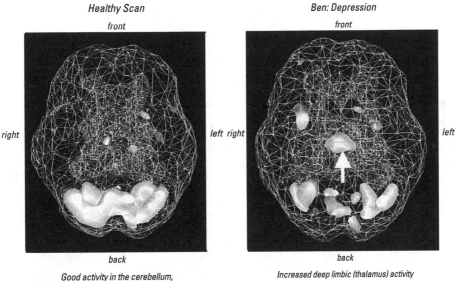

Healthy Scan

front

right   left

back

Good activity in the cerebellum,
cool everywhere else

Ben: Depression

front

right   left

back

Increased deep limbic (thalamus) activity

Obsessive-compulsive disorder (OCD) is associated with too much activity in the brain's anxiety regions. People with OCD get stuck on bad thoughts and/or repetitive behaviors, which can lead to religious obsession, ritualistic behavior, excessive worry, mistrust, and rigidity of thought. It is a very painful disorder that erodes a person's sense of emotional balance and occupies a great deal of life's precious time.

One of my patients with OCD, Seth, age thirty-two, prayed hundreds of times a day for deliverance from his tormenting thoughts. He had thoughts and images of hurting other people, and spent hours a day going through rituals to avoid all sharp objects for fear he would grab them and lash out at others, even though he had never been violent. His bad thoughts and prayers to overcome them occupied most of his days. He had little time for normal work or social interaction. Over time, with the correct medication to balance Seth's brain, his prayer life normalized and he was able to enjoy both his physical and spiritual life. His prayers are still a significant part of his life, just not hundreds of times a day.

3-D UNDERSIDE ACTIVE VIEW OF THE BRAIN

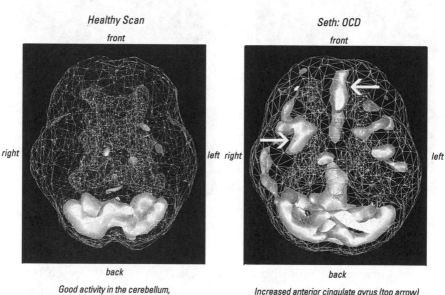

Healthy Scan

Seth: OCD

Good activity in the cerebellum,
cool everywhere else

Increased anterior cingulate gyrus (top arrow)
and basal ganglia (bottom arrow) activity

Wired for God?

There are certain brain regions that, when stimulated, cause or enhance spiritual experience. Does this prove that the brain is wired for belief in God? Does the brain's health enhance or hurt our ability to get close to God? Neurologists have known for a long time that patients with temporal-lobe epilepsy often report spiritual experiences and may be preoccupied with religious issues. Dostoevsky, Saint Paul, Saint Teresa of Ávila, and others are thought to have had temporal-lobe epilepsy, leaving them obsessed with matters of the spirit. This led scientists at the University of California, San Diego, to study epileptic patients. In 1997, a team led by Dr. Vilayanur Ramachandran believed they had discovered a "God module" in the brain, which could be responsible for our innate instinct to believe in God. Studying a group of epileptics who had profoundly spiritual experiences, the scientists located a circuit of nerves in the temporal lobes that became electrically active when the patients thought about God. The scientists said that initial results suggested that the phenomenon of religious belief could be "hard-wired" into the brain. The research team said the most intriguing explanation is that a seizure causes an overstimulation of the nerves in the God module. Do Dr. Ramachandran's experiments reveal dedicated neural machinery in the temporal lobes concerned with God and spirituality? The results certainly seem to indicate that whether a person believes in a religion or even in God may depend on the activity of this part of the brain's electrical circuitry. In similar studies by Dr. Ramachandran, electrical brain tracings over the temporal lobes showed that the epileptics and the deeply religious displayed a similar response when shown words invoking spiritual belief.

If a God module exists, it suggests that people who are atheists could have a differently configured neural circuit. Would it be surprising that God created us with a physical facility for belief? We need a mechanism to see and hear God's presence in the physical life.

Andrew Newberg, at the University of Pennsylvania, uses SPECT studies to peer into minds during meditation. Dr. Newberg and his colleagues chose to investigate the neurobiology of meditation precisely because it is a spiritual state easily duplicated in the laboratory. The study was funded by the Templeton Foundation, which is interested in fostering ties between science and religion. So far, they have scanned the brains of Buddhist monks during prolonged meditation. To photograph neural activity during meditation, the researchers injected each monk with a faintly radioactive tracer chemical that quickly infused into brain cells, where it illuminated neural activity for the SPECT camera. The images revealed distinctive changes in brain activity as the mind settled into a meditative state. In particular, activity diminished in those parts of the brain involved in generating a sense of three-dimensional orientation in space. The loss of one's sense of place, in turn, could account for a spiritual feeling of release into a place beyond space and time. This suggests that an essential element of the religious experience of transcendence may be hard-wired in the brain.

IN the next three chapters we'll take a look at five brain systems typically involved with relationships, work, and spiritual growth: the prefrontal cortex (PFC), anterior cingulate gyrus, basal ganglia, temporal lobes, and deep limbic system. The functions and problems of each area will be discussed, along with the implications of each system in regard to good, evil, love, and the health or sickness of the soul. I'll also include some case histories and SPECT examples.

Three

The Thoughtful, Compassionate Brain

The Prefrontal Cortex (PFC)

You are not supposed to kill people. You are supposed to have that thing in your head that goes off and says really bad f—— idea.

—FROM THE MOVIE *DROWNING MONA*

That still, small voice in your head that helps you decide between right and wrong.

—JIMINY CRICKET, *PINOCCHIO*

If the anterior portion of the cerebrum is wounded, then the internal senses—imagination, memory, thought—suffer; the very will is weakened, and the power of determination is blunted. . . . This is not the case if the injury is in the back of the cerebrum.

—EMANUEL SWEDENBORG, 1882

THE prefrontal cortex (PFC) is the chief executive officer of the mind. It is the internal supervisor that guides, directs, focuses, and controls thoughts and behaviors; the PFC is the most developed part of the brain, accounting for nearly all of the front 30 percent of the human brain. It occupies only 11 percent of the brain of the chimpanzee, our nearest primate cousin. *The PFC is responsible for human success.* It houses our ability to see and plan for tomorrow and to consistently match our behavior over time to reach our goals. In this chapter we will explore the functions and problems of the PFC as it relates to our ability to live and work successfully with others and to be quiet and focused within ourselves.

When the PFC works properly, we are thoughtful, empathic, compassionate, able to appropriately express our feelings, organized, and goal directed. The PFC supervises us and protects us from impulsive (acting without thinking) sin and ill-thought-out behaviors. Our conscience, sense of right and wrong, and free will are housed primarily in this part of the brain. The PFC is called the executive part of the brain because, like a business executive, it is heavily involved in planning, forethought, judgment, organization, and impulse control.

The PFC helps you think about what you say or do before you say or do it. In accordance with your experience, the PFC helps you select between alternative actions in personal, social, and spiritual situations. For example, if you are very frustrated by events in your life and think about cursing God and you have good PFC function, you are more likely to be thoughtful in your prayers. If you have poor PFC function, you are more likely to do or say something that you may regret later. Likewise, if you are a minister or elder in a church and you are counseling someone who is causing conflict in the congregation and you have good PFC function, you are more likely to think about what you have to say ahead of time and give a thoughtful response that helps the situation. If you have poor PFC function, you are more likely to do or say something that will inflame the situation, making it worse than it needs to be. The PFC helps you problem-solve, see ahead of a situation, and choose the most helpful alternatives.

The PFC helps you learn from mistakes. Good PFC function doesn't mean that you won't make mistakes. Rather, it generally means you won't make the same mistake over and over again: You learn from past experiences. For example, a man with good PFC function notices that when he has several alcoholic drinks he acts in embarrassing, thoughtless, and irritating ways, and so he stops drinking. A man with decreased PFC function doesn't

PFC—LEFT SIDE

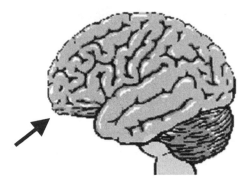

learn from past experiences and continues to drink despite the problems it causes in his life. Individuals with poor PFC function don't seem able to draw on their past experiences, and they react impulsively to satisfy their immediate wants and needs.

The PFC helps concentration and attention span. It helps you focus on important information while filtering out less significant thoughts and sensations. Good attention span is required for many things in life, such as short-term memory, learning, intimacy, and spirituality. The PFC, through its many connections within the brain, helps you keep on task and allows you to stay focused on goals until the end. The PFC sends quieting signals to the emotional and sensory parts of the brain. When you need to focus on something or someone important, like your spouse, your prayers, or tasks at work, the PFC decreases the distracting input from other brain areas, helping to inhibit or filter out distractions. When the PFC is underactive, there is less of a filtering mechanism and distractibility becomes a problem. A healthy PFC is essential to people who meditate—which requires the ability to focus and calm the mind. The PFC helps you to be able to sit still long enough to pray and to be quiet enough to hear your own inner thoughts.

Thoughtfulness and impulse control are heavily influenced by the PFC. These traits are essential for a healthy relational, emotional, and spiritual path in life. The need for forethought is found in almost all human endeavors, from pursuing an education and profession, to choosing and nurturing a mate, to dealing with children and being a positive member of a religious congregation. Without proper PFC function, impulses take over, making it difficult to act in consistent, thoughtful ways. Impulse control issues are one of the main components of sin, doing something that you know is wrong. Without full functioning of the PFC, people tend to act on the moment, without forethought or regard for consequences. The moment is what matters, not tomorrow or next week.

The PFC is also the part of the brain that allows you to express emotions, such as happiness, sadness, joy, and love. The PFC translates the feelings of the limbic system, the emotional brain, into recognizable feelings, emotions, and words, such as love, passion, or hate. Underactivity or damage in this part of the brain often leads to a decreased ability to express thoughts and feelings. Alexythymia is the inability to express emotion. Our studies have shown that it is associated with underactivity in the PFC.

Problems in the PFC lead to decreased attention span, distractibility, impaired short-term memory, decreased mental speed, apathy, decreased verbal expression, poor impulse control, mood control problems (due to its connections with the limbic system), decreased social skills, and overall decreased control over behavior. When there are problems in the PFC, the organization of daily life becomes difficult, and internal supervision—the conscience—goes awry. Here are two examples:

Brian, a forty-four-year-old, three-times-divorced physician, had moved from town to town and clinic to clinic. He was socially isolated and spiritually adrift. Although he had a high IQ, he was frequently fired from jobs for disorganization, insubordination toward his superiors, and thoughtless behavior toward patients. He was often late for appointments, and he frequently did not get his paperwork done on time. He made the same mistakes over and over, job after job, stuck in self-destructive patterns that could be traced to his childhood. He joined churches but rarely followed through on his commitments. As a child, he frequently got into trouble with both his parents and the law. He had trouble conforming his behavior to social norms.

Many people told Brian that he had a character problem. They said that he was self-absorbed and passive-aggressive. He came to see me after being fired for the third time in one year. As part of his evaluation, I ordered a SPECT study to evaluate brain function. Overall, he had very low brain activity, especially in his prefrontal cortex. As a child, he had a near-drowning incident and was unconscious for two days. I concluded that his overall poor brain activity was likely due to oxygen deprivation. I knew that Brian's problem was not his character; the problem was the organ that controls character, his brain. The hardware of his soul, his very essence, was severely damaged. And even though he could still walk, talk, and feed himself, he was clearly brain damaged and in need of treatment rather than judgment. With the appropriate therapy, Brian's condition improved. Al-

BRIAN'S SPECT STUDY

Note marked decrease in prefrontal cortex activity.

Top Down Surface View   Underside Surface View

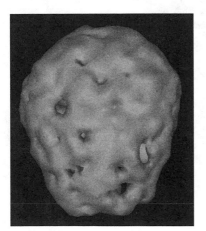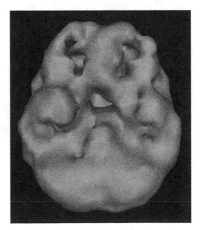

though it may never be optimal because of the damage to his brain, the improved function allowed him to remain in the same job, relationship, and church for many years.

William, a Catholic priest, came to see me after he read *Healing ADD,* my recent book on attention deficit disorder. Throughout his life he had experienced problems with concentration, focus, follow-through, and procrastination. He barely finished his studies at the seminary and had great trouble focusing his mind on his prayers or paying attention when hearing confessions. His father had many of the same problems. William's SPECT study showed decreased PFC activity. With the addition of stimulant medication, William said, "For the first time in my life I can stay focused on my prayers. My whole life I felt inferior because I couldn't meditate on God or stay focused on my prayers." After treatment, people in his congregation told him they noticed a difference and they felt that he was more present

WILLIAM'S SPECT STUDIES—UNDERSIDE SURFACE VIEWS, BEFORE AND AFTER MEDICATION

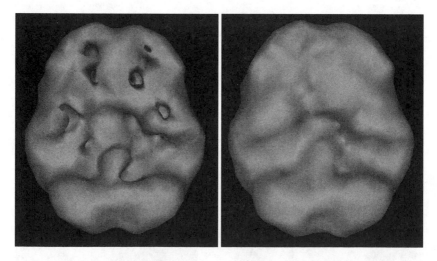

Before Treatment　　　　　　　*After Treatment*

Markedly decreased PFC　　　　　*Improved PFC*

and emotionally available to them. He reported that he felt that he was able to make a more significant spiritual impact because he could stay focused on his goals. A follow-up SPECT study showed significant improvement in his PFC.

Too little PFC activity leads to thoughtless and impulsive behavior, whereas, as we will see in the next chapter, too much activity in the PFC leads to excessive anxiety and planning, as is the case with obsessive-compulsive disorder.

Healthy Prefrontal Cortex Traits

When the PFC works properly, you have a good sense of right and wrong and you are able to match your behavior to your moral beliefs. You know what you want in life, and you are able to stay focused on the things that are most important to you. Despite distractions or obstacles, you stay on the path to your goals. You empathize with others—you are able to get outside of yourself to see another person's opinion or point of view. You are able to apologize when you make mistakes, and you see how your behavior impacts others. You are able to focus and attend to conversations, follow through on commitments and chores, and organize your actions. You feel settled, and you are able to sit still in school, in church, and elsewhere. You show thoughtfulness. You tend to have a strong conscience, neither overbearing nor hostile, and you are led by doing good for yourself and others. You are able to fully exercise free will.

Unfortunately, everyone does not have the same ability to exercise free will. This is a very controversial statement. Yet, it is clear to me that if your free will, judgment, and impulse control center (PFC) are healthy, you have better access to free will than if your free will center is underactive (as in people with attention deficit disorder) or overactive (which we see in people with obsessive-compulsive disorder). You do not have the same ability to monitor choices as others who have healthy PFCs. It does not mean you have no ability unless there is severe damage, but your ability is less.

POSITIVE PFC TRAITS

- Thoughtful and forward thinking
- Ability to express yourself clearly (in prayer and to others)
- Focused on both short- and long-term goals (can think about the present, but also has the future in mind)
- Ability to be still and pay attention to others (able to focus on others, see the needs of others, and be still enough to be reflexive and thoughtful)
- On time (for church, prayer meetings, work, dates, etc.)
- Follows through on commitments
- Learns from mistakes (learns from sins of the past)
- Strong, healthy conscience (understands right from wrong, and is able to match behavior to internal concepts of right and wrong)
- Fully able to exercise free will (good control over behavior)
- Compassionate and empathic

When I first started to image the brain, I scanned many members of my family, including my three children, myself, my aunt who had a panic disorder, and even my mother. Out of the group, my mother had the healthiest brain I had seen until then (and even now, twelve years and twelve thousand scans later). This came as no surprise because throughout my life I have benefited from a mother who was kind, compassionate, thoughtful, consistently caring, on time, and organized. Certainly she wasn't perfect, but I cannot remember times when her behavior was erratic or harsh. She was and is amazing. It's no coincidence that her loving behavior was connected to a brain that worked right. Her brain shows good, full, even symmetrical activity, especially in her PFC, even at the age of seventy.

A look at my mother's life highlights her good brain function. She has been married for fifty-two years to my father. She raised seven healthy, relatively happy, and productive children. She remains very involved in our lives; she is adored by her twenty-one grandchildren and is very active in her church. She has a myriad of friends, plays golf at a very high level, and was her club champion for many years. Sometimes I tease my mother, saying it is very hard to be raised by a woman with a healthy brain. It didn't prepare me to be married. Mom was always on time, organized, loving, firm, and consistent. I never heard her yell at or be disrespectful to my father. This did not prepare me for the real world, I tell her. How could anyone live up to such consistent behavior?

MOM'S HEALTHY BRAIN

Top Down Surface View

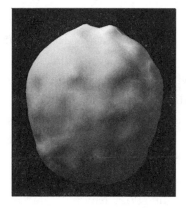

Underside Surface View

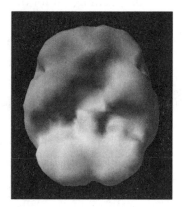

Left Side Surface View

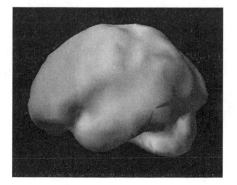

Here are several other examples of a healthy PFC at work:

BILL, JESSICA, RUSTY, JOSEPH, AND LARRY

Bill, a twenty-year-old college premed student, spent a great deal of time studying in the university library. His dorm was very distracting because of frequent parties, drug use, and lots of noise. Several of his premed friends got caught up in the distractions at school and ended up choosing easier majors. He stayed focused on his goals, disciplined in study, attending church, and being the person he wanted to be. Despite the amount of schoolwork, Bill found time to be involved at church, volunteering in the youth program.

Jessica was the mother of four-year-old twins. Despite the fact that they required a lot of attention and she was often tired, she was organized in caring for them. She had them on a schedule, got her chores done in an efficient manner, and was loving, caring, and consistent with them. She was able to provide a consistent environment for their growth. She read to them, taught them to pray, and appropriately disciplined them.

When Rusty turned forty-three, he suffered a midlife crisis triggered by the death of his older brother, who died of stomach cancer. Rusty started to wonder about the meaning of his life and if he was in the right line of work and even if he was married to the right woman. He thought about leaving home and starting a new life. Before he did anything rash, he thought through his options and sought counseling. The death of his brother had hit him hard, but he also had enough sense, thanks to healthy PFC function, to get help.

After his father died of cancer, Joseph, forty-two, wanted to feel closer to God. He decided to pray every day for twenty minutes before he went to work. He set his alarm to get up early and followed through with his plan. Several years later, he continues with the early morning prayers on a daily basis. He was able to consistently follow through with his plans.

Larry was the youth minister at a local church. He was a dedicated, kind man. He was single and often lonely. One Sunday a very shapely, attractive seventeen-year-old girl came to the youth group. She did not have a father and took an immediate liking to Larry. She flirted with him, wore low-cut dresses to church, and made suggestive comments about what she'd like him to do to her. Even though Larry was attracted to her, he politely kept his distance and made sure they were never alone together. He thought about her when they were apart, but he also thought about the many negative consequences if he returned her affection.

UNHEALTHY PFC TRAITS

- Short attention span—often derailed by internal and external distractions
- Lack of perseverance—poor follow-through, will only do things as long as they are interesting
- Lack of discipline and self-control—trouble maintaining consistent ethics and consistent regimens
- Impulse control problems—difficulty thinking ahead of situations, makes decisions based on the immediate moment rather than what is best for both the here and now and the future
- Trouble learning from experience—repeats mistakes, doesn't seem to learn from the past
- Poor judgment—makes bad decisions, based on impulse rather than thoughtfulness
- Chronic lateness, poor time management—has trouble being on time, following through on promises on time, always seems to be in a hurry
- Disorganization—the space around the person is often a mess, and his mind seems the same way
- Conflict- or negative-seeking behavior—many people with underactivity in the PFC use conflict or negativity as a form of self-stimulation
- Weak conscience—self-centered, doesn't care what others think or feel, and has a problem distinguishing between right and wrong

Looking at the examples similar to the cases above, let's see what happens with an unhealthy PFC:

JEFF, SUE, ROBERT, DONNY, WESLEY, AND JAMES

Jeff, twenty-five, was in his seventh year at college. He had changed his major several times, did drugs part of the time, and was distracted by girls and parties. He had gone to college with the intention of being a doctor but flunked out of his early biology and chemistry classes. He was unfocused on his schoolwork, often late to class, disorganized, impulsive in his actions, and self-absorbed. He was raised in church and had every intention of finding a new church in his college town, but he never got around to it.

Sue was the mother of two small children. She was disorganized and inefficient, and felt constantly overwhelmed. She was frequently irritable with the children. She complained about how overworked she was and often berated her husband for not helping, even though he worked two jobs to support them. After several years, her husband left them.

Robert, forty-five, changed his whole life in the last year. He divorced his wife of twenty years, moved to Los Angeles from Seattle to take a new job as an assistant television producer, and spent most of his retirement money. He rarely saw his three young children and got involved in intense but short-term love relationships. He initially laughed when his wife asked him to get help when he left her. He finally came to understand when he tried to return home, but his wife said getting help was prerequisite to her having anything romantic to do with him ever again.

After stressful periods in Donny's life, he would recommit himself to praying every day and attending church regularly. The commitment would last only a few weeks, and then other things would distract him and he would not follow through.

Wesley was the youth minister at a local church. He was single and often lonely. One Sunday, a pretty fifteen-year-old girl came to the youth group. She flirted with him. Wesley gave her extra attention, sent her e-mails at home, made her feel special, and after a few months started having sex with her. She became pregnant and he lost his job.

James came from the Midwest. He had been a very successful oil executive, yet his life was a mess. He had been married four times. He had multiple affairs while married to each of his wives. He had problems with his temper, said things that were inappropriate to his employees, and was estranged from all of his five children. After his current wife gave him my book *Change Your Brain, Change Your Life,* he came to my clinic. In his history I uncovered a significant brain injury that occurred when he was in college. As a defensive tackle, he was knocked unconscious during a football game. He was dizzy for a week, had headaches off and on for a year, and noticed more problems in school. His SPECT study showed marked decreased activity in his prefrontal cortex, especially on the left side.

JAMES'S SPECT STUDY—PFC INJURY
Note marked decrease in prefrontal cortex activity.

Top Down Surface View *Underside Surface View*

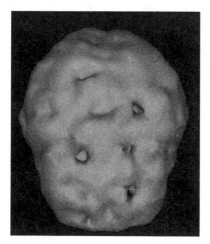
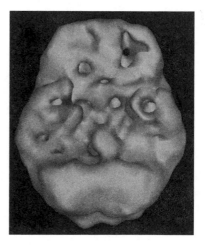

• • •

GOOD PFC function helps us see ahead of situations—we can get off the train tracks when we see the train coming. Poor PFC function doesn't allow us to see ahead or plan for the future—we don't see the train until it's about to run over us. In order for your soul to work right, the PFC has to set a good and noble course for you. Your soul must remain on course for spiritual and emotional growth, and it must have the tools to learn from mistakes and follow through to new heights. Good PFC activity allows you to focus and follow through on what is truly important in your life.

Four

The Flexible, Growth-Oriented Brain

The Anterior Cingulate Gyrus and Basal Ganglia

THERE are two highly interconnected parts of the brain that help you feel settled, relaxed, open-minded, and flexible: the anterior cingulate gyrus, which runs lengthwise through the deep regions of the frontal lobes, and the basal ganglia, two large structures deep within the brain. These two areas are the brain's major cognitive switching areas. I think of them as the brain's gear shifters, greasing human behavior, allowing us to be flexible, adaptable, and open to change as it is needed. These parts of the brain are involved in helping you shift your attention from thing to thing, move from idea to idea, and see the options in your life.

In this chapter we will explore the functions and problems of the anterior cingulate gyrus and basal ganglia as they relate to our daily interactions and spiritual and emotional growth. We will see how normal operations in these parts of the brain allow flexibility, cooperation, connection with others, and openness to emotional and spiritual growth, and how problems here cause us to be rigid, inflexible, and stuck in old thinking and behavior patterns.

Being able to appropriately shift attention allows you to move easily through your days and ultimately transition into new modes of thinking and behaving. When attention gets stuck on negative thoughts, hurts from the past, or anger, emotional or spiritual growth becomes arrested. Shifting attention and flexibility lead to an ability to adapt to new situations. Adaptability is a major reason human beings have been successful as a species. Over time, humans have been able to adapt to many changes, such as in climate, diet, social structures, and population density. Those who cannot change suffer greater risk of failure. There are many day-to-day situations in life where flexibility is essential. For example, living with a new person such as a college roommate, husband or wife, or a barrack of fellow marines requires adaptability and being able to integrate another person's habits and traits into your life. Having to have things your way and being unable to bend to another person's needs or desires can cause serious relational problems. Likewise, working at a new place of employment also requires the ability to adapt. You have to learn a new work system and figure out how to get along with different personalities and how to please a new boss.

THE ANTERIOR CINGULATE GYRUS AND THE BASAL GANGLIA

The scans show the anterior cingulate gyrus (front middle area of scan) and basal ganglia (two areas on each side of the brain 30 percent down from the front).

Underside Active View   Left Side Active View

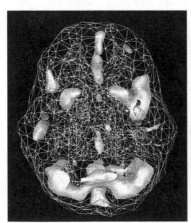
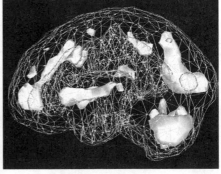

Cooperation, be it at church, on the job, or as part of a sports team, is also influenced by this part of the brain. When the anterior cingulate gyrus and basal ganglia work in an effective manner, it is easy to shift into cooperative modes of behavior. We need other people in our lives in order to be healthy. Human beings are a relational species. Cooperation enhances emotional and spiritual connection between people. Uncooperative and difficult behaviors are characteristic of people with poorly functioning gear shifters. Too much activity in the anterior cingulate gyrus and basal ganglia is usually caused by a lack of the neurotransmitter serotonin, which prevents people from properly shifting their attention, leading to rigid, contradictory, and contentious behavior. Such people also have a strong tendency to hold grudges.

Hank, forty-eight, had been angry with God since childhood. His mother had died in a car accident when he was eight years old. He prayed for God to bring her back to him, but when his mother did not return, he decided never again to talk to God. Hank was sent to see me by his marital counselor. Hank had a terrible problem with jealousy and holding on to problems from the past. When he told me about his promise not to talk to God some forty years earlier, I knew he had a problem in the brain's gear shifter, a condition that was confirmed on his SPECT scan. Balancing this part of his brain was very helpful for Hank. He was more flexible and loving toward his wife, and he was able to let go of his anger at God and return to church.

Jenny, seven, was brought to our clinic by her parents for an evaluation, including SPECT studies. Her parents had long been troubled by her irritability, worrying, and obsessive thinking. In order to do the study, we had to start an intravenous (IV) line. When my technician tried to start the IV, Jenny screamed, "No, I won't let you do it." She did not scream in protest once; rather, she screamed it at least five hundred times. She kept repeating the same thing over and over, and we knew what part of her brain was the problem by her repetitive behavior. Her scan confirmed our suspicions of significant hyperactivity in her basal ganglia and anterior cingulate gyrus. I prescribed the natural antidepressant St. John's wort, which in my experience helps calm anterior cingulate gyrus and basal ganglia hyperactivity. Within several weeks, Jenny became more flexible and cooperative and easier to be around. Her personality was softer and less intrusive, and she was better able to connect with others.

JENNY'S SPECT STUDIES BEFORE TREATMENT

Note marked hyperactivity in the anterior cingulate gyrus and basal ganglia.

Underside Active View   *Left Side Active View*

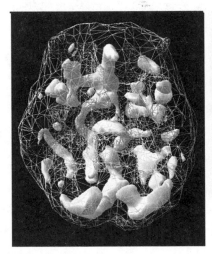 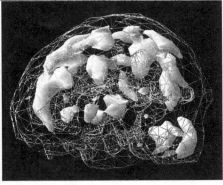

The anterior cingulate gyrus and basal ganglia have also been implicated in "future-oriented thinking," such as planning and goal setting. When they work well, people are able to plan the future in a reasonable way. When they are underactive, people have problems with motivation and get-up-and-go. When they work too hard, people plan too much, worry too much, often becoming overly serious and single-minded about whatever goals they have set for themselves. Difficulties in these parts of

JENNY'S SPECT STUDIES AFTER TREATMENT

The scans show calming of activity in the anterior cingulate gyrus and basal ganglia.

Underside Active View   *Left Side Active View*

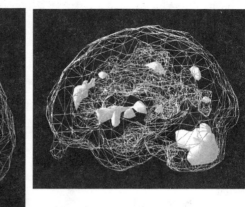

the brain can cause a person to see negative events in the future and feel very unsafe in the world.

Ten-year-old Joshua had excessive activity in these parts of the brain. He was constantly afraid. He worried about himself dying, his parents dying, and his friends dying. He was so consumed with fear that he had stopped going to school. When his parents brought him to our clinic, no obvious stress was found in his background. Yet, there was a family history of people with anxiety disorders. Joshua's SPECT study showed marked hyperactivity in the anterior cingulate gyrus and basal ganglia. After he was placed on Zoloft, a serotonin-enhancing medication, his fears subsided and he relaxed enough to return to school.

The anterior cingulate and basal ganglia, in my experience, allow a person to experience emotional growth and see different options. The people, businesses, and religious and political institutions that thrive are adaptable to change as needed. I have seen adaptability among the best ministers and religious leaders I have known. I have seen ministers with severe anterior cingulate gyrus and basal ganglia problems get stuck in outdated modes of interactions. They are the types that say "Believe what I tell you or leave the church." At the other end of the spectrum are individuals who explore alternative pathways, recognizing that new ideas protect against psychological and emotional stagnation.

The problems associated with anterior cingulate gyrus and basal ganglia hyperactivity include anxiety, obsessive-compulsive disorder, eating disorders, addictive disorders, and behavioral difficulties in children. They may hold on to hurts or grudges from the past and stubbornly cut off those they love. They may also get stuck on negative behaviors, or develop compulsions such as hand washing or excessively checking locks. One patient who had anterior cingulate gyrus and basal ganglia problems described this phenomenon to me, saying it was "like being on a rat's exercise wheel, where the thoughts just go over and over and over." Another patient told me, "It's like having a reset button in your head that is always on. Even though I don't want to have the thought anymore, it just keeps coming back." All of these disorders are associated with problems shifting attention or getting stuck. There are also a number of "subclinical patterns" associated with abnormalities in this part of the brain. The term "subclinical" relates to problem traits that do not reached the same level of intensity as a psychiatric disorder like obsessive-compulsive disorder, but still cause difficulties in a person's life. Examples of these problems include worrying, holding on to hurts from the past, automatically saying no, and unwillingness to try something new or another person's way.

Cognitive inflexibility is the root of most of these problems and has caused many wars and religious and relational battles. It is associated with this feeling: "I'm right. You are wrong. We have to do things my way. There is no other way but my way."

You'll notice this type of thinking in many oppressive or fundamentalist religions or cults. One has to conform or be excluded from the group.

Healthy Anterior Cingulate and Basal Ganglia Traits

As mentioned, the anterior cingulate gyrus and basal ganglia are the brain's gear shifters. When they function properly, people easily shift their attention from one idea to the next. They can smoothly go from thought to thought and from idea to idea as needed. They tend to be relaxed, flexible, and adaptable, and are likely to see options in tough situations; they do not get stuck in inappropriate, ineffective, or outdated modes of operating. When they face problems, they work through solutions and then let the problems go. They are usually able to forgive the mistakes of others and tend not to hold on to hurts from the past. They encourage others to help them in their daily work, but they do not rigidly control situations. They tend to be successful in interpersonal relationships, have a positive outlook, and see a hopeful future. Basically, they are able to roll with the ups and downs of life without excessive stress.

POSITIVE ANTERIOR CINGULATE AND BASAL GANGLIA TRAITS
- Flexibility, adaptability
- Ability to solve problems and let them go
- Ability to go with the flow
- Strong ability to cooperate
- Seeing things from another person's perspective
- Good at collaboration
- Ability to forgive past wrongs
- Ability to let go of hurts
- Seeing the future in a positive light
- Ability to deal with conflict
- Feeling physically relaxed
- Good motivation

Here are examples of healthy anterior cingulate gyrus and basal ganglia at work:

CHUCK, BARBARA, MALLORY, SUE AND ANTHONY, FATHER GREG, JOLENE, DAVID, AND RABBI BILL GRIMES

Chuck, a twenty-eight-year-old psychiatry resident, had just broken up with his girlfriend of four years. He was very sad at the loss and felt depressed for several weeks. When he realized the breakup was final, he saw a counselor for several sessions, took some time off from dating, and moved beyond the relationship.

Barbara was stuck in an early morning traffic jam. She was going to miss a very important meeting. She felt very upset until she realized there was nothing she could do but call the office and reschedule with apologies. She was then able to let go of being upset.

Mallory had been badly snubbed by one of her best friends, Lillie. They had been close friends since childhood, but Lillie had always been jealous of Mallory's beauty. Lillie did not invite Mallory to her parents' fiftieth wedding anniversary party, even though all her other friends were invited. When Mallory discovered this, she became very upset and called Lillie. Lillie told Mallory that she did not invite her because she didn't want someone more beautiful than she in the pictures. Mallory told Lillie that she was very hurt and didn't believe Lillie was so shallow. After several days, Mallory put herself in Lillie's shoes, felt bad that Lillie had such low self-esteem, and made a truce with her.

After drifting apart for several years, Sue and Anthony divorced after ten years of marriage. They had three children together. Despite the breakup, they were able to stay friends. They amicably mediated the divorce settlement and effectively shared custody. Over the years they were able to welcome each other's new spouses into their extended families. They could still value the good things they saw in each other.

Father Greg was the post chaplain at Fort Irwin, where I was chief of the mental health clinic. He was a unique Catholic priest, and I loved attending his services. His sermons frequently dealt with forgiveness and God's love. We became close friends during our tour of duty in the Mojave Desert. The more I knew Father Greg, the more I saw a man deeply committed to God. He was flexible and easygoing, but very committed to his principles and ideals. I frequently sent lonely and hurting soldiers for his counsel. Almost always they came away from his sessions uplifted or consoled.

Jolene was a college freshman. She was away from home for the first time, living in the dorm. Many of her classmates complained about the noise in the dorm, the hard class schedules, and the overall stress of being a college freshman. Jolene, however, thoroughly enjoyed her first year away from home. Even though she missed her family, she made friends, felt relaxed and confident about school, exercised regularly, and stayed motivated to study and do well in her classes.

David, an English teacher at a local public high school, taught and practiced meditation. He was plagued by anxiety as a teenager and saw a counselor for several years. His therapist taught him diaphragmatic breathing and simple relaxation techniques that were very helpful. Wanting to help others who struggled with the same issues, he taught a class of relaxation exercises every morning for twenty minutes. He noted that as he exercised with his students, he felt more relaxed himself.

Rabbi Bill Grimes was a positive, easygoing man. He looked toward the future with hope and had a calming presence on those around him. He was especially good in crisis situations, in which he helped people think through situations in a calm, loving way.

UNHEALTHY ANTERIOR CINGULATE GYRUS AND BASAL GANGLIA TRAITS (ALL OF THESE TRAITS HAVE TO DO WITH PROBLEMS OF SHIFTING ATTENTION)
- Worrying, rumination—the same negative thought over and over

- Holding on to hurts from the past—inability to relinquish grudges
- Stuck on thoughts—obsessions or any other thought can get stuck
- Stuck on behavior—compulsions, or having to have things done your way
- Oppositional behavior—automatic tendency to say no
- Argumentativeness—automatic tendency to disagree or argue with someone even before hearing them out completely
- Uncooperativeness—appearing selfish because you can see only your wants and needs and your point of view
- Addictive behavior—getting stuck on the need and desire for alcohol, drugs, food, gambling, etc.
- Cognitive inflexibility—rigid thought patterns
- Anxiety, nervousness—excessive worry about the future
- Panic attacks—anxiety taking control of the body
- Physical sensations of anxiety—feeling tense or revved up
- Tendency to anticipate the worst—inability to stop seeing the future in anything but a negative light
- Conflict avoidance—tendency to stay away from any interaction that brings on anxiety
- Muscle tension, soreness—from chronic anxiety

Let's see what happens with an unhealthy anterior cingulate gyrus and basal ganglia:

ELLIE, JIM, JESSICA, KENT AND NIKKI, CAPTAIN WALLACE, CHRISSY, RALPH, AND FATHER MURPHY

Ellie, a twenty-five-year-old internal medicine resident, was devastated by the breakup with her fiancé. All she could think of was their failed relationship. She was so sad that she stopped going to work. She called her ex-boyfriend hundreds of times each day, showed up at his place of work, wrote him constantly, and was almost expelled from her residency program for her erratic behavior. She was ordered by her program director to see me.

Jim was stuck in morning traffic. There was an accident on the Bay Bridge, and he was going to be late for work. He went ballistic. He honked, yelled, cursed, felt panicky, and was an emotional wreck for the rest of the day, even though he couldn't do anything about the delay.

Jessica had been hurt by one of her long-standing friends. One day at a party her friend had made a thoughtless joke at Jessica's expense (her friend may have had poor PFC activity that day). Jessica cried about the comment for days. She never talked to her friend again, even though the friend tried to apologize on many different occasions.

Kent and Nikki were divorced after six years of marriage and two children together. Their divorce was very messy: They fought over support, child custody, the property settlement, and almost anything else. Both felt injured and wanted to hurt the other. The divorce was not final for five years. They still do not speak to each other and often put the children in the middle of their many arguments. They also hate each other's new spouse.

Captain Andrew Wallace (not his real name) was the post chaplain where I was stationed in Germany during the early 1970s. He was a staunch fundamentalist minister who preached about the evils of dancing, blue jeans, and makeup. He seemed angry a lot. He was very stern with his children, who often rebelled against him. He talked incessantly about sin, the end of the world, and how people should be ready to be taken to heaven at any minute. His services were not well attended.

Chrissy was a college freshman. She was away from home for the first time, living in the dorm, and hated it. The noise bothered her. Her roommate bothered her. She complained about how far apart her classes were on campus. She called home every night for two months, complaining about school. She could not stop missing her family, friends, and home. At Thanksgiving break her parents brought her to see me. She was on the verge of developing a major depression with features of obsessiveness and anxiety. Her SPECT study showed a marked increase in anterior cingulate gyrus and basal ganglia activity.

Chrissy's SPECT Study

The scans show hyperactivity in the anterior cingulate gyrus and basal ganglia.

Underside Active View   *Left Side Active View*

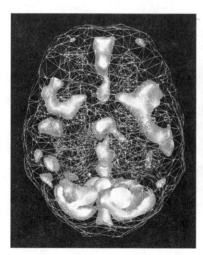
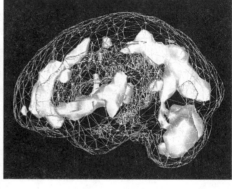

Ralph, a high-school French teacher, was not popular with any of the students. He was rigid and boring, and often seemed angry. Things had to be done his way or you would fail his class. He did not listen to students, seeming preoccupied with his own point of view, and he made the students hate French.

Father Murphy was a hostile man who drank too much and was angry and negative toward his parishioners. He predicted negative outcomes in crisis situations and always seemed to prepare people for the worst. People felt more anxious around him.

Racism and Hatred

In my experience, racism and hatred often involve dysfunction in the anterior cingulate gyrus and basal ganglia. I have scanned many angry people through the years, and many who held irrational hatred against people of different ethnic groups or religions. An overactive anterior cingulate gyrus and basal ganglia cause people to get stuck in negative patterns, as we have seen. Racial hatred, be it black versus white, Arab versus Jew, or Protestant versus Catholic, is a form of being seriously stuck in negative patterns of feelings and behaviors. I can often trace this hatred in families back through generations. Hyperactivity in these parts of the brain is often an inherited trait. Not only are people taught to hate through parental or social modeling, but their brains may be naturally predisposed to getting stuck on negative thoughts and attitudes. Harvard psychiatrist Alvin Poussaint has said that racism should be classified as a mental illness, that racists are sick. I agree. They have brains that are stuck in outmoded ways of operating and cannot shift into a healthier, kinder reality. Here's an example:

Leo

Leo, seventeen, was a high-school senior who hated anyone on an athletic team. He was uncoordinated as a child and poor at sports. He saw athletic boys as having many social advantages, especially with girls. Leo was socially withdrawn, listened to very dark music, and ruminated about violent acts toward athletes. He told a friend not to go to a football game because something bad might happen. With a rash of high-school shootings fresh in his mind, Leo's friend alerted the police. When the police searched Leo's home, they found loaded rifles and handguns, along with a drawing of potential targets at a football game. Leo was arrested. I met him through his defense attorneys. Leo was a socially anxious teen who was also depressed, oppositional toward authority, and prone to obsessive thinking patterns, especially about violence. His scan revealed severe hyperactivity in the anterior cingulate and basal ganglia regions of the brain. Leo's sense of himself was locked into the loops of dark thoughts that circled in his brain. On Zoloft, a medication to calm the hyperactive areas, Leo started to relax and feel more positive, despite his situation, letting go of some of the hatred he had toward specific groups of people.

I N order for your soul to work right, you must be able to experience emotional and spiritual growth. In addition, it is essential to stay connected to others. We are a relational species, and we need to give and receive love in order to feel complete. When the anterior cingulate gyrus and basal ganglia work well, we are able to be flexible, forgive past wrongs, and open ourselves to growth in new ways. When these parts of the brain do not work well, we end up stagnant, isolated, stuck in negativity, alone, and disconnected from those who give our lives meaning.

Five

The Spiritual
and Passionate Brain

The Temporal Lobes and Deep Limbic System

THE temporal lobes, which lie underneath your temples and behind your eyes, and the deep limbic system add the emotional spice to life. Together, they are considered to be the emotional brain, housing our passions, desires, and sense of spirituality. They either give us zest for life or drop us into the depths of despair. They contain the emotional flame that fuels our joys, but when they burn out of control, they may fire dark thoughts or cause us to react with rage toward others or ourselves. In computer terminology, these parts of the brain are an important piece of the soul's operating system. Unfortunately, they are frequently forgotten in psychiatry and rarely talked about in clinical settings (outside of temporal-lobe seizure disorders). Yet, they play an essential role in personality development, and perhaps even religious experience. In this chapter we will discuss the temporal lobes and deep limbic system. We will see how they are involved with memory, emotion, spiritual experience, social connectedness, mood stability, and temper control. At the end of the chapter, we will explore the relationships between brain trauma and emotional and behavioral problems. Due to their location, the temporal lobes are often injured in even mild brain trauma.

THE TEMPORAL LOBE

Left Side Surface View
(arrow indicates the temporal lobe)

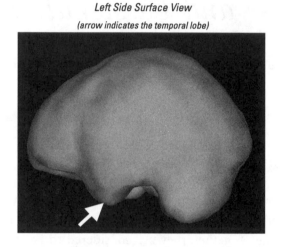

Underside Surface View
(arrow indicates amygdala
area of the temporal lobe)

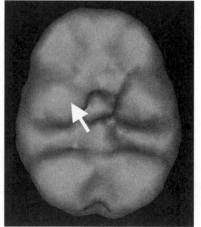

THE DEEP LIMBIC SYSTEM

Underside Active View
(arrow indicates thalamus,
deep limbic system)

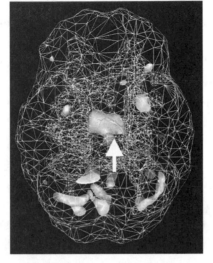

Left Side Active View
(arrow indicates thalamus, deep limbic system)

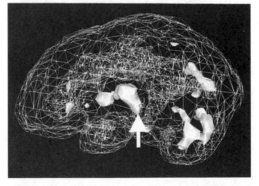

When the temporal lobes and deep limbic system work right, we have a good sense of personal history or memory, are even-keeled in emotions, have access to spiritual experience, and have control over our temper. When there are problems in these parts of the brain, our memories suffer, we either lack spiritual experience or have destructive ones, and experience mood swings and a temper that is out of control.

The dominant temporal lobe, which is usually on the left side for right-handed people, helps us to understand and process language. It is also involved with intermediate and long-term memory, and the retrieval of words. In our clinical experience, we have seen that the left temporal lobe is also involved in mood stability and temper control.

The nondominant temporal lobe, which is usually on the right side for right-handed people, is involved with reading facial expressions (sensing that someone is happy, sad, interested, or bored), reading vocal intonation or sounds ("It was the tone of your voice that made me mad"), and processing rhythm and music. It has also been implicated with intuition, such as having a sense when one of your children is suffering even though he may be in another city or state. In addition, the nondominant temporal lobe has been associated with religious experiences, such as flashes of insight and spiritual experiences like the one the Apostle Paul had on the road to Damascus.

The great Russian writer Fyodor Dostoyevsky had bouts of "temporal-lobe seizures." He felt his affliction was a "holy experience." His biographer, Rene Fueloep-Miller, quotes Dostoyevsky as saying that his epilepsy ". . . rouses in me hitherto unsuspected emotions, gives me feelings of magnificence, abundance and eternity." In *The Idiot,* Dostoevsky wrote:

> There was always one instant just before the epileptic fit . . . when suddenly in the midst of sadness, spiritual darkness and oppression, his brain seemed momentarily to catch fire, and in an extraordinary rush, all his vital forces were at their highest tension. The sense of life, the consciousness of self, were multiplied almost ten times at these moments which lasted no longer than a flash of lightning. His mind and his heart were flooded with extraordinary light; all his uneasi-

ness, all his doubts, all his anxieties were relieved at once; they were all resolved in a loft calm, full of serene, harmonious joy and hope, full of reason and ultimate meaning. But these moments, these flashes, were only a premonition of that final second (it was never more than a second) with which the fit began. That second was, of course, unendurable. Thinking of that moment later, when he was well again, he often said to himself that all these gleams and flashes of supreme sensation and consciousness of self, and therefore, also of the highest form of being, were nothing but disease, the violation of the normal state; and if so, it was not at all the highest form of being, but on the contrary must be reckoned the lowest. Yet he came at last to an extreme paradoxical conclusion. "What if it is disease?" he decided at last. "What does it matter that it is an abnormal intensity, if the result, if the sensation, remembered and analyzed afterwards in health, turns out to be the acme of harmony and beauty, and gives a feeling, unknown and undivined till then, of completeness, of proportion, of reconciliation, and of startled prayerful merging with the highest synthesis of life?"

Psychiatrist Dietrich Blumer at the University of Tennessee in Memphis is one of the world's experts on temporal-lobe epilepsy. In a 1999 *Neurology Journal* article he wrote:

[A] deepening of emotionality with a serious, highly ethical, and spiritual demeanor has been described by clinicians as a positive personality change among patients with chronic medial temporal-lobe epilepsy. Some of these patients tend to be particularly orderly and detailed in their speech and actions (viscosity) and often experience a relative decrease in sexual interest and arousal. These personality changes, distinct from personality changes noted in any other individuals, are subtle in the majority of patients with chronic epilepsy. Patients with the described personality changes may also develop intermittent symptoms of an interictal dysphoric disorder (depression), with episodes of irritable moods that contrast with a predominantly good-natured attitude and for which the patients will be remorseful.

At Laurentian University in Sudbury, Canada, Dr. Michael Persinger has established a lab to induce religious experiences. His subjects are asked to don a motorcycle helmet equipped with electromagnets that produce a magnetic field causing bursts of abnormal activity (overactive neutrons) in the temporal lobe of the brain. Dr. Persinger has noted that induced activity in this part of his subjects' brain causes spiritual and supernatural experiences. People report feeling a sense of presence in the room, which they describe as God, angels, or aliens, or an out-of-body or near-death experience. According to Dr. Persinger, the sense of self, or who you are, in the left hemisphere of the temporal cortex is matched by a corresponding sense of self in the right hemisphere of the temporal cortex. When these two hemispheres become disoriented, there will be a sense of another self. When the emotional brain is also stimulated, feelings will be enhanced, causing intense spiritual feelings. A number of events can trigger these spiritual or supernatural experiences, such as very stressful events—like a car accident, surgery, a decrease in oxygen to the brain at very high altitudes, extreme changes in blood sugar levels, many hours of sleeplessness, temporal-lobe seizures, drugs, or trances from repetitive acts like chanting or dancing and meditation. It is possible that the temporal lobes are God's neural machinery for communicating with us. We can say that Saint Paul had a temporal-lobe seizure on the road to Damascus or that God used Paul's temporal lobe to get his attention and communicate with him. The temporal lobes are involved with receptive language, and this is a major part of the brain that receives and integrates information.

The inside of the temporal lobes, called the medial aspect, and the deep limbic system lie near the center of the brain. Considering their size—about that of a walnut—they are packed with functions critical for human behavior and survival. From a developmental standpoint, the emotional brain is an older part of the mammalian brain that enabled animals to experience and express emotions. It freed them from the stereotypical behavior and actions dictated by the brain stem, found in the older reptilian brain. The subsequent development of the surrounding cerebral cortex in higher animals, especially humans, gave them the capacity for problem solving, planning, organization, and rational thought. Yet, in order for these functions to occur, one must have passion, emotion, and the desire to make it happen. The deep limbic system adds the emotional spice to the cerebral cortex, if you will, in both positive and negative ways.

This part of the brain helps to set a person's emotional tone. When it is less active, there is generally a positive, more hopeful state of mind. When it is heated up, or overactive, negativity can take over. Due to this emotional shading, the deep limbic system and medial temporal lobes provide the filter through which you interpret the events of the day. It tags or colors events, depending on your emotional state of mind. When you are sad (with an overactive deep limbic system), you are likely to interpret neutral events through a negative lens. For example, if you have a neutral or even positive conversation with someone whose deep limbic structure is "negatively set," he or she is likely to interpret the conversation in a negative way. When this part of the brain is "cool," or functions properly, a neutral or positive interpretation of events is more likely to occur. Emotional tagging of events is critical to survival. The valence, or charge, we give to certain events in our lives drives us to action (such as approaching a desired mate) or causes avoidance behavior (withdrawing from someone who has hurt you in the past). These areas of the brain store highly charged, both positive and negative, emotional memories. If you have been traumatized by a dramatic event, such as being in a car accident or watching your house burn down, or if you have been abused by a parent or a spouse, the emotional component of the memory is connected to the deep limbic system of the brain. On the other hand, if you have won the lottery, graduated magna cum laude, or watched your child's birth, those emotional memories are stored here as well. The total experience of our emotional memories is responsible, in part, for the emotional tone of our mind. The more stable, positive experiences we have, the more positive we are likely to feel. The more trauma in our lives, the more emotionally set we become in a negative way. These emotional memories are intimately involved in the emotional tagging that occurs.

The deep limbic structures are also intimately involved with bonding and social connectedness. When the deep limbic system of animals is damaged, they do not properly bond with their young. In one study of rats, when the deep limbic structures were damaged, mothers would drag their offspring around the cage as if they were inanimate objects. They would not feed and nurture the young as they would normally do. This system affects the bonding mechanism that enables you to connect with other people on a social level; your ability to do this successfully in turn influences your moods. When we are bonded to people in a positive way, we feel better about our lives and ourselves. This capacity to bond then plays a significant role in the tone and quality of our moods.

The deep limbic system tends to be larger in women. This may account for the reality that women in overwhelming numbers are the primary caretakers for children and the elderly. The larger limbic size seems to make emotional connections easier for women. Women tend to have more friends; they go to church, and they pray—what I call bonding with God—more than men. Women have a stronger nesting instinct than men, which appears to reflect a great biological need to have their houses in order. When a couple moves, it is generally the woman who feels unsettled until everything is put away. Women are usually primary caretakers for the home and take on the bulk of housework. Unfortunately, with the larger limbic size comes a greater incidence of depression. After puberty, females are three times more likely to develop depression than males. In a study by Mark George at the National Institute for Mental Health, published in 1996, when both male and female adult subjects were asked to think of nothing, men's brains were more active in the more primitive physical activity centers of the brain (cerebellum), while women's brains were more active in the emotional and bonding centers of the brain (limbic system). This study seems to indicate that, left to themselves, men will think about sex, their golf swing, or their jump shot, whereas women will think about their spouse, children, or parents.

The deep limbic system, especially the hypothalamus at the base of the brain, is responsible for translating our emotional state into physical feelings of relaxation or tension. The front half of the hypothalamus sends calming signals to the body through the parasympathetic nervous system. The back half of the hypothalamus sends stimulating or fear signals to the body through the sympathetic nervous system. The back half of the hypothalamus, when stimulated, is responsible for the fight-or-flight response, a primitive state that gets us ready to act when we are threatened or scared. This "hard-wired response" happens immediately upon activation, such as seeing or experiencing an emotional or physical threat. In this response the heart beats faster, breathing rate and blood pressure increase, the hands and feet become cooler to shunt blood from the extremities to the large muscles (to fight or run away—the fight-or-flight response), and the pupils dilate to see better.

This "deep limbic" translation of emotion is powerful and immediate. It happens with overt physical threats and also with more covert emotional threats. This part of the brain is intimately connected with the prefrontal cortex and seems to acts as a switching station between running on emotion (the deep limbic system) and rational thought and problem solving with our cortex. When the limbic system is turned on, emotions tend to take over. When it is cooled down, more activation is possible in the cortex. Current research on depression indicates increased deep limbic system activity and shutdown in the prefrontal cortex, especially on the left side.

The temporal lobes and deep limbic system are largely responsible for moving memories into long-term storage, and they help you recognize the people you love, along with those you'd like to forget. The temporal lobes and deep limbic system have been labeled the "interpretative cortex," because through an almond-shaped structure called the amygdala, they help you take in and integrate the current world based on your past experiences. The amygdala receives information from the five senses (sight, hearing, touch, taste, and smell), integrates it with past knowledge, and sends out signals to the body. When the amygdala and deep limbic system fire appropriately, we tend to react to the world in a logical, thoughtful way. When these areas are overactive, we tend to be too reactive to the situations in our lives; when they are underactive, we tend to act inappropriately.

Temporal-lobe and deep limbic problems have been associated with aggression, either directed toward others or turned against the self in suicidal thoughts or actions. One of the most important outcomes of my brain-imaging work has been the discovery of left-temporal-lobe abnormalities to violence, including dark and evil thoughts. Many of our patients were sent to our clinic after committing such acts as murder, arson, spousal abuse, rape, and bombing had left-temporal-lobe abnormalities. I have also seen a correlation with temporal-lobe problems and sensitivity to slights, mild paranoia, reading difficulties, and emotional instability.

The temporal lobes have also been implicated in problems with facial recognition and social skill difficulties. In addition, it is clear that poorly functioning temporal lobes have some relationship to amnesia and dementia. Unexplained headaches or abdominal pain is also common in temporal-lobe abnormalities, as are periods of anxiety or fear for no particular reason. Abnormal sensory perceptions, visual or auditory distortions, feelings of déjà vu (the feeling you have been somewhere before even though you never have) or jamais vu (the feeling you have never been to a familiar place), religious or moral preoccupation, periods of excessive writing, and seizure problems have also been seen with problems in this part of the brain.

Do you know people who see every situation in a bad light? That actually could be a temporal-lobe and deep limbic system problem because, as mentioned, these systems tend to set our emotional filter, and when they are working too hard, the filter is colored with negativity. One person could walk away from an interaction that ten others would have labeled as positive but which he or she considers negative. And since the temporal lobes and deep limbic system affect motivation, people sometimes develop an "I don't care" attitude about life and work; they don't have the energy to care. Because they feel hopeless about the outcome, they have little willpower to follow through with tasks.

Healthy Temporal-Lobe and Limbic Traits

When the temporal lobes and deep limbic system function properly, people tend to be emotionally stable. They are able to clearly process and understand what others say. They can retrieve words for conversations. They tend to accurately read the emotional states of others. They have good control over their tempers. They have access to accurate memories, and because of their memory, they have a sense of personal history and identity. As mentioned, the temporal lobes and deep limbic system have been implicated in spiritual experience. It is possible that positive spiritual experiences are received by healthy temporal lobes. A personal sense of closeness to God may be housed in the temporal lobes. When these systems function properly, people tend to be happy, positive, and able to connect with other people. They tend to filter information in an accurate light, and they are more likely to give others the benefit of a doubt. They are able to be playful, and they tend to draw people toward them with their positive attitude.

POSITIVE TEMPORAL-LOBE AND DEEP LIMBIC SYSTEM TRAITS

- Good memory
- Mood stability
- Word retrieval
- Accurate reading of social situations
- Personality stability
- Control over temper
- Access to spiritual experience
- Positive mood and emotional tone
- Positive internal filter
- Access to positive memories
- Promotes bonding with others

Here are several examples of healthy temporal lobes at work in the lives of everyday people.

HEATHER, BILL, KENT, SANDRA, AND JEFFREY

Heather was the business manager for a large medical clinic. She managed eight doctors and thirty employees. Despite the constant stress inherent in running a medical clinic (I know from personal experience that managing physicians is never an easy task), her mood was even, her temper under control, and she had a very good memory for details.

Bill was the father of a challenging child. His daughter Kerry had been diagnosed with attention deficit disorder, and she tended to be oppositional and conflict seeking. She frequently tried to push his buttons so he would get angry at her. Remembering the past, Bill kept the volume of his voice low and never yelled at her. He had good control over his temper and helped Kerry through firm, consistent discipline.

Kent was adept at reading social situations. He came from a

large contentious family and was often called upon to be the peacemaker when problems occurred between his siblings. He was the best in his family at understanding the turmoil without overreacting, using words to explain what he saw and communicating solutions in a thoughtful way. His even temper allowed him to step back from the turmoil and help others.

Sandra was a deeply religious Christian woman. She prayed every day for forty-five minutes and often felt the presence of God in her daily life. Her prayer time and sensitivity to God allowed her to feel that the Holy Spirit led her day-to-day actions. She sensed when others needed her help, and she was a leader in her church. Others sought her for counseling and felt she had many intuitive insights. Her behavior was consistent, and she was a positive force in her congregation for many years.

Jeffrey was sixteen years old when he was referred to me. He had had sixteen surgeries to repair his face from a severe dog attack when he was four years old. He was referred to me to help him with anxiety about the general anesthesia used for the surgeries. In the last two surgeries the anesthesia had made him sick, and he was starting to feel panicked about an upcoming surgery, his seventeenth. After all, how many people with sixteen surgeries wouldn't be anxious about the seventeenth one. In working with Jeffrey, I found him to be one of the kindest, most loving, and intelligent teenagers I had ever met. Despite having multiple facial scars, he had a girlfriend, he was popular at school, he could laugh at himself, he was diligent, and he cared deeply about his own family. He had reasons to be negative and depressed, but he wasn't. It took us only three hypnotic sessions to calm his anxiety about the surgeries. I saw him several more times, just to try to understand his healthy attitude. From our sessions it was clear he had a close relationship with God. He believed that everything in life, even the dog attack, happened for a reason. He trusted that God would take care of him, in this life and beyond.

• • •

HEALTH professionals often see amazing children like Jeffrey dealing as best they can with chronic medical problems. We also see ill children or teens who become depressed, angry, noncompliant, and negative with only minor medical problems. What is the difference? One difference is how the brain's temporal lobes and limbic system are set. If they are calm, people tend to be positive, happy, and hopeful. When they are overactive, people tend to be sad, negative, and irritable.

UNHEALTHY TEMPORAL-LOBE AND DEEP LIMBIC SYSTEM TRAITS
- Aggression, internally or externally directed
- Dark or violent thoughts
- Sensitivity to slights, mild paranoia
- Word-finding problems
- Reading difficulties
- Emotional instability
- Difficulty reading social cues
- Difficulty recognizing tone of voice
- Memory problems (amnesia)
- Headaches or abdominal pain without a clear explanation
- Anxiety or fear for no particular reason
- Abnormal sensory perceptions, visual or auditory distortions
- Feelings of déjà vu or jamais vu
- Periods of spaciness or confusion
- Religious or moral preoccupation
- Hypergraphia (excessive writing)
- Seizures
- Moodiness, irritability, depression
- Increased negative thinking
- Negative peception of events
- Flood of negative emotions
- Social isolation

Looking at examples similar to the cases above, let's see what happens with an unhealthy temporal lobes and deep limbic system:

BARBARA, DICK, RENEE, JOHN, AND IAN

Barbara was a hospital administrator. The constant stress of her job caused frequent headaches, mood swings, and temper problems both at home and at work. She lasted only a year in her job.

Dick was the father of an ADD child. His son, Joshua, was difficult. Joshua had trouble with his behavior at school, did poorly with other children, and was defiant at home. He constantly pushed his father's buttons. Dick couldn't stand Joshua's behavior, constantly berating him and often striking him in anger. I met Dick and Joshua after they were referred to me by the court system. The teacher had reported the bruises Dick left on Joshua, and child protective services contacted the police to have Dick arrested. Dick's SPECT study showed marked decreased activity in the left temporal lobe and left prefrontal cortex.

DICK's SPECT STUDY

Underside Surface View   *Left Side Surface View*

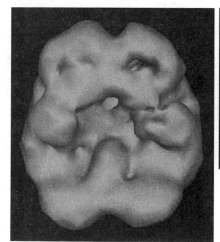
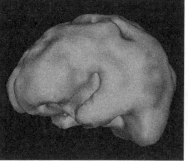

Decreased left-temporal-lobe activity

Decreased left-temporal-lobe and prefrontal cortex activity

Renee, twenty-two, was poor at reading social situations. She frequently misinterpreted her family's actions and often felt as though others were out to hurt her. Her negative attitude caused her to lose jobs and to be unable to live on her own, even though she wanted to very badly. Her parents brought her to see me after several suicide gestures.

John worried about the devil every day. He worried about the devil tempting him, his mother, and his brother. He saw signs in the environment—shadowy figures and images that moved in paintings—that reminded him of the devil. He was so preoccupied with the devil that he went to church every day and could not work consistently. His mother brought him to see me after she heard me lecture. She felt he might have temporal-lobe problems. She was right: He had severe decreased activity in his right temporal lobe.

Ian, age seven, had religious preoccupations, even though his parents were not particularly religious or churchgoing people.

John's SPECT Study

Underside Surface View

Right Side Surface View

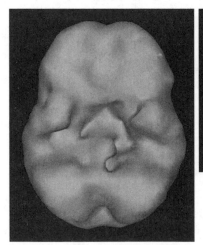

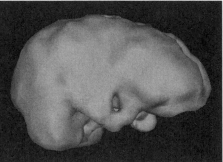

Decreased right-temporal-lobe activity

Decreased right-temporal-lobe activity

He worried about the end of time, going to hell, evil people, and God's wrath. He wondered if he would kill himself (at age seven) and had many suicidal fantasies. When he drew pictures of himself hanging from a tree, his parents brought him to see me.

ON one of the occasions I appeared on Leeza Gibbons's television show, we did a segment on amnesia. Three couples appeared on the show. With one couple, the wife had a "status epilepticus" seizure episode (seizures that don't stop) and remained unconscious for three weeks. When she woke up, she had lost complete memory of sixteen years of her life, including her children's childhood and the time she met and married her husband. When she woke from her coma, she had no idea who the handsome man in the room was. She had a brain scan, which showed serious damage in her left temporal lobe. She wrote a touching book about her experience, *Past Remembering* (Jill Robinson). Of the two other couples on the show, the husband in one couple and the wife in the other had serious brain injuries, with loss of consciousness from car accidents. When both people woke from their comas, they had amnesia for the time that they met and married their current spouses. When I first heard about the program, I thought it must have been staged. In over twenty years of clinical practice I had never seen such a thing. How can you get three couples together who had such an unusually terrible experience? Can you imagine? Waking up in a hospital and not knowing the person you are supposed to go home with? On second thought, I suppose that some couples I know might find it beneficial to forget the hurts of the past and make a new start. As I got to know the couples on the show, I realized their problems were real, not made for television. The whole show was fascinating, but the next day was even more interesting. I taped the show in Hollywood on a Tuesday. On Wednesday I was back in my office in Northern California, sitting at the imaging computer terminal, when one of the doctors in my clinic introduced me to a sixty-two-year-old college professor who had fallen off his roof the prior year. He had been unconscious and developed amnesia about a seven-year period, the time he met and married his wife. What are the odds of that happening? Given that I had just spent the day before with three couples who had the same experience, I could really understand what this couple was going through. He had significant damage to his PFC and the inside part of both of his temporal lobes.

BRAIN INJURY SPECT STUDY

Top Down Surface View   *Underside Surface View*

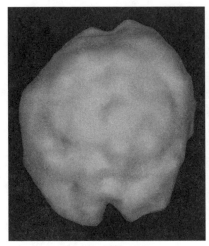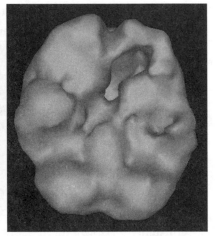

Decreased PFC activity   *Decreased PFC and temporal-lobe activity*

The temporal lobes and deep limbic system are an amazing part of the soul's operating system. In order to have memory, a personal sense of self, emotional stability, and control over anger and rage, these areas need to be healthy. Losing full access to these areas through brain trauma, dementia, or toxic exposure to drugs can seriously impair your ability to be who you really are, color your thoughts and experiences with sadness and negativity, and disrupt the very connections you have in life with others and even with God. Let's take a deeper look at one of the most common causes of temporal-lobe dysfunction, brain trauma.

How Mild Traumatic Brain Injuries Can Disrupt the Brain-Soul Connection

One of the most important lessons I've learned through our brain-imaging work is that brain injuries, even "mild" ones, matter more than most people think, including physicians. Brain SPECT imaging is often able to show areas of damage that are not seen on anatomy studies like CAT scans or MRI studies. We can see contra-coup injuries (opposite parts of the brain damaged by the same injury) and old injuries (even damage from birth or forceps deliveries). Why are brain injuries so important? Some basic brain facts are in order here.

- Your brain is very soft, similar in consistency to soft butter or custard, and so it is easily bruised or damaged.
- Your skull is really hard. Inside your skull there are many ridges, rough areas, and sharp bony edges.
- Your brain is confined in a closed space. When you experience a blow to the head, there is no place for the brain to go, so it ends up slamming against the walls, ridges, and sharp bony edges of the skull, ripping small blood vessels, causing micro-hemorrhaging (bleeding) and small areas of scar tissue to form over time.
- You do not have to lose consciousness in order to have a significant brain injury. Consciousness is controlled by structures deep in the brain stem. There may be a significant injury to the cortex or surface of the brain, sparing the brain stem, and no subsequent loss of consciousness.

A concussion, or "mild traumatic brain injury," is far more than just a "bump on the head." According to the American

Academy of Neurology, "There is no such thing as a minor concussion." A study from UCLA Medical Center, published in the May 2000 issue of *Neurotrauma,* revealed that researchers found the "level of glucose use in people who suffered mild concussions was similar to that in comatose, severely brain-injured patients . . . Even mild head injuries result in major changes to the brain's metabolism and could make victims susceptible to more serious damage from a repeated blow." According to lead researcher Dr. Marvin Bergsneider, "It fits with what clinicians see. We know that just because people are walkie-talkies—because they can walk and talk—that that's not the full story . . . Many people blow that [concussions] off as being innocuous. What this study indicates is that clearly concussions can be serious."

Concussions occur when the head either accelerates rapidly and then is stopped or is spun rapidly. The violent shaking causes the brain cells to undergo metabolic changes. The damaged brain cells fire all their neurotransmitters at once in an unhealthy cascade, flooding the brain with chemicals, deadening certain receptors linked to learning and memory, and disrupting the cells' ability to transmit signals. Although often there are no immediate symptoms and nothing irregular shows up on the CAT scan or the MRI, subtle changes occur. Over a period of a few weeks or even months, the individual may become tearful, angry, irritable, have trouble thinking clearly or concentrating, or suffer from headaches, confusion, blurred vision, memory loss, nausea, and sometimes unconsciousness. Other devastating symptoms can occur as if in slow motion. There may be personality changes, temper problems, dark thoughts, or difficulty expressing emotions or understanding others.

There are a number of brain areas especially vulnerable to injury. These include:

- The temporal lobes, which house memory, receptive language, temper control, and mood stability

- The limbic system, which can cause problems with depression, negativity, and libido
- The PFC, where judgment, concentration, attention span, impulse control, organization, planning, and expressive language are centered
- The anterior cingulate gyrus, the brain's "gear shifter," where damage causes people to get stuck on negative thoughts or behaviors
- The parietal lobes, at the top back part of the brain, which coordinate and interpret sensory information from the opposite side of the body. They also handle directions, construction, and advanced mathematics.
- The occipital lobes, which can cause problems with visual processing

Brain injuries can interrupt, delay, or alter social and intellectual development. In both children and adults, traumatic brain injuries can cause physical difficulties such as severe headaches, dizziness, fatigue, and diminished motor skills. They can also create mental difficulties such as memory loss, difficulty in concentrating, depression, hypersensitivity to noise, and photophobia (hypersensitivity to light). Often the most difficult problem for families to handle is the emotional and social difficulties that may arise after a concussion, such as increased incidence of psychiatric problems. Psychiatric problems are common after traumatic brain injury, even when the injury is relatively mild. A high percentage of those suffering even a mild concussion experience depression within the first two years. In addition, there is an increased incidence of substance abuse, marital problems, job-related problems, and incarceration and other legal problems.

A number of years ago I wrote a newspaper article on brain injuries. The day the article appeared in the paper, I received a call from a distraught mother. Four years earlier her sixteen-year-old son had sustained a brain injury from a bicycle accident. The front tire of his bicycle hit a curb, and he flipped over the handlebars onto the left side of his face. He was unconscious for about thirty minutes. Over the next several months his personality changed. He went from being a straight-A student and a sweet young man to someone who had no interest in school and was easily angered and depressed. He also started drinking alcohol on a regular basis. Three years later he shot and killed himself. The mother blamed herself for his downward spiral. No one told her that a minor brain injury could ruin her son's life. My article helped her understand the terrible tragedy. Likely he injured the left temporal lobe.

Here are two other examples of brain injury–induced character problems.

DANNY

Danny, age eleven, was a loving child who was doing well in fifth grade and got along well with other children. Over Easter break he was involved in an automobile accident while riding with his mother to a family gathering. Danny had been wearing a seat belt, but the left side of his head slammed against the rear side window. He was unconscious for several minutes. Over about twelve weeks, Danny's behavior began to change. He became negative, irritable, temperamental, and oppositional. He blurted out in class, and he had trouble paying attention in school. Homework was hard, where before it had been very easy. Over the next year he lost friends and started to feel alone and isolated. He would impulsively say things that hurt their feelings. A year after the accident, Danny's mother knew something was wrong. She brought him to a therapist who thought the problem was psychological, a result of the accident. The therapist thought that Danny suffered from post-traumatic stress disorder, but the counseling didn't help. His pediatrician thought he was just being difficult and recommended firmer discipline, which didn't help. Reluctantly the pediatrician diagnosed Danny with ADD and tried Ritalin. It didn't help. In fact, it seemed to make him moody and more aggressive. By the age of fifteen, when he came to our clinic for evaluation, Danny was failing in school and had many behavioral problems at home. I felt that he may have had a chronic postconcussive syndrome, secondary to the accident. His brain SPECT study revealed marked decreased activity in the prefrontal cortex and temporal lobes. I placed him on a small dose of Neurontin, an anticonvulsant, to stabilize his temporal lobes and Adderall to help him focus. The medication evened out his mood, and he did better in school. He was able to rebuild friendships.

DANNY'S SPECT STUDY
Decreased PFC and temporal-lobe activity

Underside Surface View   *Left Side Surface View*

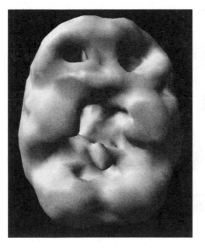 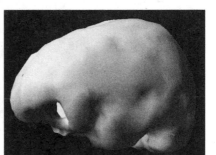

STEVEN
I have seen a number of roofers through the years. As you can imagine, brain injuries are a common occupational hazard for

this group. Steven, thirty-eight, was brought to see me by his wife, who was on the verge of divorcing him. He had sustained a serious brain injury three years prior to our first appointment, falling twenty-five feet from a roof onto the left side of his head, and was knocked unconscious for about twelve hours. From a loving, conscientious husband and father Steven turned into an irresponsible, uncaring, and temperamental individual. He had struck his wife twice during arguments. His wife wanted to leave him, but she felt badly about abandoning someone who was damaged. He refused help until she threatened to leave him. His SPECT study showed serious damage to his left temporal lobe and left parietal lobe. On an anticonvulsant, his mood and temper were much better.

STEVEN's SPECT STUDY

Underside Surface View

Left Side Surface View

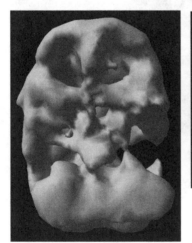

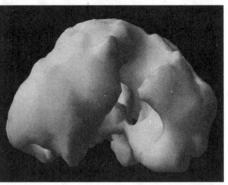

Marked decreased left-temporal- and parietal-lobe activity

Marked decreased PFC
and temporal-lobe activity

After seeing these scans, I would not let my children hit soccer balls with their heads, play tackle football, or snowboard without a helmet. I encourage my own kids to play tennis, golf, Ping-Pong, and track. Your brain matters. Protect it.

•   •   •

IN the last three chapters we have explored the function and problems of the five brain systems most intimately involved with the brain-soul connection. These chapters lay the foundation for the book and help us understand ourselves and others through the lens of new brain science and, as you will see, set the stage to develop strategies in Part 2 to optimize the hardware of the soul.

Six

The Good, Bad, and Emotionally Ugly

Brain and Personality Development

Our character is who we are in the world over time. It is our nature. It is how we are day to day. It represents a consistent set of thoughts, feelings, and actions. When we do something in character, it is consistent with our past behaviors. When we do something that is out of character, it is significantly different from how we acted in the past. A healthy character has enduring traits that allow us to move our lives forward in a productive way; an unhealthy character consists of long-standing qualities that are self-destructive and interfere with our progress and effectiveness as human beings.

Character and morality are intertwined. Morality or moral behavior is tied to social mores regarding what is right, fair, and good versus what is wrong, unfair, or evil. It is the judgment we as individuals and society in general place on specific behaviors. A moral person is thought to be someone who does the right thing, acts fairly, and avoids doing harm without necessary reason (such as in war). An amoral person is someone who doesn't care if he does the right thing, can be unfair in an interaction without it bothering him, and can hurt others for his own gain.

A healthy sense of morality drives us to follow rules of good conduct, to do what is right, and to care about others and ourselves. A weak or badly formed sense of morality reveals someone who is selfish, self-centered, and erratic in his approach to what's right and what's wrong. Character and moral development are lifelong processes. They develop slowly over time and lead to our individual growth and maturity. Healthy character and moral development are highly dependent on healthy brain development and function.

How you become the person you are is determined by several interdependent factors, including brain function, modeling behavior after others, past and current stresses, and memories. You need a healthy brain to be your best, and at the same time, your thoughts, feelings, and interactions can enhance or hurt brain function. Nowhere is this more true than in character and moral development. Without healthy brain function we cannot do the things that are most human, such as make plans, control our instincts, and give and receive love. Yet, even with a healthy brain, we must have positive role models to train our neurons in love, fairness, and doing the right thing. We must also be free from intense painful stress, which negatively affects the brain, and we must have accessible memories of positive, loving experiences.

A Healthy Brain: The Foundation of Good Moral Character

Who we are, in large part, is shaped by brain function. A healthy brain allows us to act in consistently positive ways. Having a healthy brain allows us to learn by appropriate modeling from our parents, siblings, and teachers; it allows us to learn from the mistakes we make in life so that we do not have to repeat them over and over; and it allows us to notice the behaviors that makes us happy and those that don't. So it follows that an action or behavior that interferes with brain function can also interfere with character. Damage to the brain from infection, trauma, malnutrition, or exposure to toxins such as alcohol or drugs can damage our character. In a number of recent studies poor brain function has been associated with amoral behavior. From the laboratory of neuroscientist Antonio Damasio came a study of two men who had damage to their prefrontal cortices. They had serious problems conforming their behavior to social mores and ended up as isolated and ineffectual individuals. Psychologist Adrian Raines found that people who chronically broke societal rules also had poor activity in the prefrontal cortex.

The Prefrontal Cortex (PFC): The Moral Center

The prefrontal cortex (PFC), the most developed part of the brain, plays a leading role in character and moral development. It allows us see beyond ourselves and enables us to empathize with others. It allows us to anticipate the future so that we can appreciate the consequences of our actions and be socially responsible. The health of the prefrontal cortex heavily influences thoughtfulness and impulse control. A healthy PFC helps you think about what you say and do before you say or do it. For example, you may have a negative thought about your child, but you stop yourself from expressing it immediately because you know it might hurt the situation. If, on the other hand, you had problems with your PFC such as poor impulse control, you may not be able to keep yourself from blurting out your opinion before you had a chance to think about its effect. The PFC is also part of the brain that helps you learn from mistakes and correct behavior that doesn't work for you. Good PFC function prevents you from having to repeat the expression "Why do I always do that?" over and over again.

Being able to keep your head in tense emotional situations prevents you from getting into disputes and reacting too quickly to insults. Here again, the PFC plays a role. The PFC translates feelings from the deep limbic system, or the emotional brain. Good PFC function makes for tempered reactions and thoughtful judgments, allowing the use of tact and forethought in heated moments.

The PFC is not fully formed until we are in our early to mid-twenties. This may be one of the most important reasons that parents and teenagers struggle with each other. As children grow, parents expect more and more from them, yet most teens do not have adult brain capacity until they are in their twenties. Many teens may, in fact, be "acting their age" when they are struggling to do the right thing. Teenage brains are very vulnerable to toxic exposure, and the developing teen brain can become derailed by substance abuse. A teen in the midst of normal development can too easily become stuck in an immature mode of operation if he or she is exposed to toxic substances that impede brain growth. An eighteen-year-old who has been drinking regularly since the age of fourteen typically acts as if he is fourteen or fifteen. A twenty-two-year-old who has been smoking marijuana regularly since age sixteen is likely to be acting as if she is sixteen or seventeen.

Attention deficit disorder (ADD), an inherited brain disorder, occurs as a result of neurological dysfunction in the prefrontal cortex. People with ADD often have poor impulse control and long-standing difficulty paying attention to the routine tasks of life, such as homework, chores, organizing paperwork, planning, and managing time. They tend to be restless and easily distracted, and must struggle to learn new things unless they are very interested in the topic. Because of the learning struggles and impulsivity, it's harder for people with ADD to develop the consistent, thoughtful tendencies that make for a healthy character. People with ADD tend to be about three to five years behind in emotional development. For instance, a young man of sixteen with ADD who wants to get his driver's license may have to delay driving because he may in fact have the emotional maturity of a boy of thirteen and as yet be unable to make prudent decisions about safety and responsibility.

Due to poor activity in the PFC, people with ADD tend to unconsciously seek conflict or look for problems where none exist as a way to stimulate activity in this part of the brain. They don't know that they do it, and they deny it, but they do it just the same. Using anger, emotional turmoil, and negative emotion for self-stimulation can get people into trouble, damage relationships, and hurt the immune system. The high levels of adrenaline produced by conflict-driven behavior decrease the immune system's effectiveness and increase the body's vulnerability to illness.

The good news is that ADD can be treated. When the right medication is prescribed to address problems in the prefrontal cortex, people with ADD can become more thoughtful and empathic, and can develop better planning skills. This is why early treatment of ADD is crucial to moral and character development.

Prefrontal cortex problems may also be associated with conduct disorder. As its name implies, children with conduct disorder have long-standing difficulties following rules. They may have a pattern of aggressive behavior, bullying, fighting, destroying property, lying, and stealing. New York child psychiatrist Rachel Klein conducted a study in which she compared children with ADD to a group of children with conduct disorder who did not have ADD. When she put the children with ADD on medication, they improved. There are innumerable studies that show medication works for ADD, but it's interesting to note that when she put the children with conduct disorder on the same medication, they also improved. It may be that the children with conduct disorder who received medication had more access to their frontal lobes and therefore more availability of the forethought necessary to make decisions about their actions.

Left Versus Right

The left and right hemispheres of the brain often have a different perspective on life, especially in the prefrontal cortex. In many studies, healthy activity in the left prefrontal cortex has been associated with a positive outlook, found in people who approach life with happiness and zest. Decreased activity in this part of the brain due to illness or damage has been associated with depression, pessimism, anger, and irritability. Increased activity in the right prefrontal cortex has been seen in people who tend to be pessimistic, negative, and withdrawn, whereas decreased right prefrontal cortex activity has been associated with people who tend to joke a lot, deny any problems that might be present, and feel inappropriately positive in negative situations. Clearly, balance is needed for health.

NANCY

Nancy, a forty-year-old homemaker and mother of three, came to see me with her husband. They were on the verge of divorce. Nancy said that she had big problems with anger and impulse control. Her husband said she was the most negative person he had ever met. He said that she complained incessantly, was often angry and aggressive with the children, and would cry for little or no reason. Nothing seemed to make her happy. In her history I discovered a bad diving accident when she was twenty years old. In Corona del Mar, a quaint beach town an hour south of Los Angeles, she had been diving with college friends off a thirty-foot rock formation just off shore. That day the tide was out and the water was shallower than she was used to. Diving headfirst into the shallow water, she hit her head on the rocky ocean floor and knocked herself unconscious for several hours. Her friends saved her life, but she was never the same after the incident. She dropped out of college a semester later and noted increased irritability and decreased ability to think. She had been dating her husband-to-be at the time, and even though he noticed the change, he still wanted to be with her.

Nancy's SPECT study showed severe damage to the left prefrontal cortex, decreased left-temporal-lobe activity, and increased deep limbic activity. The prefrontal- and temporal-lobe problems were likely a direct result of the brain injury. The deep limbic hyperactivity likely occurred because the prefrontal cortex, which has many inhibitory fibers directed at the deep limbic areas, was no longer able to suppress it. Through a combination of medication and biofeedback we were able to enhance activity in the PFC and temporal lobes and calm the limbic hyperactivity. Nancy became more positive and better able to be a positive participant in her marriage and with her children.

NANCY'S SPECT STUDY

Top Down Surface View

Left Side Surface View

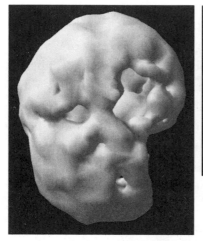
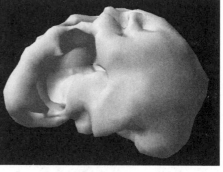

Underside Surface View

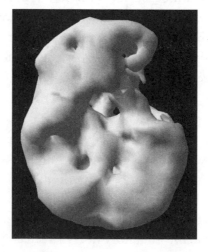

Note marked decreased left PFC, parietal lobe, and temporal lobe activity.

The SPECT pictures were very helpful for Nancy and her husband. She could see the damage in her brain and was more highly motivated to get help, rather than just seeing me under the threat of divorce. Her husband, who had been chronically angry at her for being such a negative influence on the children and him, developed more empathy for her and became much more supportive.

Integrating the Past and Present: Memories Make Us Who We Are

The temporal lobes and deep limbic system, which process and help store memories, are also involved in character development. The sum of our memories and experiences is responsible for our sense of identity and connectedness to those around us, as well as our character. The temporal cortex is heavily involved with storing and retrieving long-term memories, allowing us to integrate present sensory information with past knowledge. How we interpret and react to present-day events and how well we learn from our mistakes depend greatly on what we recall from the past. For example, if you become involved in a negative romantic relationship, your memory helps you to remember the unpleasant experiences and change for the better the next time around. But if you have a poor memory of previous experiences and events, you are more likely to repeat mistakes. If you have a bad experience at a particular church, it is only natural that you would attend another church, where you would be more sensitive to slights—you take the past hurts with you. If you fall into a disagreement with a parishioner at the new church, you may overreact and move on to yet another church with increased defensiveness, likely repeating the same series of events.

Emotional stability is heavily influenced by the dominant temporal lobe, usually the left side for right-handed people. The ability to consistently feel stable and positive, despite everyday ups and downs, is important for the development of character. Some would say consistency is the hallmark of good character. Decreased activity in this part of the brain leads to fluctuating, inconsistent, or unpredictable moods and behaviors. We must be able to control our conduct before we can exercise free will and make real choices about what we want to do. Problems in the temporal lobes have been associated with aggression, suicidal feelings, and violent and evil thoughts. A person with temporal-lobe problems may be frightened by his thoughts, yet be unable to control them. Temporal-lobe problems may also cause sensitivity to slights or criticism, and mild paranoia, which can ruin relationships with others.

The deep limbic system is responsible for our emotional tone, for filtering the way we see events, and for coloring our perceptions of the world. Bonding may be difficult for people with problems in the deep limbic system. Our memories can "set" the way in which we look at present-day events. Someone who has experienced a number of traumas or losses, who has suffered abuse in childhood or mourned the early death of a parent, may appear to have overall negative outlook on life, whereas someone with more positive life experiences is likely to feel more optimistic. A persistent negative or gloomy outlook, which often develops in someone with depression, can drive others away. A person immersed in negativity may be less able to share in others' concerns, increasing isolation and thus loosening the social connections necessary to feeling good about oneself and helping others.

Seeing the Other Side: Problems with the Anterior Cingulate Gyrus

An overactive anterior cingulate gyrus can cause problems with rigidity and inflexibility, or not being able to "go with the flow." People who suffer from an overactive anterior cingulate gyrus may become very upset when things are not done exactly as they wish or when plans are not followed precisely as defined. It is difficult for people with this problem to see things from another person's point of view or to welcome others' input and assistance. Along with the prefrontal cortex, the anterior cingulate system also aids us in being able to see options. When we are unable to see options, we have a hard time choosing the most logical, thoughtful response to situations. Getting stuck in an idea, a belief, or a plan, and having no sense of options, can lead to hostility and lack of cooperation in relationships, families, businesses, religious groups, even among nations.

Flexibility and cooperation are vital to being able to empathize with others. Empathy is the foundation for a developed moral character. Without it, we can't feel how others respond to our actions, or we may not care. With it, we are able to sense vicariously what others feel when we connect with them and in so doing build lasting emotional bonds.

What Is Empathy, and How Does It Develop?

Empathy is our ability to sense what others feel. Just as we know from experience that a slap on the hand can hurt someone physically, experience also teaches us that a cruel remark can hurt someone emotionally. We don't unnecessarily slap people or make cruel jokes at others' expense because we *feel* for other people. We want to treat people kindly just as we wish to be treated. It's this sense of connection—to ourselves, to other people, to our communities, and to humanity—that makes us want to do right and allows us to be successful in the world. We're happier when we are connected; we are able to our pursue goals more freely. Think about the people who do well at work. They're not just the people who do their jobs well; they are the people who are able to form bonds and stay connected. They recognize the contributions others make to their achievements and acknowledge them, making them great business partners, co-workers, and employers. In his wonderful book *Love and Survival,* Dean Ornish suggests that people who have more satisfying connections are also likely to be physically healthier and to live longer.

As we are learning, the health of our prefrontal cortex and anterior cingulate gyrus is especially important to the development of a sense of empathy. When your anterior cingulate system works too hard, you can see only your own thoughts. It's as if your brain is in a tunnel with no windows or doors and you can see only your position in life. Because you are narrowly focused on getting what you want, you may appear selfish. But when your anterior cingulate gyrus is calmed down, you are better able to see things from a perspective outside your own and to respond to others' input and suggestions.

Similarly, the prefrontal cortex allows you to see beyond your own wants and needs and to appreciate others' feelings. Geoff was a brilliant doctor before he was involved in a skiing accident in which he hit a tree with his head and was unconscious for several days. His SPECT study revealed serious damage to his prefrontal cortex. After the accident he still had his medical knowledge, but he seemed to his family, friends, and colleagues like a different person. He was temperamental with patients and alienated his friends with his erratic and irritable behavior. After he was fired from a teaching job, one of his assistants helped him move. She stored some of his belongings in her own home and took things to the city dump for him that he said he no longer wanted. A month after he left, he complained that she stole some of his records and filed court papers against her. In her mind she was helping someone in pain and couldn't believe that he would sue her because he had lost his records. She knew he was struggling, had empathy for him, and tried to help, but in the end felt betrayed by him. She felt as though she never wanted to help anyone again. She wrote to me after reading my book *Change Your Brain, Change Your Life,* saying she had greater empathy for the man, but she was haunted by those burdensome memories and wasn't sure she'd want to help others.

Why Do Some People Appear to Have More Empathy than Others?

It may be that some people, like Mother Teresa or Nelson Mandela, have an amazing capacity for compassion and empathy because they have healthier prefrontal cortices than others, along with positive life programming to make a difference. Our life experiences directly affect our brain's health, our sense of caring, and in turn our moral development. Simply put, how we are treated and how we experience others being treated affects our ability to relate to other people. Let's say your father was a minister. He was a warm and caring pastor who sacrificed to give to others. He spent his free time working on projects that fed the hungry. He was on the board of numerous nonprofit organizations that tirelessly labored for social justice. But he never spent any time with you. Deprived of emotional connection with the father who gave so much to others may have left you with less empathy than others. On the other hand, suppose your father was a caring minister who took you on his rounds to visit the sick, who spent time talking with you about your concerns, and took you out to throw a baseball or get an ice-cream cone every once in a while. By example and by interaction, you became a more caring person.

The people close to you influence your outlook, your values, how you spend your time, and how you treat other people. In other words, who you hang out with matters. If you are consistently in the company of someone who gossips, for example, it's likely you'll gossip. If you live with someone who is depressed, in my experience you are likely to become depressed. Spending time with positive, uplifting people will make you feel positive and hopeful. If you want to improve your attitude and conduct, spend time with someone whose conduct and values you admire. Emulate his or her behavior, and you will likely find it rubs off! You'll notice yourself avoiding actions and statements that might cause disapproval in the person you admire. By the same token, you find yourself naturally guided toward better, more life-affirming, behavior.

How to Make Your Child a Republican or a Democrat

Do you want your child to share your values? Talk to him. If you're a Republican and you want your children to be Republican, spend time with them, listen to them, speak nicely to them, and show them compassion. Children adopt the values of parents with whom they have a strong bond. If you're a Republican and you want your children to become Democrats, neglect them, don't talk to them, and criticize them constantly. Be indifferent or angry with them and they will take a position opposite yours. Children become bonded to us when we spend time with them every day. They are more likely to choose our values when we have a good relationship with them, and they are more likely to choose the opposite values if we have a bad or distant relationship with them. You cannot have a good relationship with your child if you don't spend time with him or her. One study reported that "on average parents spend less than seven minutes a week talking with their children." That's pretty frightening when you consider how much time children spend watching TV. Think about the competition. Television screens flash at a concentration frequency of about thirty cycles per second, drawing and commanding your attention. When the number of hours of exposure is great, your brain is repeatedly receiving messages from that medium, and they become hard-wired into your brain. You are conditioned to accept what you see, including negative images of violence or unrealistic images of beauty. What you tell your kids may be one thing, but what they see may be another.

In a study published in the *Journal of the American Medical Association* in 1997, Michael Resnick, Ph.D., and colleagues at the University of Minnesota reported that teenagers who felt loved and connected to their parents had a significantly lower incidence of teenage pregnancy, drug use, violence, and suicide.

Firm parenting is as critical to character development as bonding. The brain needs direction, boundaries, consequences for unacceptable actions, and positive reinforcement. The brain learns best in an environment of love, support, and clear direction. Studies on effective parenting all point in the same direction. The parents who raise the healthiest children are those who are firm and kind. Permissiveness is bad for children. Parents who are permissive and unable or unwilling to be firm in disciplining raise children who have social and academic problems. Parents need to set clear guidelines of acceptable behavior and reinforce those guidelines through positive reinforcement and consequences.

For instance, one night while in a restaurant I watched how parents can actually encourage dysfunction in their child's brain. A three-year-old boy was running around the restaurant. He was loud, obnoxious, defiant, and hyperactive. The mother was very frustrated and repeatedly redirected her son. The father just let him run wild. Whenever the mother tried to discipline her son, the father told her to lay off him. "Boys will be boys," he said. The boy, and his parents, got many evil looks from others at the restaurant that night. Children (and their brains) need a firm hand. They need direction and consequences. Parents need to provide prefrontal cortex supervision for them until they can provide it for themselves. When you tell a child to do something, he needs to know that you mean it and that you'll back it up. He needs a bit of anxiety in order to stimulate growth in his prefrontal cortex. Not too much anxiety or it will disrupt his development, but enough anxiety to know that you are serious and that you mean what you say.

When We Struggle with Character Problems

Our character can be defined in part by the way we interact with others. When the way in which we interact with others doesn't work, when we notice a pattern of multiple relationships and multiple disconnections, a personality disorder may at the root of the problem. The term "personality disorder" implies inflexible and long-standing patterns of experience and behavior that impair healthy functioning. They can be the source of great personal pain for the suffering person. A personality disorder can sabotage relationships, prevent the realization of desired goals, and impede our moral development and spiritual health. When we are preoccupied, for example, with intrusive thoughts, deep fears of abandonment, or feelings of paranoia or superiority, it's hard to reach beyond the self to the expansive concerns of spirit and morality. It's hard to be our best selves. A person with a personality disorder may feel inexplicably isolated from a sense of well-being, of closeness to others and to God. It may be hard for someone with a personality disorder to feel empathy and thus to feel part of a reciprocally loving community. Feelings of isolation and disconnectedness can lead to a sense of life being meaningless and to devaluation of one's own individual contributions. This sense of aloneness and lack of purpose can place people with personality disorders at higher risk for suicide. Personality is what we present to the outside world. It is not the true self, which is broader and deeper than the outward appearance of self. When we think of working on aspects of the personality, we think not of correcting flaws but of opening doors to greater joy and connectedness.

Traditionally, personality disorders have been resistant to psychotherapy. Traditional psychiatric thought has focused on the developmental causes of these disorders rather than brain abnormalities. It has been my experience that many people labeled as personality disordered are really brain disordered. The implications for treatment are immense—do we talk someone through their difficult behaviors or try to change their brain? Probably we do both.

Personality Disorders Interfere with Character

ANTISOCIAL PERSONALITY DISORDER

Antisocial personality disorder is characterized by a long-standing pattern of disregard for the rights of others and may be an extension of conduct disorder seen in adolescence. The likelihood of developing antisocial personality disorder seems to have increased in young children with conduct disorder and ADD. People with antisocial personality disorder frequently break rules, fight, and develop relationship and work problems. With little or no empathy, they may steal, destroy property, and manipulate or deceive others for their own ends, and thus they are overrepresented in our nation's prisons. They tend to be impulsive and lacking in forethought. Traditionally, these people are thought of as evil, bad, and sinful, but the work of psychologist Adrienne Raine of the University of Southern California has seriously challenged this notion. Dr. Raine found that, compared to a group of healthy men, the MRI scans of the men with antisocial personality disorder showed decreased brain cell density in the PFC. They are likely dealing with less access to the brain part that controls conscience, free will, right and wrong, and good and evil. A fascinating additional finding of Dr. Raine's work showed that people with antisocial personality disorder also had slower heart rates and lower sweat gland activity than the control group. Lower heart rates and sweat gland activity are often associated with low anxiety states (just picture how your hands sweat and your heart races when you are anxious). Could this mean that people with this type of difficult temperament do not have enough internal anxiety? Could the PFC be involved with appropriate anxiety? Intriguing questions. For example, most people feel anxious before they do something bad or risky. If I needed money, and got the thought in my head to rob the local grocery store, my next thoughts would be filled with anxiety:

"I don't want to get caught."
"I don't want to be thought of as a criminal."
"I could lose my medical license."

The anxiety would prevent me from acting out on the bad thoughts. But what if, as Dr. Raine's study suggests, I do not have enough anxiety and I get an evil thought in my head like "Go rob the store." With poor PFC activity (a poor internal supervisor, or conscience, with little to no anxiety), I am more likely to rob the store without considering all of the consequences to my behavior. There is an interesting treatment implication to be learned from this work. Typically, psychiatrists try to help lessen a person's anxiety, but maybe we have it backward. Perhaps people with antisocial personality disorder should be treated to increase their anxiety. And maybe that's what spiritual leaders had in mind when they talk about hellfire and damnation. There are a certain percentage of us who need to be scared into behaving right, who need more anxiety, who need to know that hell exists.

NARCISSISTIC PERSONALITY DISORDER

People with narcissistic personality disorder (NPD) believe that they are special and more unique or gifted than other people. They require constant admiration and recognition for their achievements. A sense of entitlement derived from a bolstered sense of superiority may lead people with narcissistic personality disorder to place great demands on others, expecting their needs to be met immediately, regardless of the inconvenience. Although they may appear confident, they may in fact have very low self-esteem, which they attempt to boost by association with others they imagine being as gifted as they. They may seek connections exclusively with those whom they perceive to be special and form alliances solely to advance their careers or other endeavors. Although lacking empathy and the ability to listen patiently to others' concerns, a person with narcissistic personality disorder may spend an inordinate amount of time thinking about what others think of her or him. People with narcissistic personality disorder may belittle or envy others' achievements and be unwilling to acknowledge contributions others make to their own successes. A person with narcissistic personality disorder may appear rude, condescending, and arrogant, criticizing others while being unable to tolerate criticism himself or herself. A person with NPD often seesaws between a depressed mood, because of feelings of shame or humiliation, and grandiosity. As with other personality disorders, a person with narcissistic personality disorder may suffer from additional problems such as anorexia, substance abuse, anxiety, and depression. People with narcissistic personality disorders may have overactive cingulate systems that prevent them from seeing outside themselves and taking a broader perspective. Poor prefrontal-lobe activity may cause the lack of empathy so pronounced in this disorder.

A feeling of social connectedness is the basis of a healthy soul and character. Clinging to the notion that you might be better than others, somehow more privileged or entitled, erects barriers between you and the people to whom you want to get close and makes it impossible to empathize with others' needs. Protecting yourself with such distancing tactics as criticism, disinterest in others' problems, belittling others, or refusing to acknowledge their accomplishments makes it tough to develop a sense of security and companionship, of being loved. It's very hard to make moral decisions from this place, from the position of "What I need is most important." Persistent focus on yourself, your appearance, how others see you, and the neediness that accompanies these anxiety-provoking concerns takes you away from your true self, the self that can focus on what you really care about and what you want your life to be about. Because people with narcissistic personality disorder may sometimes accomplish external goals, it can be hard to discern the reasons for a lack of connectedness and a hollow spiritual life. Identifying with others, being able to be humble, grateful, and kind, to listen, and to truly appreciate others' caring and contributions to your life readies you to receive spiritual learning.

BORDERLINE PERSONALITY DISORDER

Instability in relationships, impulsivity, and low self-esteem characterizes borderline personality disorder. People with borderline personality disorder may switch attitudes toward others, identifications, values, and goals quickly. For example, someone with borderline personality disorder may worship a new friend or lover and then drop him or her quickly, complaining that the new friend wasn't caring enough. Professional goals and interests, as well as mood, may change suddenly. Highly reactive and impulsive, such people may experience periods of extreme irritability, anger, or anxiety. They may engage in self-destructive behaviors such as drinking heavily, driving fast, overspending, bingeing on food, or having unsafe sex. People with borderline personality disorder may feel periods of great emptiness and engage in suicidal or self-mutilating behaviors. Boredom may be intolerable to someone with this disorder, and consequently he or she may perpetually seek stimulation. Childhood abuse or neglect or the early loss of a parent may be found in family histories of people with this disorder.

The biological underpinnings of borderline personality disorder are complex. People with borderline personalities may have a combination of prefrontal-lobe problems, which accounts for impulsivity, conflict- and stimulation-seeking behaviors, and the tendency to intensely value or devalue individuals. Anterior cingulate problems may also exist, evidenced by obsessive thinking, cognitive inflexibility, and a very strong tendency to hold on to grudges and past hurts. There may also be temporal-lobe abnormalities. The left temporal lobe is involved with aggressive behaviors toward the self and others.

Consistency and control over impulsivity are necessary to developing and sticking to character goals. When you are controlled by your emotions, constantly reacting to outside events in the heat of the moment, you cannot develop an overall sense of who you are, what you want, and how you will get what you want. Contemplation is important to developing a sense of right and wrong, what is good and bad for you and for others. Likewise, being enslaved by impulses and reactions denies you the opportunity to build a strong sense of self-esteem. When you can control what you do, you feel greater certainty about your identity. It's rewarding to be able to clarify your personal values and to stick to them, to know that you and you alone are in charge of your life.

It's hard to build a sense of security and of being loved when you find yourself attaching unrealistic expectations to people to whom you're attracted and then ending friendships before they've had a chance to develop. Social connectedness takes work: It implies forgiving and flexibility. It's important for all of us to try to develop greater empathy for others by asking ourselves about another's point of view and not automatically assuming we know what others feel and think.

Practical Applications

One of the most exciting aspects of the research into the connection between the brain, soul, and spiritual health is the revision we can begin to make in our understanding of character traits once considered to be moral or psychological flaws. In my experience, most people want to be good, to be loved, and to feel a sense of connection in the world. We are beginning to understand that some of the behaviors that prevent us from being our best selves may have underlying biological causes. Knowing the root causes of negative behavior doesn't excuse bad behavior or diminish the need for moral and spiritual teachings. Rather, it allows us to better understand difficult behaviors and develop more tools to aid people who are suffering, who choose help.

To optimize character and moral development, we must optimize brain function. In addition, clearly stated moral teachings act as a guide for the nervous system to know right and wrong. Some people with lower prefrontal cortex activity need anxiety (consequences such as the idea of hellfire and damnation) in order to follow the straight and narrow, and all of us need connectedness with others in order to learn. In summary, a healthy brain is essential to healthy morality and character development (hardware), along with proper guidance and modeling (software).

Seven

In God's House

Brain Health and the Sunday Sermon

DOES talking about the brain belong in church? Can we discuss the brain in the quiet of the temple? Should ministers, priests, rabbis, and other religious leaders learn about the brain? Is it sacrilegious to point to brain abnormalities as part of the reason people struggle with difficult behavior? I have been asked these questions many times by my deeply religious friends and colleagues. When some of them heard the title of this book, they warned me that I would be making enemies by talking about religious issues and brain science in the same book. I was encouraged to stick to safer topics. However, the connection between God and humanity, good and evil, and the brain is very easy for me. After all, I am a brain scientist, with a B.A. in biology from a Bible college. What could be more natural? What is unnatural to me is ignoring people with brain problems, even when they occur at church.

Does Talking About the Brain Belong in Church?

Houses of worship are very important people places. We go to our churches, synagogues, mosques, or temples to worship, pray, learn, and find fellowship. The organ that allows us to do all of those things is the brain. When the brain works right, we can participate in our religious and spiritual communities; when the brain doesn't work right, it is very hard to maintain a positive presence in the sanctuary.

Through the years one of my clinics' largest referral sources has been churches and religious leaders. I have many relationships with forward-thinking pastors, priests, and rabbis who understand the brain-soul connection and send us children, adults, couples, families, and ministers struggling with behavioral or emotional problems. I have frequently spoken at churches about the brain's connection to our daily lives and how behavior becomes problematic when the brain's functioning goes awry. Understanding this connection is important to obtaining proper treatment, as well as to a deeper understanding and forgiveness. If we are all sinners (very true in my experience of others and myself), and sin, as we have seen, can be related to brain problems, then forgiveness and treatment may go hand in hand.

Over the last seven years Dr. Earl Henslin, a well-known Christian psychologist and author, has sent scores of patients to my clinics. He says that healing the brain is an important first step in helping people heal their relationship with God. When a person can understand his or her problem through the lens of brain science, and see it on a SPECT scan, healing begins. This knowledge brings understanding, which is a catalyst for forgiveness and openness to change. Completing the circle, openness and forgiveness bring God back into a person's life anew. Earl once told me about Dave, a married forty-year-old father of three children and pastor of a small church. Dave struggled with depression, anxiety, and sexual addiction to pornographic material. He had problems getting along with the church's board and was on the verge of divorce when he came to see Dr. Henslin. He didn't want to lose his family or his position in the church, but his behavior and feelings were out of control. After Earl evaluated him, he told Dave that he thought he was suffering from several brain-related problems, including deep limbic (depression), basal ganglia (anxiety), and anterior cingulate gyrus (getting stuck on pornographic material) problems. As part of the therapy, Dr. Henslin referred Dave for a SPECT study to look at the underlying brain issues. Dave left his first session with Earl feeling more hopeful than he had in quite some time. He was expecting this great Christian psychologist to chastise him for his sinful behavior. Instead, he found potential explanations and hope for healing. Earl perfectly predicted Dave's scan. Dave had excessive activity in the deep limbic area, basal ganglia, and anterior cingulate gyrus. His emotional brain was working too hard, leading to negativity, and he became stuck in negative patterns of behavior. With the help of antidepressant medication and intensive psychotherapy, Dave was able to give up his obsession with pornographic material, and his mood, anxiety, and social effectiveness significantly improved at home and at church. Subsequently, we have seen many other good people from Dave's church.

DAVE's SPECT STUDY

Underside Active View

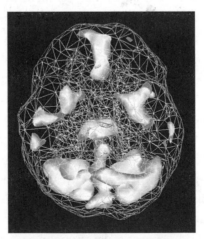

Increased deep limbic, basal ganglia, and anterior cingulate activity

Earl developed a lecture titled "Spirituality, Emotions, and Brain Chemistry." He showed some overheads of my clinic's scans as he did the presentation and said the impact was amazing. After the presentation, he stayed to answer individual questions for over an hour. One woman patiently waited until everyone had left. When he got to her, she just started to sob.

At the last minute in his lecture, Earl had decided to share a story about a man who had fallen from a jungle gym and injured his prefrontal cortex in childhood. Subsequently, this man had problems with focus and impulsivity. Earl described the change in the man's life once he was scanned and could see the damage to his prefrontal cortex. He realized that it was not a matter of more prayer or Bible study; it was a brain problem. After taking stimulant medication for his prefrontal cortex, for the first time in his life this man could actually pray and study the Bible without being distracted and follow through on things he had not been able to finish. With tears in her eyes, the woman told Earl about her elementary-school-age son, who had also fallen from a jungle gym. She was now homeschooling him because his rages at school were such that the public school could not handle him. Her tears flowed because she had been blaming herself all these years for her son's injury. In therapy, with a professional who obviously did not understand the brain-soul connection, she had been told that her son's rages were due to her unresolved anger toward her own mother that was unconsciously transferred to him. Earl reassured her that her son's problems were likely from the fall, with the accompanying temporal-lobe and prefrontal cortex problems. She felt a wave of guilt lift from her soul after talking with Earl.

If religious leaders are going to talk about their congregant's behavior (both positive and negative) in the weekly sermon and in individual counseling, then they should also talk about the brain. When educated religious leaders acknowledge the brain's role in behavior, it gives members of the congregation permission to seek help for themselves and their loved ones. God heals in many ways. Doctors and their medicines are one of the ways. By connecting behavioral problems solely to a weak will or sinful behavior, the people in the congregation who need help just end up trying harder to fix their "weak nature" but succeeding less. Clearly, religious leaders need education about the brain-soul connection.

Let's look at each brain system as it relates to God's house and priests, ministers, rabbis, and believers.

Brain Issues in God's House

PREFRONTAL CORTEX ISSUES

A religious leader with a healthy PFC (the brain's supervisor) helps God's house run in an efficient and effective manner. Services start on time. The church is well organized. The minister shows empathy, thoughtfulness, and consistent behavior. The religious leader plans for the future and follows through on projects. The parishioners with healthy PFC activity are involved with their church, follow through on projects, are disciplined in prayer, and learn from the mistakes they make.

PFC problems are often at the heart of sinful behavior. When people lack forethought, judgment, and impulse control, serious problems arise. Religious leaders and students with PFC problems say things impulsively and may even act out misdeeds, such as stealing from the offering or engaging in sexual indiscretions. They may be late to services, inattentive in meetings, and disorganized in how they handle the day-to-day management of the house of God. Likewise, congregants with PFC problems exhibit more sinful, hurtful behavior.

ANTERIOR CINGULATE GYRUS AND BASAL GANGLIA ISSUES

As a reminder, the anterior cingulate gyrus and basal ganglia are the parts of the brain involved with cognitive flexibility and relaxation. A religious leader with a healthy anterior cingulate gyrus and basal ganglia allows open-mindedness, cooperation, and flexibility in God's house. Ministers tend to be forgiving and relaxed, and see the future in a positive light. Congregants with healthy anterior cingulate gyrus and basal ganglia activity tend to be flexible, adaptable, and accepting. They tend to be cooperative in group situations and are open to new ways of doing things.

Anterior cingulate gyrus and basal ganglia problems are frequently linked to sin. When people get stuck on negative thoughts and behaviors or they are cognitively inflexible or rigid, disaster is just around the corner. Religious leaders with these problems hold tightly to their own opinions, to the detriment of themselves and others. Life in the church or at school has to be their way or they become upset. They leave little room for the wants, desires, and needs of others; rather, they tend to be argumentative and oppositional. More extreme cases may even break away from their church and start a new movement because they could not compromise with the ideas of others. They may preach eternal damnation for those of different belief systems. They frequently appear selfish. It is as though their mind gets locked in a tunnel without windows or doors and they can see only their own ideas. They tend to be unforgiving and worry too much about the future. These people may have problems with addiction, such as substance abuse problems, sexual addictions, or gambling. The shame associated with these problems for ministers of God may be so overwhelming as to lead to suicidal behavior. Likewise, congregants with anterior cingulate gyrus and basal ganglia problems exhibit more sinful, difficult behavior. In direct contrast to most religious teachings, they tend to hold on to grudges. They may have obsessive thoughts (religious and otherwise) and compulsive, ritualistic behaviors. They also tend to be oppositional and argumentative at church meetings or functions. They worry and experience excessive guilt. They may have problems with addictions, such as gambling. I once treated a man who was an elder in his church. He had stolen over $100,000 from church funds to support his gambling habit. The church pastor loved this man and wanted to find an alternative to legal action, so he made a deal with the man to see me for treatment and pay back the money. His SPECT study showed severe increased activity in the anterior cingulate gyrus and basal ganglia. He cooperated with treatment, which consisted of psychotherapy, medication, and attendance at Gamblers Anonymous meetings, and paid back the money over the next twelve years.

COMPULSIVE GAMBLER'S SPECT STUDY

Left Side Active View

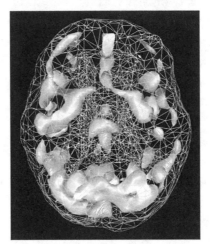

Increased anterior cingulate
and basal ganglia activity

TEMPORAL-LOBE AND LIMBIC ISSUES

Religious leaders with healthy temporal lobes and limbic systems show emotional consistency, temper control, and an overall positive attitude. They have good memories for details of the lives of people in their congregation and also for the church's past. They are able to read social situations and know when the congregation is paying attention to their sermons and when they seem disinterested. Sophisticated religious leaders enhance temporal-lobe function by emphasizing music (music is processed in the temporal lobes). They see the spiritual value of music in worship and make it an important part of the worship service. Healthy temporal lobes and a balanced limbic system allow religious leaders greater access to spiritual experience. They more easily feel the presence of God, and through prayer and meditation they are able to sense God's direction for the congregation.

Temporal-lobe and limbic system problems are often involved in sinful behavior: When people are temperamental, anxious, aggressive, and misread social situations, problems more easily occur. Religious leaders with temporal-lobe and limbic system problems may act irrationally, exhibit temper tantrums to their families or church members, forget important obligations, or put a negative spin on most thoughts. The negativity can be pervasive and drive people away from the church. In a similar way, God's people with temporal-lobe and limbic system problems can have serious problems. I have seen these areas contribute to violent behavior toward the self and against others. Assault, murder, rape, arson, and other criminal behaviors are often associated with problems in this part of the brain. Suicidal behavior, one of the ultimate sins that used to be considered unforgivable in many religions, is often associated with severe problems in this part of the brain.

Sermon Issues, Perceiving God, and the Brain

Can your priest, rabbi, or minister's weekly sermon be affected by brain function? I think so. Preachers who exhort the love of God likely have cool limbic systems; ministers who preach God's wrath likely have limbic systems that are often associated with negativity. Hellfire and damnation preachers often have hot limbic systems (negativity) as well as hot anterior cingulate gyri, which can prevent them from forgiving behavior. Sermons that are logical, thoughtful, and well planned show PFC input. Sermons that are ill-prepared, disjointed, and rambling may be prepared with little PFC input. Sermons that make the same point over and over and over again may have too much anterior cingulate gyrus input.

How one sees or perceives God is also likely influenced by brain health. In my experience, people who have a healthy limbic system tend to see God as loving, warm, present, and compassionate. A dysfunctional limbic system leads to feelings of insecurity, negativity (God doesn't like me), and distance from and abandonment by God. People with a healthy anterior cingulate gyrus tend to see a forgiving God who cares for their anxieties and worries. Heightened activity in this part of the brain leads people to perceive God as a grudge-holding, unforgiving, inflexible, and rigid God who is ready to beat you with a spiritual stick and damn your eternal soul to hell. A healthy PFC helps people focus on God. In contrast, an unhealthy PFC causes people to miss God's guidance because they are distracted with irrelevant things.

Is it possible that some people actually chose their specific religion based on brain compatibility or need? Maybe. Although I am not aware of any studies to prove my hypothesis, I have seen that converts to the Catholic, Lutheran, and Episcopal faiths tend to be more "anterior cingulate" in brain function. They seem to like rituals and consistency in worship. People who need PFC stimulation seem to feel more at home in Pentecostal churches. There is little doubt that the excitement, joyful singing, loud praises to the Lord, and intense sermons will stimulate even the most distracted parishioner to stay awake and pay attention in church. Many people with temporal-lobe sensitivity who experience mystical or spiritual experiences may gravitate to Evangelical or Pentecostal worship services. The experiences are more commonplace in these groups and thus more accepted, and even admired, by others.

Are There Health Benefits to Going to Church?

Research strongly suggests that going to church and being part of a body of believers has health benefits for both brain and body. The John Templeton Foundation at Harvard Medical School and David Elkins, Ph.D., president of the Humanistic Psychology Division of the American Psychological Association, have noted:

- The mortality rate for men who attend church is 25 percent lower than those who don't. For women it is 35 percent lower.
- Hip-fracture patients who attend church on a regular basis walk longer distances and have less depression at discharge than those who don't.
- Patients who depend on their faith for strength are three times more likely to survive open-heart surgery.
- Because people who attend church are about ten times less likely to smoke, they suffer markedly lower rates of coronary artery disease, lung cancer, and chronic obstructive pulmonary disease than others.
- In general, people who attend church have stronger immune systems than those who don't, which contributes to their overall better health. In a 1997 study reported in the *International Journal of Psychiatry in Medicine,* research on seventeen hundred adults found that those who attend religious services were less likely to have elevated levels of interleukin-6, an immune substance prevalent in people with chronic diseases.
- Religious patients spend half as long per stay in the hospital as nonreligious patients. In a Duke University study, devout patients recovering from surgery spent an average of eleven days in the hospital, compared with nonreligious patients who spent twenty-five days.
- People with strong religious faith recover from depression 70 percent faster than those without a strong religious

faith. A 1997 Columbia University study published in the *Journal of the American Academy of Child and Adolescent Psychiatry* reported that women with religious mothers are 60 percent less likely to be depressed in ten years than women whose mothers aren't so reverent. Daughters belonging to the same religious denomination as their mothers are even less likely (71 percent) to suffer from depression; sons were 84 percent less likely.

- When asked what was the most important factor in helping them cope with illness and recovery, 42 percent of hospitalized patients cited their religious faith.
- The Alameda County Study, which follows nearly seven thousand people, showed that worshipers who participated in regular church-sponsored activities are markedly less stressed over finances, health, and other daily concerns than nonreligious people.

ONCE again, we see that having a healthy brain enhances life, even spiritual life. At the same time, having a spiritual or soulful approach to life also enhances the brain. It is a circle. The brain and soul need each other to work right, and it seems they both do better in church, synagogue, mosque, or temple.

Eight

Lead Us Not into Temptation

**Brain-Soul Connections and Disconnections for
Parents, Bosses, Community, Church,
and World Leaders**

LEADERS affect our souls. They affect how we grow, how we work, how we love, and how we worship. A healthy brain enhances leadership abilities. An unhealthy brain can wreak havoc in leaders and potentially cost people their jobs, sanity, lives, and even eternal souls. People who lead—such as parents, teachers, coaches, work supervisors, ministers or religious leaders, and politicians—are found in every walk of life. A healthy brain helps leaders to be thoughtful, goal directed, empathic, flexible, steadfast, respectful, and emotionally stable. A leader with a challenged brain is a prescription for disaster.

Effective leaders, in whatever position they hold (parenting, business, ministry, etc.), show a consistent set of traits. As you will recognize, they have brain systems that are intact. They have good prefrontal cortex traits, such as being goal directed, forward thinking, attentive, good at follow-through, firm, thoughtful, empathic, and consistent. They have good anterior cingulate and basal ganglia traits, such as being flexible, adaptable, and capable of change as needed. They have good temporal-lobe and limbic function, manifested by being positive, stable, and having good memories. They remember the past, learn from their mistakes, and connect with others.

When any of these systems are problematic, there can be leadership problems. Let's look at the pathology in each system and see how the brain can influence leadership.

The PFC and Leadership

As we've seen, the PFC is the supervisor. It watches, guides, and protects behavior. Problems in this part of the brain may lead to a multitude of leadership problems. Here are common PFC problems and their impact on leadership skills.

A lack of forward thinking can cause major problems. A mother's lack of forethought may cause her to be what I call a "fast-food mother." Mothers with PFC problems lack forethought in planning meals. When the children get hungry, they start to plan dinner. Since it occurs at the last minute, they often go to McDonald's, Jack in the Box, Wendy's, and other fast-food restaurants. A lack of planning among clerics may lead to poor sermons dashed off at the last minute or poor planning for religious holidays. A coach who doesn't think ahead often doesn't coach for long because ill-prepared teams tend to lose more than others. A teacher with poor planning skills will teach the bare minimum and does not adequately prepare students for the next step in their education.

A short attention span can cause many leadership problems. When leaders fail to pay attention to important issues at hand, things can get out of control. Tasks go undone at home or at church; distractions take people away from their primary purposes. People can take serious advantage of you. I have treated a number of business executives with ADD. It seemed an inordinate number of them had employees who embezzled significant funds from them. One of my patients, who ran an $800 million business, developed a major depression after his chief operating officer was found to have embezzled $3 million. He never saw it coming because he was paying attention to personal things outside of work. Parents who do not pay attention to their children can also have serious problems. We see that drug abuse and antisocial behavior is much more common in parents who do not adequately supervise their teenage children.

Impulse control problems are common among ineffective leaders. They tend to not fully think about what they say before they say it, or think about what they do before they do it. They tend to say things that hurt other people's feelings, to act without thinking. Sexual harassment suits are often brought against people with impulse control problems. Other leaders with these problems may act abusively toward their families, or they may have affairs with employees, members of the congregation, or members of their political staff. They may overreact and chastise an employee in front of other employees. As coaches, they may lose control at a ball game and make fools of themselves in front of a community or even a national audience. They may start an ill-advised war without thinking through all the consequences of their behavior.

I have treated a number of leaders who were conflict driven or negative seeking. They tended to pick fights with other leaders and subordinates. When I was an army psychiatrist, I treated the commanding officer of an infantry company at the request of the post general. He received more complaints from his men than any officer I had ever met. He focused on the negative, picked on his men, and constantly fought with one or more of the other company commanders in our division. It was not surprising to me that he had experienced a significant frontal-lobe injury in the past. Since I treat many patients with ADD, I commonly see adult ADD parents who pick on their spouses and children. Conflict-driven behavior is very common in ADD children and adults. When the family leader is conflict driven, everyone in the family suffers.

Weak conscience, also characteristic of PFC problems, can be devastating to a leader. Good leaders have integrity. People can trust them. When leaders betray trust, lie, steal, or cheat, they set a very bad example and tone for the family, congregation, or organization.

Dr. B, a hospital medical director, displayed many PFC problems. His patients didn't like him because of his abrasive manner. The hospital staff avoided him. He frequently blurted out awful comments to the physicians and nurses, calling them incompetent and unethical and making other derogatory remarks in front of staff and patients. Several female staff members filed complaints of sexual harassment against him. The day he was fired, the hospital administrator came to work early. When she walked into her office, she found her secretary performing oral sex on Dr. B behind her desk. Dr. B was referred to me as part of a medical board investigation. He had a history of a head injury playing football in high school. When I scanned him, he had very poor activity in his PFC.

DR. B's SPECT STUDY

Underside Surface View

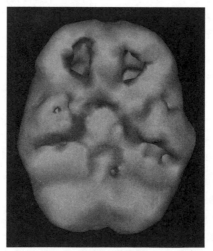

Decreased PFC activity

The Anterior Cingulate Gyrus, Basal Ganglia, and Leadership

Healthy activity in the anterior cingulate gyrus and basal ganglia is related to cognitive flexibility, adaptability, the ability to see options and solve problems, cooperation with others, and the ability to see things from another person's perspective. These structures help people with collaboration, forgiveness, seeing the future in a positive light, and having the ability to deal with conflict. Excessive activity in the anterior cingulate gyrus and basal ganglia in a leader wreaks havoc for the people under their care. Here are just some of the ways.

Anxiety and worry are common when there is hyperactivity in the anterior cingulate gyrus and basal ganglia. These traits seriously impair leadership. When a leader worries or suffers from anxiety, he or she becomes tied up in negative thoughts and frozen with fear. Doubt creeps into decisions, and the future looks scary. Leaders with anxiety tend to predict failure and infect the people they lead with feelings of insecurity. They may talk incessantly about their fears and worry others, or they may start to hide from their charges, leaving others to wonder what is wrong. Here is an example: Father Timothy suffered from anxiety. He had panic attacks and social anxiety. Whenever an attack came over him, he had to leave the situation immediately. He drank to get the anxiety under control. Sometimes he would leave the confessional in the middle of hearing someone's confession for fear of having another attack. Many of his parishioners felt that he didn't like them and stopped attending church. His diocese sent him to see me. After he started treatment, he sought out a number of the parishioners who had left the church in order to make amends.

Holding on to hurts or grudges seriously undermines leadership, whether it is parental, work related, or in the political or religious arena. I am certain that wars have been fought because one or both political leaders had excessive anterior cingulate gyrus and basal ganglia activity. Holding on to hurts from the past can cause generational hatred and may even infect our

DNA. Grudges cause people to be blind to good family or political negotiations and settlements. I often see this played out in families going through a divorce. There is often so much animosity that people go out of their way to hurt one another, even if they hurt the children and their own financial or physical health as well. Likewise, people with excessive activity in these parts of the brain hold on to opinions excessively and see things only from their own point of view. It is very hard to lead if you cannot compromise, cooperate, or trust.

In my experience in dealing with hatred and racism, both as a military and civilian psychiatrist, there were severe problems shifting attention and people got stuck in negative thought patterns. Through the years I have had the opportunity to scan a number of White Supremacists, skinheads, and KKK members. Almost invariably they had excessive activity in the anterior cingulate gyrus and basal ganglia.

Additionally, problems in this part of the brain cause people to be oppositional, argumentative, inflexible, and react negatively to the ideas and suggestions of others. They tend to be uncooperative and disagree or argue with someone even before hearing them out completely. These traits ruin a leader. The leader appears selfish and self-centered, and cannot show empathy for the people he or she leads. They alienate those they lead. When parents act this way, children look forward to moving out as soon as possible. When the boss at work acts this way, there is a high turnover of employees. When church or political leaders act this way, they have a high incidence of disloyalty and betrayal among their staff.

Leaders who have problems in these parts of the brain often bring disasters into their families. In one of the saddest cases I have evaluated a thirteen-year-old boy murdered his father. The boy and his younger sister had been severely emotional and physically abused by him. He also sexually abused his daughter. From the history, it was clear that the father had a terrible problem with his anterior cingulate gyrus. He was obsessive, rigid, and explosive when things did not go his way. He would hold grudges for years and regularly bring up the children's past misdeeds. After the teenager couldn't take the abuse anymore, especially the sexual abuse of his sister, he murdered his father by shooting him in the head as he came out of his sister's room. When I did a SPECT study of the teenager, I found that he had one of the hottest brains I had ever seen, especially in the area of the anterior cingulate gyrus. Likely, he inherited the pattern from his father and the severe abuse made it much worse, causing him to be unable to get the abuse out of his head or to come up with a better solution than shooting his father and ruining his own life.

The Temporal Lobes and Deep Limbic System and Leadership

As noted, healthy activity in the temporal lobes and deep limbic system help people to have a good memory, mood stability, temper control, word retrieval, accurate reading of social situations, personality stability, increased access to spiritual experience, and positive mood and emotional tone. These characteristics are essential in leadership. Effective leaders have to be able to remember the past to see developing trends and learn from prior mistakes. Mood stability and temper control are helpful to maintain an even leadership style where people trust you and are not afraid that you may explode at any time. Word retrieval helps leaders express their ideas and give appropriate directives. Reading social situations is essential to building alliances with the people you lead, as well as with other leaders. Access to spiritual experience is essential to religious leaders but also, many would argue, to family and political leaders as well. A positive mood and emotional tone helps leaders maintain emotional balance and well-being and keep them on track to help people in a positive way. Problems in the temporal lobes or deep limbic system can cause serious leadership problems. Here are a few examples.

Memory problems can seriously impair a person's ability to

lead. If leaders forget important experiences from the past they are likely to make the same mistakes over and over and lead their charges into troubled waters. Memory problems decrease a leader's sense of continuity and can cause problems with following through on important issues. A CEO of a large company in the Bay Area did not remember some high-level meetings where new business strategies were discussed, even though they were going to cost the company several hundred thousand dollars. When the new strategies backfired, the board of directors chastised him. He blamed his subordinates for doing things behind his back. Yet, the minutes of the meetings about the new strategies clearly showed him present. Several members of the board of directors noted other issues with his memory and sent him to my clinic for evaluation. His SPECT study showed early evidence of Alzheimer's disease (decreased activity in the parietal and temporal lobes).

CEO's SPECT Study—Early Alzheimer's Disease

Top Down Surface View   *Underside Surface View*

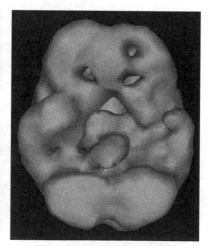

Decreased parietal-lobe activity   *Decreased temporal-lobe activity*

Memory problems cause problems with parents. They may forget to pick up the children at school or forget they made an important promise to a child. Memory problems can impair pastors. They may forget the names of people in their congregation or forget important meeting obligations. Memory problems can impair teachers or coaches as they may forget important information to teach or ignore important trends that are happening in an athletic game.

Moodiness and temper problems have been common to many leaders throughout history, but these are surely not helpful traits. Moodiness leads to unpredictability and mistrust. Temper problems scare people and cause them to hide or withhold information from leaders. Paranoia is often part of temporal-lobe problems. A paranoid leader is dangerous and can lead his family, country, or church to destruction. I treated a man who became paranoid after his father died. He started to feel that people were out to hurt him. He mistrusted his wife and his teenage son. They became afraid of him and started to ignore him, fueling the mistrust further. He alienated everyone in his family except his mother, who brought him to see me. His SPECT study showed marked decreased activity in his left temporal lobe. His paranoia diminished after he was placed on an anticonvulsant. He was then able to reconnect with his family.

Difficulty reading social cues also causes leadership problems. Effective leaders are good at reading the emotional states of those around them. When you misread signals, your behavior appears erratic and insensitive and pushes people away, eroding support. A professor in my psychiatry residency program had problems reading social cues, which ruined his effectiveness as a teacher. Even though he was a smart, well-read man, he continually misread social situations. Every time a resident would question something he said, the professor seemed to feel threatened; he became defensive and had a temper tantrum. None of the residents approached him for counsel. Our learning experience was diminished because he misread social situations.

Should We Scan Political Candidates?

What do political candidates' past indiscretions mean? Does past drug or alcohol abuse mean anything? How about prior temper problems, extramarital affairs, or financial problems? Maybe nothing. They may just be overblown issues in the otherwise normal lives of powerful political men and women. We all make mistakes. However, the symptoms may mean a lot, such as evidence of underlying brain dysfunction. Sometimes people with temper problems have underlying brain problems that are associated with emotional rigidity, holding grudges, and obsessive thoughts. Sometimes alcohol and cocaine have lasting negative effects on brain function. Sometimes an extramarital affair or financial problems may indicate an underlying attention deficit disorder.

Is the brain health of a political candidate a fair topic in an election year? Should we even go so far as to do brain scans of high-level political candidates? Should this information be released to the public like the results of a physical examination? Some people think that discussing brain-health issues is an invasion of a candidate's privacy; some think that performing brain scans on would-be high-level political candidates is a silly idea. Not me. I want our elected leaders to be some of the brain-healthiest people in the land. How do you know about the brain health of a presidential candidate unless you look? As we have seen, the brain is involved in everything we do: how we think, how we feel, how we act, how we get along with others, how we negotiate, how we pay attention at meetings, and how we turn away the advances of White House interns.

President Woodrow Wilson is a dramatic example of how brain problems can affect politicians and political power. Wilson suffered a right-hemisphere stroke during the Versailles Peace Conference, shortly after World War I. Even though the stroke didn't paralyze him, the people who knew him saw an immediate negative change in his personality. He was irritable, inflexible, and spiteful, whereas before he was forward thinking and able to compromise. He also became less sociable. Several weeks after the first stroke, he had another one that paralyzed his left side. Despite his obvious infirmity, he denied having any problems (denial is very common in right-hemisphere problems). Those around him became very distressed. He fired his secretary of state for trying to discuss his medical situation with the cabinet. His stroke may have been involved in setting the stage for World War II. After his stroke, he could no longer argue effectively for the League of Nations.

Two presidents in the recent past have shown clear brain pathology. President Ronald Reagan's Alzheimer's disease was evident during his second term in office. Nonelected staff members were covering up his forgetfulness and directing the country's business. We had a national crisis that few people were aware of. Brain studies have shown predictive value five years before Alzheimer's disease becomes evident. No one talked about the brain problems of President Clinton, but we suffered through his poor judgment, impulse control problems, not learning from mistakes, and excitement-seeking behavior—all problems that point to prefrontal cortex problems.

A national leader with brain problems can potentially cost millions of lives. President Slobodan Milosevic of Yugoslavia was a recent historical example. Both of his parents committed suicide, he has had reported bouts of depression, and it was said that he drank alcohol heavily, all signs that point to brain problems. He was found to be unreasonable and unreliable in negotiations, and he had a severe lack of concern for many people in his country. He cost millions of people their homes and many their lives.

With SPECT we can see healthy or diseased prefrontal lobes (the judgment center), temporal lobes (a main memory center), and parietal lobes (main association area). If we have the tools, shouldn't we look? On the ballot we could see a presidential candidate's name along with a picture of his or her brain, and the opponent's name along with a picture of his or her brain. This is potentially important information to put into the election equation.

Ensuring that our elected officials have healthy brains may be more than an interesting topic of conversation. A president with brain problems could wreak all sorts of havoc on current and future life in the United States and the world at large. Maybe we shouldn't leave the health of our leaders to chance. Maybe we should think about looking, starting now.

Are there downsides to looking at the brain scans of political candidates? Yes. We would lose a lot of potential candidates. No longer would they be able to withhold information about drug use or memory problems. There are also a number of truly great presidents that likely would have been kept out of office. Abraham Lincoln had a brain injury when he was twelve years old, he suffered from severe bouts of depression, and he had illusions (temporal-lobe phenomena). John Kennedy used painkillers while in office, a fact that would have affected his brain. Ulysses Grant indulged in substantial amounts of alcohol before and during his presidency.

Despite the downsides of scanning political candidates, the stakes now are far too high to dismiss the idea. A president with a brain problem can demoralize the nation's soul (as happened during the William Clinton–Monica Lewinsky scandal) and even threaten the human race's very existence (Adolf Hitler).

2

Optimizing the Brain-Soul Connection

Nine

Amen Brain System Checklist and Strategies to Optimize Each Brain Area

My hope at this point is that I have convinced you of the brain-soul connection. The brain and soul need each other reciprocally to be healthy and happy. In this part of the book I will give you a lot of ideas and exercises to optimize the brain-soul connection. Understanding the brain-soul connection is the first step in becoming your best self. Optimizing the brain is the next important step to healing the hardware of the soul. To do this, you need to understand your brain's vulnerabilities and develop strategies to overcome them. Unfortunately, the day-to-day use of functional brain imaging in clinical practice is still seven to fifteen years away. Based on our very large database of twelve thousand scans, I developed a questionnaire to evaluate the five brain systems discussed in this book. This questionnaire has gone through many revisions; I'm sure it will go through more. We use this questionnaire as part of our clinical evaluation of patients at the Amen Clinics to evaluate each of the five systems discussed in the book.

Self-report questionnaires have certain advantages and limitations. They are quick, inexpensive, and easy to score. One of the dangers is that people may fill them out as they want to be perceived. For example, some people mark all of the symptoms as a frequent problem, in essence saying, "I'm glad to have a problem so that I can get help, be sick, or have an excuse for the problems I have." Some people are in total denial. They do not want to see any personal flaws, and they do not consider any symptoms as problematic, saying, "I'm okay. There's nothing wrong with me. Leave me alone." In our clinical experience, most people gauge themselves with reasonable accuracy. Self-report bias is one of the reasons that it is important to have another person fill out the questionnaire as well. This will give you and others a more complete picture.

This questionnaire is a valuable tool to help determine if there are problems in the prefrontal cortex, anterior cingulate gyrus, basal ganglia, temporal lobes, or deep limbic system. It provides the basis for targeted interventions. A person may have more than one type of problem; some people have even four or five problems areas.

It's important to note that this (or any) questionnaire is never meant to be used alone. It is not meant to provide a diagnosis, but rather it serves as a guide to help people begin to identify problems and get further evaluation if needed.

AMEN BRAIN SYSTEM CHECKLIST

Please rate yourself on each of the symptoms listed below, using the following scale. If possible, to give you the most complete picture, have another person who knows you well (such as a spouse, lover, or parent) rate you as well.

0	1	2	3	4	NA
Never	Rarely	Occasionally	Frequently	Very Frequently	Not Applicable/ Not Known

Other Self

____ ____ 1. Fails to give close attention to details or makes careless mistakes.

____ ____ 2. Trouble sustaining attention in routine situations (i.e., homework, chores, paperwork).

____ ____	3.	Trouble listening.
____ ____	4.	Fails to finish things.
____ ____	5.	Poor organization for time or space (such as backpack, room, desk, paperwork).
____ ____	6.	Avoids, dislikes, or is reluctant to engage in tasks that require sustained mental effort.
____ ____	7.	Loses things.
____ ____	8.	Easily distracted.
____ ____	9.	Forgetful.
____ ____	10.	Poor planning skills.
____ ____	11.	Lack clear goals or forward thinking.
____ ____	12.	Difficulty expressing feelings.
____ ____	13.	Difficulty expressing empathy for others.
____ ____	14.	Excessive daydreaming.
____ ____	15.	Feeling bored.
____ ____	16.	Feeling apathetic or unmotivated.
____ ____	17.	Feeling tired, sluggish, or slow moving.
____ ____	18.	Feeling spacey or "in a fog."
____ ____	19.	Fidgety, restless, or trouble sitting still.
____ ____	20.	Difficulty remaining seated in situations where remaining seated is expected.
____ ____	21.	Runs about or climbs excessively in situations in which it is inappropriate.
____ ____	22.	Difficulty playing quietly.
____ ____	23.	"On the go" or acts as if "driven by a motor."
____ ____	24.	Talks excessively.
____ ____	25.	Blurts out answers before questions have been completed.
____ ____	26.	Difficulty awaiting turn.
____ ____	27.	Interrupts or intrudes on others (e.g., butts into conversations or games).
____ ____	28.	Impulsive (saying or doing things without thinking first).
____ ____	29.	Excessive or senseless worrying.
____ ____	30.	Upset when things do not go your way.

_____ _____ 31. Upset when things are out of place.

_____ _____ 32. Tendency to be oppositional or argumentative.

_____ _____ 33. Tendency to have repetitive negative thoughts.

_____ _____ 34. Tendency toward compulsive behaviors.

_____ _____ 35. Intense dislike for change.

_____ _____ 36. Tendency to hold grudges.

_____ _____ 37. Trouble shifting attention from subject to subject.

_____ _____ 38. Trouble shifting behavior from task to task.

_____ _____ 39. Difficulties seeing options in situations.

_____ _____ 40. Tendency to hold on to own opinion and not listen to others.

_____ _____ 41. Tendency to get locked into a course of action, whether or not it is good.

_____ _____ 42. Needing to have things done a certain way or you become very upset.

_____ _____ 43. Others complain that you worry too much.

_____ _____ 44. Tend to say no without first thinking about question.

_____ _____ 45. Tendency to predict fear.

_____ _____ 46. Panic attacks.

_____ _____ 47. Symptoms of heightened muscle tension (headaches, sore muscles, hand tremor).

_____ _____ 48. Periods of heart pounding, rapid heart rate, or chest pain.

_____ _____ 49. Periods of trouble breathing or feeling smothered.

_____ _____ 50. Periods of feeling dizzy, faint, or unsteady on your feet.

_____ _____ 51. Periods of nausea or abdominal upset.

_____ _____ 52. Periods of sweating, hot or cold flashes.

_____ _____ 53. Tendency to predict the worst.

_____ _____ 54. Fear of dying or doing something crazy.

_____ _____ 55. Avoid places for fear of having an anxiety attack.

____ ____ 56. Conflict avoidance.

____ ____ 57. Excessive fear of being judged or scrutinized by others.

____ ____ 58. Persistent phobias.

____ ____ 59. Low motivation.

____ ____ 60. Excessive motivation.

____ ____ 61. Tics (motor or vocal).

____ ____ 62. Poor handwriting.

____ ____ 63. Quick startle.

____ ____ 64. Tendency to freeze in anxiety-provoking situations.

____ ____ 65. Lacks confidence in their abilities.

____ ____ 66. Seems shy or timid.

____ ____ 67. Easily embarrassed.

____ ____ 68. Sensitive to criticism.

____ ____ 69. Bites fingernails or picks skin.

____ ____ 70. Frequent feelings of sadness.

____ ____ 71. Moodiness.

____ ____ 72. Negativity.

____ ____ 73. Low energy.

____ ____ 74. Irritability.

____ ____ 75. Decreased interest in others.

____ ____ 76. Decreased interest in things that are usually fun or pleasurable.

____ ____ 77. Feelings of hopelessness about the future.

____ ____ 78. Feelings of helplessness or powerlessness.

____ ____ 79. Feeling dissatisfied or bored.

____ ____ 80. Excessive guilt.

____ ____ 81. Suicidal feelings.

____ ____ 82. Crying spells.

____ ____ 83. Lowered interest in things usually considered fun.

____ ____ 84. Sleep changes (too much or too little).

____ ____ 85. Appetite changes (too much or too little).

____ ____ 86. Chronic low self-esteem.

_____ _____ 87. Negative sensitivity to smells/odors.

_____ _____ 88. Frequent feelings of nervousness or anxiety.

_____ _____ 89. Short fuse or periods of extreme irritability.

_____ _____ 90. Periods of rage with little provocation.

_____ _____ 91. Often misinterprets comments as negative when they are not.

_____ _____ 92. Irritability tends to build, then explodes, then recedes, often tired after a rage.

_____ _____ 93. Periods of spaciness or confusion.

_____ _____ 94. Periods of panic and/or fear for no specific reason.

_____ _____ 95. Visual or auditory changes, such as seeing shadows or hearing muffled sounds.

_____ _____ 96. Frequent periods of déjà vu (feelings of being somewhere you have never been).

_____ _____ 97. Sensitivity or mild paranoia.

_____ _____ 98. Headaches or abdominal pain of uncertain origin.

_____ _____ 99. History of a head injury or family history of violence or explosiveness.

_____ _____ 100. Dark thoughts, may involve suicidal or homicidal thoughts.

_____ _____ 101. Periods of forgetfulness or memory problems.

Answer Key

For each of the areas listed below, add up the number of answers that were scored as three or four and write them on a separate sheet of paper. A cutoff score is provided with each type. Then go to the sections that apply to your specific issues for the medications, nutritional interventions, and supplements that may help to optimize each area.

Prefrontal cortex dysfunction, questions 1–28:

Highly probable	8 questions with 3 or 4
Probable	6 questions with 3 or 4
May be possible	4 questions with 3 or 4

Anterior cingulate system hyperactivity, questions 29–45:
    Highly probable   10 questions with 3 or 4
    Probable   7 questions with 3 or 4
    May be possible   4 questions with 3 or 4

Basal ganglia hyperactivity, questions 46–69:
    Highly probable   10 questions with 3 or 4
    Probable   7 questions with 3 or 4
    May be possible   4 questions with 3 or 4

Deep limbic system hyperactivity, questions 70–88:
    Highly probable   10 questions with 3 or 4
    Probable   7 questions with 3 or 4
    May be possible   4 questions with 3 or 4

Temporal-lobe dysfunction, questions 89–101:
    Highly probable   8 questions with 3 or 4
    Probable   6 questions with 3 or 4
    May be possible   4 questions with 3 or 4

Brain System Strategies

Here are strategies to optimize each area of the brain. Many more will be given throughout the rest of the book.

PREFRONTAL CORTEX ISSUES

If your score in the PFC indicates problems, there are a number of things to do to optimize this part of the brain. Problems in this part of the brain can be associated with the diagnosis of attention deficit disorder (ADD), brain trauma, or toxic exposure. ADD is commonly divided into two main categories, ADD with hyperactivity and impulsivity (Type 1) and ADD without hyperactivity and impulsivity (Type 2). Type 1 is often identified early in life, especially in boys. The level of hyperactivity, restlessness, and impulsivity causes them to stand out from others. Brain studies of this subtype reveal decreased activity in the prefrontal cortex and premotor cortex in response to an intellectual challenge, most likely due to low dopamine availability in the deeper structures of the brain. Type 1 ADD is usually very responsive to stimulant medications such as methylphenidate (Ritalin, Concerta), dextroamphetamine (Dexedrine), magnesium pemoline (Cylert), and Adderall (a combination of amphetamine salts). These medications enhance PFC activity and prevent brain shutdown, allowing a person to have more access to this part of their brain. Type 2, or inattentive ADD, often becomes apparent later in childhood or early adolescence. The symptoms must be present for at least six months and must not be related to a depressive episode or the onset of marijuana usage. Marijuana use can often make a person seem as though they have ADD without hyperactivity. It is important to screen for usage in teenagers or adults.

Girls with ADD are frequently missed because they are more likely to have the nonhyperactive form. The severity of both of these disorders is rated as mild, moderate, or severe. Even though Type 2 ADD folks have many of the same symptoms of the people with Type 1 ADD, they are not hyperactive and may appear hypoactive. Additional symptoms for this subtype include excessive daydreaming, frequent complaints of being bored, appearing apathetic or unmotivated, appearing frequently sluggish or slow moving, or appearing spacey or internally preoccupied—the classic "couch potato." Most people with Type 2 ADD are never diagnosed. They do not exhibit enough symptoms that "grate" on the environment to cause others to seek help for them. Yet, they often experience severe disability from the disorder. Instead of help, they get labeled as willful, uninterested, or defiant. As with Type 1 ADD, brain studies in patients with Type 2 ADD reveal a decrease in brain activity in the frontal lobes of the brain in response to an intellectual challenge. Again, it seems that the harder these people try to concentrate, the worse it gets. Type 2 ADD is also usually responsive to stimulant medications.

Nutritional intervention can be especially helpful in this part of the brain. For years I have recommended a high-protein, low-carbohydrate diet that is relatively low in fat to my patients with ADD. This diet has a stabilizing effect on blood sugar levels and helps both with energy level and concentration. Unfortunately, the great American diet is filled with refined carbohydrates, which has a negative impact on dopamine levels in the brain and concentration. With both parents working outside of the home, there is less time to prepare healthy meals, and fast foods have become more the norm. The breakfast of today typically involves foods that are high in simple carbohydrates, such as frozen waffles or pancakes, Pop-Tarts, muffins, pastry, rolls, or cereal. Sausage and eggs have gone by the wayside in many homes because of the lack of time and the perception that fat is bad for us. Even though it is important to be careful with fat intake, the breakfast of old is not such a bad idea, especially where ADD or other dopamine-deficient states exists. The major sources of protein I recommend include leans meats, eggs, low-fat cheeses, nuts, and certain beans. These are best mixed with a healthy portion of vegetables. The ideal breakfast is an omelette with low-fat cheese and lean meat, such as chicken. The ideal lunch is a tuna, chicken, or fresh fish salad with mixed vegetables. The ideal dinner contains more carbohydrates, such as bread or potatoes, with lean meat and vegetables. Eliminating simple sugars (such as cakes, candy, ice cream, and pastries) and simple carbohydrates that are readily broken down into sugar (such as bread, pasta, rice, and potatoes) will have a positive impact on energy level and cognition. This diet is helpful in raising dopamine levels in the brain. It is important to note, however, that this diet is not the ideal diet when there are cingulate or overfocus issues, which usually stem from a relative deficiency of serotonin. Since serotonin and dopamine levels tend to counterbalance each other, whenever serotonin is raised dopamine tends to be lowered and when dopamine is raised serotonin is lowered.

Nutritional supplements can also have a positive effect on brain dopamine levels and help with focus and energy. I often have my patients try L-tyrosine (500–1,500 milligrams two to three a day). This supplement helps to increase dopamine and blood flow in the brain, and many of my patients report that it helps with energy, focus, and impulse control. In addition, exercise boosts blood flow to this part of the brain.

ANTERIOR CINGULATE GYRUS ISSUES

People with anterior cingulate gyrus hyperactivity, usually due to deficiencies in the neurotransmitter serotonin, tend to have trouble shifting their attention from thought to thought and end up "stuck" on particular thoughts or behaviors. This brain pattern is often associated with worrying, moodiness, emotional rigidity, and irritability, and may present itself differently among family members. For example, a mother or father with anterior cingulate gyrus hyperactivity may experience obsessive thoughts (repetitive negative thoughts) or compulsive behaviors (hand washing, checking, counting, etc.). The son or daughter may be oppositional (get stuck on saying "no," "no way," "never," "you can't make me do it"). Another family member may find change very hard to accept.

The best medications for this problem tend to be the "anti-obsessive antidepressants." These medications increase the availability of serotonin in the brain, and they are often helpful in calming the anterior cingulate gyrus and basal ganglia hyperactivity. They are typically marketed as antidepressants. They also tend to calm limbic hyperactivity as well. These serotonergic-enhancing medications are also used to treat eating disorders, obsessive-compulsive disorder, oppositional defiant disorder, PMS (overfocused type), excessive worrying, temper problems associated with things not going a person's way, and other anterior cingulate and basal ganglia problems listed in this book. At the time of this writing, there are ten medications commonly used to increase serotonin in the brain. These medications include Effexor (venlafaxine), Prozac (fluoxetine), Paxil (paroxetine), Zoloft (sertraline), Anafranil (clomipramine), Desyrel (trazodone), Serzone (nefazodone), Celexa (citalopram), Remeron (mirtazapine), and Luvox (fluvoxamine).

In our experience, however, people who have temporal-lobe problems may experience an intensity of angry and aggressive feelings on serotonin-enhancing medications. Therefore, we are careful to screen for these before placing someone on these medications. If there are side effects of any medication, it is important to contact your doctor and discuss them. In contrast to the stimulants, these may take several weeks to several months to be effective and even three to four months to see the best benefit. The most common side effect of these medications is sexual dysfunction. Sometimes adding gingko biloba or buprion counteracts these problems.

There are two ways that food can increase serotonin levels. Carbohydrate-containing foods such as pasta, potatoes, bread, pastries, pretzels, candy, and popcorn increase L-tryptophan levels (the natural amino-acid building block for serotonin) in the blood, resulting in more L-tryptophan available to enter the brain, where it is converted to serotonin. The calming effect of serotonin can often be felt in thirty minutes or less by eating these foods. Cerebral serotonin levels can also be raised by eating foods rich in tryptophan, such as chicken, turkey, salmon, beef, peanut butter, eggs, green peas, potatoes, and milk. Many people unknowingly trigger cognitive inflexibility or mood problems by eating diets that are low in L-tryptophan. For example, the high-protein, low-carbohydrate diets that I recommend for low dopamine states (related to prefrontal cortex underactivity) often make anterior cingulate gyrus problems worse. L-tryptophan is a relatively small amino acid. When you eat a high-protein diet, the larger amino acids more successfully compete to get into the brain, causing lower levels of brain serotonin and more negative emotional reactiveness.

Nutritional supplements such as St. John's wort, L-tryptophan, and 5-HTP are helpful for anterior cingulate gyrus overactivity. St. John's wort comes from the flowers of the St. John's wort plant (wort is Old English for plant). It got its name from the fact that it blooms around June 24, the feast day of Saint John the Baptist, and from the red ring that forms around the flowers when they are crushed and looks like the blood of the beheaded John the Baptist. St. John's wort seems to be best at increasing serotonin availability in the brain. The starting dosage of St. John's wort is 300 mg a day for children, 300 mg twice a day for teens, and 600 mg in the morning and 300 mg at night for adults. Sometimes I will prescribe as much as 1,800 mg for adults. The bottle should say that it contains 0.3 percent hypericin, which is believed to be the active ingredient of St. John's wort. I have done a number of before-and-after SPECT studies with St. John's wort. It clearly decreases anterior cingulate gyrus hyperactivity for many patients; it also helps with moodiness and trouble shifting attention. Unfortunately, I have also seen it decrease prefrontal cortex activity. One of the women in the study said, "I'm happier, but I'm dingier." When anterior cingulate symptoms are present with PFC symptoms, it's important to use St. John's wort with a stimulating substance like L-tyrosine or a stimulant such as Adderall. It has been reported that St. John's wort increases sun sensitivity (you could get sunburned more easily and need to be careful in the sun). *Also, don't use it if temporal-lobe symptoms are present without first stabilizing the temporal lobes.*

L-tryptophan (the amino-acid building block for serotonin) and 5-HTP (also a serotonin building block) are other ways of increasing cerebral serotonin. L-tryptophan was taken off the market a number of years ago because one contaminated batch, from one manufacturer, caused a rare blood disease and a number of deaths. The L-tryptophan actually had nothing to do with the deaths. L-tryptophan is a naturally occurring amino acid found in milk, meat, and eggs. I have found it very helpful for patients in improving sleep, decreasing aggressiveness, and improving mood control. In addition, it does not have side effects, which is a real advantage over the antidepressants. L-tryptophan was reapproved by the Food and Drug Administration and is now available in many stores and by prescription. I recommend L-tryptophan in doses of 1,000–3,000 milligrams taken at bedtime. One of the problems with dietary L-tryptophan is that a significant portion of it does not enter the brain. It is used to make proteins and vitamin B_3. This necessitates taking large amounts of tryptophan.

5-HTP is a step closer in the serotonin production pathway. It is also more widely available than L-tryptophan and is more easily taken up in the brain. Seventy percent is taken up into the brain, as opposed to only 3 percent of L-tryptophan. 5-HTP is about five to ten times more powerful than L-tryptophan. A number of double-blind studies have shown that 5-HTP is as effective as antidepressant medication. 5-HTP boosts serotonin levels in the brain and helps to calm anterior cingulate gyrus hyperactivity (greasing the anterior cingulate gyrus, if you will, to help with shifting of attention). The dose of 5-HTP for adults is 50–300 mg a day. Children should start at half a dose. Take 5-HTP and L-tryptophan on an empty stomach. The most common side effect of 5-HTP is an upset stomach. It is usually very mild. Start slowly and work your way up slowly.

There have also been some recent studies with Inositol, from the B vitamin family, which you can get in a health food store. In doses of 12–20 milligrams a day it has been shown to decrease moodiness, depression, and overfocus issues.

Do not take St. John's wort, L-tryptophan, or 5-HTP with prescribed antidepressants unless under the close supervision of your physician.

BASAL GANGLIA SYSTEM ISSUES

The basal ganglia are a set of large structures toward the center of the brain that surround the deep limbic system. The basal ganglia are involved with integrating feelings, thoughts, and movement, along with helping to shift and smooth motor be-havior. In our clinic we have noticed that the basal ganglia are involved with setting the body's idle or anxiety level. When they work too hard, people have problems with anxiety, nervousness, panic, fear, and physical tension.

Anti-anxiety medications are often very helpful for severe basal ganglia problems. Nervousness, chronic stress, panic at-tacks, and muscle tension often respond to medications when other techniques are ineffective. There are five classes of med-ication helpful in treating anxiety.

Benzodiazepines are common anti-anxiety medications that have been available for many years. Valium, Xanax, Ativan, Serax, and Tranxene are examples of benzodiazepines. The are several advantages to these medications. They work quickly, they generally have few side effects, and they are very effective. On the negative side, long-term use can cause addiction. In the panic attack plan I give my patients, I often prescribe Xanax as a short-term anti-anxiety medication to use in conjunction with the other basal ganglia prescriptions. BuSpar is often very effec-tive in treating long-term anxiety. It also has the benefit of not being addictive. On the negative side, it takes a few weeks to be effective, and it must be taken all of the time to maintain its effectiveness. It has been shown to have a calming effect on ag-gressive behavior. Certain antidepressants, such as Tofranil (imip-ramine) and the MAO inhibitor Nardil, are especially helpful for people with panic disorders. I have found these medications to be helpful in patients who have both limbic system and basal ganglia problems. Focal basal ganglia abnormalities, like focal limbic system changes, are often helped with nerve-stabilizing medications, such as Lithium, Tegretol, or Depakote. I have found these medications to be very helpful for some patients. The last class of medications I find helpful in severe cases of anx-iety are antipsychotic medications such as Risperdal, Zyprexa, or Seroquel. Because of their side effects, I usually save these medications until I have tried other options. When psychotic symptoms are present, these medications are often lifesaving.

What you eat has an important effect on your basal ganglia. If your symptoms reflect heightened basal ganglia activity and anxiety, you'll do better with a balanced diet that does not allow you to get too hungry during the day. Hypoglycemic episodes make anxiety much worse. If you have low basal ganglia activity and low motivation, you will likely do better with a high-protein, low-carbohydrate diet to give yourself more energy during the day. It is also often helpful to eliminate anxiety-producing chemicals such as caffeine and to eliminate alcohol, since alcohol-withdrawal symptoms often induce anxiety.

Some herbal preparations, such as kava extract and valerian root, have also been reported to help anxiety and likely have a calming effect on the basal ganglia. The B vitamins, especially vitamin B_6 in doses of 100–400 milligrams, are also helpful. If you take B_6 in these doses, it is important to also take a B complex vitamin as well. My patients have also found the scents from the essential oils chamomile and lavender to be helpful.

DEEP LIMBIC SYSTEM ISSUES

The deep limbic system lies near the center of the brain. It is about the size of a walnut. This is the part of the brain that sets a person's emotional tone, or how positive or negative you are. The limbic system also affects motivation and drive. It helps get you going in the morning and encourages you to move throughout the day. It controls the sleep and appetite cycles of the body. It affects the bonding mechanism that enables you to connect with other people on a social level; your ability to do this successfully, in turn, influences your moods.

Mood problems often occur when the limbic system of the brain is overactive. Clinical depression, manic-depressive disorder, and severe PMS are more severe problems than the garden variety most people experience in the form of bad moods. For complete healing to take place, the addition of antidepressant medication or appropriate herbal treatment may be needed. A sure sign that the prescribed medications are really treating the depression is that the deep limbic system activity normalizes. Whenever limbic activity normalizes, there is a corresponding decrease in the patient's symptoms.

In recent years, new antidepressants with wider applications and often fewer side effects than the original antidepressants have entered the market. Some of the new pharmaceuticals are important because they have the additional benefit of affecting the subclinical patterns the rest of us are more likely to experience at some time in our lives, such as moodiness and negativity. In treating clinical depression, it is important to use enough medication for a long enough period of time. Often, antidepressants take two to four weeks to become effective. The medications used for limbic hyperactivity include standard antidepressants, such as Tofranil (imipramine), Norpramin (desipramine), and Pamelor (nortriptyline), the newer antidepressants such as Prozac (fluoxetine) and Wellbutrin (buprion), and the stimulants.

Over the past decade there has been significant research on food, nutrients, and depression. The results surprise many people. We have been inundated by nutritional experts and news reporters who tell us we should eat low-fat, high-carbohydrate diets. "Low fat" is everywhere. Unfortunately, low fat is not the complete answer. In two studies in the *American Journal of Psychiatry,* men who had the highest suicide rates had the lowest cholesterol levels. Our brain needs fat in order to operate properly. Certainly, some fats—such as the omega-3 fatty acids found most prevalently in fish—are better for us than others. Protein is also essential to a healthy "deep limbic diet." Proteins are the building blocks of brain neurotransmitters. Low levels of dopamine, serotonin, and norepinephrine have all been implicated in depression and mood disorders. It is essential to eat enough protein in balanced amounts with fats and carbohydrates. Too much protein for some people may actually restrict the amount of "brain proteins" to cross into the brain. Not enough protein will leave you with a brain-protein deficit. Here are some clues.

Low serotonin levels are often associated with worrying, moodiness, emotional rigidity, and irritability (a combination of deep limbic and anterior cingulate problems). To enhance serotonin levels, eat balanced meals with carbohydrate snacks (such as crackers or bread). Exercise can be a tremendous help, along with nutritional supplementation with the amino acid L-tryptophan. There have been some recent studies with Inositol, from the vitamin B family, which you buy in a health food store. In doses of 12–20 milligrams a day, it has been shown to decrease moodiness and depression. As mentioned above, St. John's wort is a mild antidepressant that works by decreasing anterior cingulate and limbic hyperactivity.

Low norepinephrine and dopamine levels are often associated with depression, lethargy, trouble focusing, negativity, and mental fuzziness. To enhance norepinephrine and dopamine levels, it is better to have protein snacks (such as meat, eggs, or cheese) and to avoid simple carbohydrates, such as bread, pasta, cakes, and candy. Also, I often have my patients take natural amino acids such as tyrosine (1,000–1,500 milligrams a day) for energy, focus, impulsivity and DL-phenylalanine (400 mg three times a day on an empty stomach) for moodiness and irritability.

I have also found SAMe helpful for limbic problems. SAMe is involved in the production of many important brain compounds, such as neurotransmitters. It donates "methyl" groups to these compounds so that they can function properly. Normally, the brain manufactures all the SAMe it needs from the amino acid methionine. In depression, however, this synthesis has been found to be impaired. Supplementing the diet with SAMe has been found to increase the neurotransmitters involved in depression and improve cell membrane fluidity. SAMe is one of the best natural antidepressants; a number of recent studies have shown that it is as effective for some people as antidepressant medication. SAMe has also been found helpful for people who suffer from fibromyalgia, a chronic muscle pain disorder. People who have bipolar disorder or manic-depressive illness should not take SAMe. There have been a number of reported cases of SAMe causing manic or hypomanic episodes (excessively up or happy moods, extreme impulsivity in sexuality or spending money, pressured speech, or decreased need for sleep). I think these reports highlight the fact that SAMe is an effective antidepressant, since all of the prescription antidepressants have that capability as well. The standard dosage of SAMe for adults is 200–400 mg two to four times a day, and for children it is half that. One of the problems with SAMe is that it is expensive, as expensive as many of the newer antidepressants. Insurance companies do not, in general, cover herbal or supplemental treatments, making SAMe even more expensive than prescription medication for most people. Over time, the cost is likely to come down.

TEMPORAL-LOBE ISSUES

In my clinical experience, temporal-lobe symptoms are much more common in psychiatry than most people think. These include periods of panic or fear for no specific reason, periods of spaciness or confusion, dark (suicidal or homicidal) thoughts, significant social miscuing or withdrawal, frequent periods of déjà vu, irritability, rages, and illusions (such as seeing shadows out of the corner of the eye). Temporal-lobe dysfunction may be inherited or it may be caused by some sort of brain trauma.

Strategies geared toward temporal-lobe stabilization and enhancement have proven valuable for the health of the soul. From a medication standpoint, I have seen antiseizure (also called anticonvulsant) medications to be the most helpful. One of the mechanisms these medications are thought to work through is by enhancing the amino acid gamma-aminobutyric acid (GABA). GABA is an essential neurotransmitter in the brain. It is formed in the body from glutamic acid. Its function is to decrease neuron activity and inhibit nerve cells from overfiring or firing erratically. Temporal-lobe symptoms are often responsive to anti-seizure medication, such as Depakote, Neurontin, Topamax, Gabitril, Trileptal, or Tegretol. Temporal-lobe symptoms are often made worse by serotonergic medications such as Prozac, Paxil, Zoloft, etc.

GABA can also be taken as a supplement. It acts like a mild anticonvulsant and also as an anti-anxiety agent. In the herbal literature it is reported to work in much the same way as diazepam (Valium), chlordiazepoxide (Librium), and other tranquilizers, but without fear of addiction. I have seen it have a nice calming effect on people who struggle with temper, irritability, and anxiety (all which may be temporal-lobe symptoms). The doses of GABA range from 250 to 2,000 mg a day for adults, half that for children.

Ten

Healing the
Hardware of the Soul

Exercises to Focus on Eternal Values
and Direct Your Thoughts and Actions

OPTIMIZING your life has a positive impact on brain function. As brain function impacts behavior, so too does behavior impact the brain. There is scientific evidence that living a positive, spiritual life improves brain function. As with computers, hardware problems in the brain can be helped by special programming techniques or software. In this chapter, we will look at how to improve brain function through psychological, social, and spiritual interventions. We will look specifically at:

- How to enhance prefrontal cortex function by focusing on eternal values for your life and developing your own One-Page Miracle for the Soul (page 150),
- How to direct thoughts to enhance brain activity and calm the emotional areas of the brain,
- How to direct behavior to optimize brain function.

You are not stuck with the brain patterns you were born with. Through directed brain exercises you can actually enhance brain function and encourage your soul's capacity for goodness.

Focusing on Eternal Values—Living Intentionally

A prudent man gives thoughts to his steps.

— PROVERBS 14:15

What are your day-to-day goals?
What do you want out of life?
What has lifelong value for you?

Asking yourself these questions and using the answers to guide your life empowers your prefrontal cortex to work at its highest level. Forward thinking is a PFC function. The PFC allows us to see beyond the moment and plan for tomorrow, next week, next month, and next year. It helps us to be successful as human beings by anticipating the future and matching our behavior, over time, to get what we want. The PFC is the reins that guide behavior. When the PFC works properly, we are no longer driven by pure instinct to desires in the here and now, but rather we can control impulses and direct our behavior in a positive direction for the long term. Sin often occurs from a lack of forethought or judgment. Spending money excessively, adulterous affairs, road rage, child abuse, and drug abuse are just a few examples of misguided behavior.

In my psychotherapy practice I am amazed at how seldom people take advantage of the PFC's amazing planning ability. In order to be successful in life, you first have to decide what you want. Yet, judging from my experience, few people know their own values and what they want in life. They live in the moment and never set clear goals for each of the major areas of their lives. Sure, if I ask my patients what they want in life, they may say things like financial security, health, and loving relationships, but few people ever delineate those goals into a detailed mission statement for their lives. Personally and professionally, I have found developing and revising life mission statements to be an incredibly helpful exercise. I think of it as a PFC exercise because it puts the planning part of our brain into high gear.

Through the years I have developed a specific exercise for my patients. GOALS is the file name for this exercise, which has been on my computer for over twenty years. When I saw how effective this exercise was in directing and changing behavior, I retitled it the One-Page Miracle. As I further worked on the spiritual aspect of the exercise I renamed it again: the One-Page Miracle for the Soul (OPMS). This exercise is very simple, yet if you do it as I suggest, it will have a profound impact on your life. It forces you to look at what has eternal value for your life, rather than momentary value.

Simply stated, the OPMS it is a mission statement for your life based on clearly stated values. It is a clear description of what you want in your relationships, work, finances, physical health, and emotional and spiritual health. The OPMS plants your desires into your PFC. It transforms you from an instinct-driven person into a thoughtful and goal-directed individual. In my experience, the most successful people are those who used their PFC to see beyond the here and now. This form of goal setting is so basic to success it is a wonder that we do not teach it in schools.

Before I give you specific directions on how to develop your own OPMS, answer the following twelve questions to help clarify your own values. Share your answers with a friend. Hearing these answers out loud will help you fully think through them.

1. On a separate piece of paper, rank the following ten values in order of their importance to you (1 = most important, 10 = least important).

   Personal wisdom
   Wealth
   Fulfilling relationships
   Fame
   Individual accomplishments
   Legacy
   Honesty/integrity

Faith in yourself
Faith in a higher power
How you appear to others

2. What are you now doing to accomplish or enhance the first five items you placed on the list?
3. Think of yourself lying in your coffin at the end of your life. What was really important to you in your life? What has eternal value for you?
4. Are you giving enough time and effort to those people or things that really matter to you? Or are you spending the bulk of your time on things of lesser personal value?
5. What developmental period of life—adolescence, young adulthood, middle age, etc.—are you in? How have your personal goals changed from the previous period? How do you think they'll change ten years from now?
6. Reflect on your emotional development as a child in your family. Do you think it has impaired or enhanced your development? In what ways?
7. Reflect on your spiritual development. Do you think it has impaired or enhanced your development? In what ways?
8. Name five people whom you look up to and admire. Describe the traits you admire and the ways you would like to be like them.
9. Name five people you know whom you do not admire. Describe the specific things about them that turn you off.
10. List five experiences in which you felt like a failure. Have you been more likely to repeat your failures or your successes?
11. List five experiences in which you felt successful in the past. Remember these experiences, and dwell on them.
12. There are four major areas in your life:
    a. relationships (with spouse or lover, children, family, friends)
    b. work/finances (your job, school if you are a student,

or tasks at home if you're a homemaker, current and future finances, etc.)

c. personal life (the part of your life that applies just to you outside of relationships or work: physical and emotional health, interests, intellectual growth, etc.)

d. spiritual (your essence, your soul, your personality and character, the part of you known only to yourself and to God)

How significant/important is each area to you? Rank each area on a 1 to 10 point scale, giving 10 points to areas that are all-consuming and 1 point to areas that have little significance to you. How much time do you give to each area? Does this reflect its importance to you?

With the above information in mind, you are ready to develop your OPMS. It will help guide nearly all of your thoughts, words, and actions. As an example, my own OPMS appears on page 153.

TAKE out another sheet of paper and clearly write out your major goals. Use the following main headings: Relationships, Work/Finances, Self, and Soul. (You can use the worksheet on page 155.)

- Under Relationships, write the subheadings of spouse/lover, children, family, and friends.
- Under Work/Finances, write current and future work and financial goals.
- Under Self, write physical health, emotional health, interests, and intellectual growth.
- Under Soul, write what you want for your spirit, your relationship with God, your personality and character, for that part of you that no one else sees but you and God.

Next to each subheading, detail succinctly what's important to you in that area; write what you want, not what you don't want or what you think others want of you. Be positive and use the first person. Also, write what you want with confidence and the expectation you will make it happen. Keep the paper with you so that you can work on it over several days. After you finish with the initial draft (you'll frequently want to update it), place this piece of paper where you can see it every day, such as on your refrigerator, by your bedside, on the bathroom mirror, or on your desk at work. In that way, every day you will focus your eyes (and PFC) on what's important to you. This exercise will help direct your behavior to what you want. Your life will become more self-aware, and you will spend your energy on goals that are important to you.

I separate the areas of relationships, work, self, and soul in order to encourage a more balanced approach to life. Burnout occurs when our lives become unbalanced and we overextend ourselves in one area while ignoring another. For example, in my practice I see that a common cause of divorce is one person working so much that little energy is left over for his or her spouse.

A 47-year-old physician, author, husband,
and father of three children and five stepchildren.

ONE-PAGE MIRACLE FOR THE SOUL

What Do I Want? What Am I Doing to Make It Happen?

Relationships

Wife: I want to share my life, love, joys, sorrows, and physical body with Lisa. I treat her as though she is treasured, loved, and considered in most things I do.

Children: I want an active, loving relationship with my children. I am involved in their lives and listen to their ideas, wants, and needs. I notice their good behavior. I am firm and fair with them.

Friends: I cherish friendships. I nurture my relationships with special friends and cultivate new friendships as I meet people special to me.

Family: I am actively involved with members of my family (my closest friends). I love and cherish my parents and siblings, and I want to be present for them when needed.

Work/Finances

Current: I always want to do my best for my patients. I want to change the way the world views psychiatric illness and teach people and my colleagues how to look at the brain and look into the hardware of the soul. I want to be the best teacher I can be so people will easily understand the message. I engage in activities to keep my employees and clinics healthy.

Future: I want to stay on top of developments in my field and be part of new developments.

Finances: I save 15–20% of my net income to invest in retirement funds so I can take a break when I need to. I invest money for my children and teach them how to invest and save money for themselves.

Self

Physical: I eat a diet that helps me feel better and live longer. I play three hours of table tennis a week for exercise and the challenge. I maintain my weight between 160 and 165 pounds.

Emotional: I want to be relaxed, even tempered, and see the future in a positive way.

Interests: History of exploration and penguins.

Soul

Spirit: I have a positive, helpful spirit and attitude.

Relationship with God: I want to feel God's presence in my life and encourage it by going to church and praying daily.

Character/Personality: I want to live with integrity, meaning, competence, and connection.

Your name: _____

ONE-PAGE MIRACLE FOR THE SOUL
What Do I Want? What Am I Doing to Make It Happen?

Relationships

Spouse/lover: _____

_____

Children: _____

_____

Friends: _____

_____

Family: _____

_____

Work/Finances

Current: _____

_____

Future: _____

_____

Finances: _____

_____

Self

Physical: _____

_____

Emotional: _____

_____

Interests: _____

_____

Soul

Spirit: _____

_____

Relationship
with God: _____

_____

Character/
Personality: _____

_____

Start every day by reading your OPMS. It will help you focus your time and energy on things that matter to you. It will help you keep your life on track. How is it going to be at the end of your life? Will you have worked toward goals that were important to you? Or will you have lived from moment to moment? The PCF and OPMS can guide you to the place you want to be.

Directed Thinking

Finally, brothers, whatever is true, whatever is noble, whatever is right, whatever is pure, whatever is lovely, whatever is admirable—if anything is excellent or praiseworthy—think about such things. Whatever you have learned or received or heard from me, or seen in me—put it into practice. And the God of peace will be with you.
—Paul the Apostle, writing in Philippians 4:8–9

Cognitive therapy, or therapy for your thoughts, has proven to be a very helpful tool in treating a wide variety of psychological problems from depression and anxiety disorders to eating disorders and even marital or vocational problems. Most mental health professionals believe that psychologist Albert Ellis or psychiatrist Aaron Beck invented cognitive therapy. That's true as far as twentieth-century psychology goes, yet it is clear in the Bible that the Apostle Paul had laid down the principles for cognitive therapy thousands of years before Ellis or Beck. Philippians 4:8–9 is a very clear statement on the most helpful way to think and behave. Paul understood the power of moment-by-moment thoughts on your life. What you allow to occupy your mind will sooner or later determine your feelings, your speech, and your actions.

Did you know that every time you have a thought, your brain releases chemicals? That's the beauty of the brain: You have a thought, your brain releases chemicals, electrical transmissions go through your brain, and in a circular fashion you become aware of what you're thinking. If you can picture in your mind's eye the weight and power of thoughts, you will agree that they are real and they have a real impact on how you feel and how you behave. Every time you have an angry, unkind, sad, or cranky thought, your brain releases negative chemicals that activate your deep limbic system and make your body feel bad. Think about the last time you were mad. How did you feel? When most people are angry their muscles become tense, their hearts beat faster, their hands start to sweat, and they may even begin to feel a little dizzy. Your body reacts to every negative thought you have.

Mark George, M.D., demonstrated this phenomenon in an elegant study of brain function at the National Institute of Mental Health. He studied the activity of the brain in ten normal women under three different conditions. He studied these women when they were thinking neutral thoughts, happy thoughts, and sad thoughts. During the neutral thoughts, nothing changed in the brain. During the happy thoughts, each woman demonstrated a cooling of her deep limbic system. During the sad thoughts, each woman's deep limbic system became highly active. Here is powerful evidence that your thoughts matter!

Every time you have a good thought, a happy thought, a hopeful thought, or a kind thought, your brain releases chemicals that calm your deep limbic system and help your body feel good. Think about the last time that you were happy. How did you feel? When most people are happy their muscles relax, their hearts beat slower, their hands become dry, and they breathe slower. Your body also reacts to your good thoughts.

Your body reacts to every thought you have. We know this from lie detector tests. During a lie detector test, a person is hooked up to equipment that measures hand temperature, heart rate, blood pressure, breathing rate, muscle tension, and how much the hands sweat. The tester then asks questions, like "Did you do that?" If the person did a bad deed, his body is likely to have a "stress" response and to react in the following ways: hands get colder, heart beats more rapidly, blood pressure goes up, breathing quickens, muscles tighten, and hands sweat more. Almost immediately the subject's body reacts to his thoughts, whether he says anything or not. The deep limbic system is responsible for translating our emotional state into physical feelings of relaxation or tension. The opposite is also true. If he did not do the thing the tester asked about, it is likely that his body will experience a "relaxation" response and react in the following ways: hands become warmer, heart rate slows, blood pressure decreases, breathing slows and deepens, muscles relax, and hands become drier. No matter who you are, your body reacts to what you think. This happens not only when you're asked about telling the truth; your body reacts to every thought you have, whether it is about work, friends, family, or anything else.

Thoughts are powerful. They can make your mind and body feel good or they can make you feel bad. That is why emotional upset can manifest itself in physical symptoms, such as headaches or stomachaches. An ecosystem contains everything in the environment, like the water, the land, the cars, the people, the animals, the vegetation, the houses, the landfills, etc. Now, think of your body like its own personal "ecosystem." A negative thought is like pollution to your system. Just as pollution in the Los Angeles basin affects everyone who goes outside, so too do negative thoughts pollute your deep limbic system, your mind, and your body.

Thoughts are usually automatic. They just happen. Since they just happen, they are not necessarily correct, nor do your thoughts always tell the truth. They often lie to you. Most of us believe our thoughts and do not know how to challenge them or direct them in a helpful direction.

You can train your thoughts to be positive and hopeful or you can just allow them to be negative and upset you. Once you learn about your thoughts, you can chose to think good thoughts and feel good or you can choose to think bad thoughts and feel terrible. Through cognitive, or thought, therapy you can learn how to change your thoughts and the way you feel. One way to learn how to change your thoughts is to notice them when they are negative and talk back to them. When you just think a negative thought without challenging it, your mind believes it and your body reacts to it.

Children have trouble understanding the principle of directed thoughts (indeed, so do many adults). As a child psychiatrist, I needed an analogy to help children understand and correct negative thoughts. I started to call these "automatic negative thoughts" ANTs, named after the little red or black creepy, crawly things that invade the kitchen. Having bad thoughts is like having an ANT invasion in your head. When you feel sad, blue, anxious, or mad, there is often an ANT invasion fueling the bad feeling. You need a strong, internal anteater to get rid of the ANTs and the bad feelings that follow the ANTs. The kids loved the analogy. Whenever you notice these ANTs, you need to crush them or they'll ruin your relationships, your self-esteem, your personal power, and even your soul. One way to crush these ANTs is to write them down and talk back to them. You do not have to accept every thought that goes through your mind. You need to identify the ANTs, write them down, and talk back to them in order to take away the power they have over your life.

I've identified nine different ANT species, or ways that your thoughts can lie to you to make situations out to be worse than they really are. When you identify the type of ANT, you begin to take away its power over you. I have designated some of these ANTs as red because these ANTs are particularly harmful to you.

ANT #1: ALWAYS THINKING

These ANTs occur when you overgeneralize and think that something that happened once will "always" repeat itself. For example, if someone at church disappoints you, you might think to yourself "People at church *always* let me down," or "*Everyone* who goes to church is a hypocrite." Even though these thoughts are erroneous, they have tremendous power. They might even have the power to keep you away from church. Whenever you think in words like always, never, no one, everyone, every time, everything, those are examples of "always" thinking ANTs and almost always wrong. Here's another example: If your child disobeys you, you might think to yourself "He always disobeys me and never does what I ask," even though most of the time he's an obedient child. But just the thought "He always disobeys me" is so negative that it makes you feel angry and upset, activating your limbic system, and may cause you to act badly toward him. Here are other examples of "always" thinking ANTs:

"She's always gossiping."
"No one at church cares about me."
"You never listen to me."
"Everyone takes advantage of me."
"Every time I start something I get interrupted."
"I never get a break."

"Always thinking" ANTs are very common. Watch out for them.

ANT #2 (RED ANT): FOCUSING ON THE NEGATIVE

These ANTs occur when you focus only on what's going wrong in a situation and ignore everything that could be construed as positive. This ANT can take a positive spiritual experience, relationship, or work interaction and taint it. For example, you feel a deep desire to help a neighbor in need. You have the means and knowledge to help, but as you prepare to step in you remember a time that the neighbor disappointed you. Even though there were many positive experiences with your neighbor, you become focused on the negative event. The negativity causes you to pause in your effort to help and then you get distracted by other things and forget to help. Or, imagine you have a wonderful date with someone you just met. Everything goes well—you are attracted to her spirit, her mind, her values, and her looks, except she was ten minutes late for the date. If you chose to focus on her being late, you can ruin a potentially wonderful relationship. Or say you go to a new church or synagogue. It is a very fulfilling experience, but someone makes too much noise and distracts you during part of the service. If that is what you focus on, you might not go back and lose out on a wonderful opportunity for fellowship.

Your deep limbic system can learn a powerful lesson from the Disney movie *Pollyanna*. In the movie, Pollyanna came to live with her Aunt Polly after her missionary parents died. Even though she had lost her parents, she was able to help many "negative people" with her attitude. She introduced them to the "glad game," to look for things to be glad about in any situation. Her father had taught her this game after she experienced a disappointment. She had always wanted a doll, but her parents never had enough money to buy it for her. Her father sent a request for a secondhand doll to his missionary sponsors. By mistake, they sent her a pair of crutches. "What is there to be glad about crutches?" they thought. Then they decided they could be glad because they didn't have to use them. This very simple game changed the attitudes and lives of many people in the movie. Pollyanna especially affected the minister. Before she came to town he preached hellfire and damnation, and he did not seem to be very happy. Pollyanna told him that her father said that the Bible had eight hundred "Glad Passages," and that if God mentioned being glad that many times, it must be because He wants us to think that way. Focusing on the negative in situations will make you feel bad. Playing the glad game, or looking for the positive, will help you feel better.

ANT #3 (RED ANT): FORTUNE-TELLING

These ANTs occur when you predict that bad or negative things will happen in the future. Fortune-telling ANTs underlie most anxiety disorders, especially people who have panic attacks. Predicting the worst in a situation causes an immediate rise in heart and breathing rate. Just having these thoughts make you feel tense. I call "fortune-telling" red ANTs because when you predict bad things, you can make them happen. Say you are driving to work and you predict that you'll have a bad day; the first bad thing that happens reinforces your belief, and the rest of the day goes downhill. Fortune-telling ANTs hurt your peace of mind. Of course, you should plan ahead and prepare for bad things to happen, but overfocusing on them will ruin your health.

I have struggled with fortune-telling ANTs throughout my life. I know how they can cause a pervasive sense of fear and anxiety. When I first started my brain-imaging research, I decided to study the brain patterns of my own family, including my mother, my aunt, my wife, all three of my children, and myself. I wanted to see if the patterns I was seeing correlated with the people with whom I had the most intimate knowledge. I quickly learned that getting my own brain scanned was not an easy experience. Even with all that I have intellectually accomplished in my life, I was still very anxious going through the procedure. What if something was wrong with my brain? What if my brain showed the pattern of a murderer? What if nothing was there at all? I never felt more naked than after my scan, when my own brain activity was projected onto a computer screen in front of my colleagues. At the moment, I would have rather been without clothes than without the covering of my skull. I was relieved to see very good activity in nearly all of my brain. I saw an area of overactivity, however, that stood out like a red Christmas tree lightbulb in the right side of my basal ganglia, the part of the brain that often sets off anxiety. It was working too hard. The little Christmas tree lightbulb made sense to me.

Even though I do not have a clinical disorder, such as panic disorder, my whole life I have struggled with minor issues of anxiety. I used to bite my nails, and sometimes still do when I feel anxious. I used to find it very difficult to ask for payments from patients after therapy sessions. I also had a terrible time speaking in front of large groups (which I now love). My first appearance on television was terrible. My hands sweated so much that I unknowingly rubbed my hands on my pants throughout the interview. Right before my second television interview, on the nationally syndicated *Sonja Live* program on CNN, I nearly had a panic attack. While I was sitting in the "green room" in the CNN studio in Los Angeles waiting to go on the air, my mind became flooded with fortune-telling ANTs. I started to predict disaster for myself. I thought I would make a fool of myself. I might forget my own name. Say something stupid. Stutter, stumble over my words. And basically make an idiot of myself in front of 2 million people. Thankfully, in time I recognized what was happening to me. I started to chuckle to myself. "I treat people who have this problem. Breathe with your belly and kill the ANTs."

ANT #4 (RED ANT): MIND READING

Mind-reading ANTs occur when you think that you know what others think even when they haven't told you. Mind reading is a common cause of trouble between people. You know that you are mind reading when you have thoughts such as, "He doesn't like me." "They were talking about me." "They think I will never amount to much." "God is mad at me." I tell people that a negative look from someone else may be nothing more than a sign that he is constipated! You don't know. You cannot read anyone else's mind, including God's mind. You never really know what others are thinking. Even in intimate relationships, you cannot fully read your partner's mind. When there are things you don't understand, clarify them and stay away from mind-reading ANTs. They are very infectious and stir up the soul and trouble between people.

Here is an example of something that happened one Mother's Day in my home. We were having a party to celebrate our mothers. There were seven women and me. As it turned out, toward the end of the party the Los Angeles Lakers' playoff game was on television. I watched it for a bit in the family room, where everyone was, but decided to watch it in the den. About twenty minutes later, one of our guests came into the den to talk to me. She said she wanted to apologize for offending me. She had made a joke about a picture of mine in the paper. I actually thought her comment was funny. She said she felt terrible about the comment and was working on her "foot-in-mouth disease." I told her I wasn't offended, but she persisted in how insensitive she was. I told her that she couldn't read my mind. I wasn't insulted and she could feel badly if she wanted to, but not on my account. I am really glad she checked out the comment and wish she wasn't so hard on herself.

Here's another example of mind reading: During my psychiatric training program I was taking a six-week rotation in drug and alcohol abuse treatment at the National Naval Medical Center in Bethesda, Maryland. I sat in on many group sessions. There was always one counselor who made me feel uncomfortable. He seemed to be an angry man who spent most of the sessions confronting the patients: "You hate me, don't you?" "You think this program is a bunch of bull." "You don't really want to get better!" It seemed that no matter what the patients said, the counselor responded in an angry, mind-reading way. I did not think he was very successful in helping others heal.

ANT #5: THINKING WITH YOUR FEELINGS

These ANTs occur when you believe your negative feelings without ever questioning them. Feelings are very complex and are often based on powerful memories from the past. Feelings sometimes lie to you. Feelings are not about truth—they are about feelings. But many people believe their feelings even though they have no evidence for them. "Thinking with your feelings" thoughts usually start with the words "I feel." For example, "I feel like you don't love me." "I feel stupid." "I feel like a failure." "I feel nobody will ever trust me." Whenever you have a strong negative feeling, check it out. Look for the evidence behind the feeling. Do you have real reasons to feel that way? Or are your feelings based on events from the past?

ANT #6: GUILT BEATINGS

Guilt is generally not a helpful emotion, especially for your deep limbic system. In fact, guilt often causes you to do those things that you don't want to do. Guilt beatings happen when you think with words like "should," "must," "ought," or "have to." Here are some examples: "I ought to spend more time at home." "I must spend more time with my kids." "I should have sex more often." "I have to organize my office." Guilt-inducing behaviors are common in many religious institutions. "Live your life this way or else bad things will happen to you" is a frequent message. Unfortunately, guilt often backfires. Because of human nature, whenever we think that we "must" do something, no matter what it is, we don't want to do it. It is better to replace "guilt beatings" with phrases like "I want to do this . . ." "It fits with my goals to do that . . ." "It would be helpful to do this. . . ." So, in the examples above, it would be helpful to change those phrases to "I want to spend more time at home." "It's in our best interest for my kids and I to spend more time together." "I want to please my spouse by making wonderful love with him (or her) because he (or she) is important to me." "It's in my best interest to organize my office." Get rid of this unnecessary emotional turbulence that holds you back from achieving the goals you want. Of course, there are things that you should not do. Moral teaching is very important. Yet, when the goal of teaching is to produce guilt, it is often counterproductive.

ANT #7: LABELING

Whenever you attach a negative label to yourself or to someone else, you bring your ability to take a clear and fresh look at the situation to a screeching halt. Negative labels are very harmful, because whenever you call yourself or someone else a "jerk," "arrogant," or "irresponsible" you lump that person in your mind with all of the "jerks" or "arrogant people" that you've ever known and you become unable to deal with them in a reasonable way.

ANT #8: PERSONALIZATION

Personalization occurs when innocuous events are taken to have personal meaning: "My boss didn't talk to me this morning. She must be mad at me." Or, one feels he or she is the cause of all the bad things that happen: "My son got into an accident with the car. I should have spent more time teaching him to drive. It must be my fault." There are many other reasons for behavior besides the negative explanations an abnormal limbic system picks out. For example, your boss may not have talked to you because she was preoccupied, upset, or in a hurry. You never fully know why people do what they do. Try not to personalize their behavior.

ANT #9 (THE MOST POISONOUS RED ANT): BLAME

Blame is very harmful. When you blame something or someone else for the problems in your life, you become a victim of circumstances and you cannot do anything to change your situation. Many relationships are ruined by people who blame their partners when things go wrong. They take little responsibility for their problems. When something goes wrong at home or at work, they try to find someone to blame. They rarely admit their own problems. Typically, you'll hear statements from them like:

"It wasn't my fault that . . ."
"That wouldn't have happened if you had . . ."
"How was I supposed to know . . ."
"It's your fault that . . ."

The bottom-line statement goes something like this: "If only you had done something differently, I wouldn't be in the predicament I'm in. It's your fault, and I'm not responsible."

Whenever you blame someone else for the problems in your life, you become powerless to change anything. The "Blame Game" hurts your personal sense of power. Stay away from blaming thoughts and take personal responsibility for changing the problems you have.

Summary of ANT Species

1. "Always" thinking: thinking in words like always, never, no one, everyone, every time, everything
2. Focusing on the negative: seeing only the bad in a situation
3. Fortune-telling: predicting the worst possible outcome to a situation
4. Mind reading: believing that you know what another person is thinking, even though they haven't told you
5. Thinking with your feelings: believing negative feelings without ever questioning them

6. Guilt beatings: thinking in words like should, must, ought, have to
7. Labeling: attaching a negative label to yourself or to someone else
8. Personalization: innocuous events are taken to have personal meaning
9. Blame: blaming someone else for your problems

In order to keep your brain functioning at a high level, it is important to have good emotional and thought management. Whenever you notice an ANT entering your mind, train yourself to recognize it and write it down. When you write down automatic negative thoughts (ANTs) and talk back to them, you begin to take away their power and gain control over your moods. Kill the ANTs by feeding your internal anteater.

The *Kill the Ant/Feed Your Anteater* exercise is for whenever you need to control your mind. It is for times when you feel anxious, nervous, depressed, or frazzled. It is for times when you need to be your best. Whenever you feel depressed or anxious, fill out the *Anteater* form below.

EVENT: Write out the event that is associated with your thoughts and feelings.

_____

_____

_____

_____

ANT (Write out the automatic negative thoughts.)	*Species of ANT* (Identify the type of irrational thought.)	*Kill the ANT* (Talk back to the irrational thoughts.)
_____	_____	_____
_____	_____	_____
_____	_____	_____
_____	_____	_____

_____   _____   _____
_____   _____   _____
_____   _____   _____
_____   _____   _____

_____   _____   _____
_____   _____   _____
_____   _____   _____
_____   _____   _____

ANT	Species of ANT	Kill the ANT
You never listen to me.	Always Thinking	I get frustrated when you don't listen to me, but I know you have listened to me and will again.
The minister doesn't like me.	Mind Reading	I don't know that. Maybe he's just having a bad day. Ministers are people, too.
I'll stutter if I do the reading at church.	Fortune-Telling	I don't know that. Odds are I will do fine.
I'm unlovable.	Labeling	Sometimes I do things that push others away, but I can find love and be in a loving relationship.
It's your fault we have these problems.	Blame	I need to look at my part of the problems and find ways to make the situation better.

Your thoughts really matter. They can either help or hurt your deep limbic system. Left unchecked, ANTs will cause an infection in your whole body system. Whenever you notice ANTs, you need to crush them or they'll affect your relationships, your work, and your entire life. First you need to notice them. If you can catch them at the moment they occur and correct them, you take away the power they have over you. When a negative thought goes unchallenged, your mind believes it and your body reacts to it.

ANTs have an illogical logic. By bringing them into the open and examining them on a conscious level, you can see for yourself how little sense it really makes to think these kinds of things to yourself. You take back control over your own life instead of leaving your fate to hyperactive limbic-conditioned negative thought patterns.

Sometimes people have trouble talking back to these grossly unpleasant thoughts because they feel that such obvious age-old "truisms" simply must be real. They think that if they don't continue to believe these thoughts, then they are lying to themselves. Once again, remember that to know what is true and what is not, you have to be conscious of the thoughts. Most negative thinking is automatic and goes unnoticed. You're not really choosing how to respond to your situation; it's being chosen for you, by bad brain habits. To find out what is really true and what is not, you need to question it. Don't believe everything you hear—even in your own mind!

I often ask my patients about their ANT population. Is it high? Low? Dwindling? Or increasing? Keep control over the ANTs in order to maintain a healthy deep limbic environment.

Directed Actions

The Apostle Paul's plea to "think about such things" is followed by a second exhortation, "put into practice" what you have learned. Actions over time determine character. A positive character leads to a healthy life. An erratic or negative character leads to a chaotic life. Acting right is important in shaping optimal brain function. Each day, before you do anything or say anything ask yourself if it fits the goals you have. Direct your thoughts and behaviors.

Can positive behavior change the brain? Two UCLA studies in particular looked at the brain-behavior connection in people with obsessive-compulsive disorder (OCD). They randomly separated patients with OCD into two groups, a medication treatment group and a behavior modification treatment group. They performed PET studies (a nuclear medicine brain study like SPECT) before and after treatment. In general, the medication group, which was treated with Prozac, showed calming of activity in the basal ganglia, one of the parts of the brain implicated in getting stuck on negative thoughts or behaviors. The behavior modification group showed exactly the same thing. When behavior therapy worked for the OCD patients, there was calming in the same part of the brain.

The behavior therapy was done by placing the patients in a stressful situation and showing them that nothing bad would result from it. This therapy is intended to "desensitize" a person to the thing or action she fears. A patient who fears dirt, for example, might be asked to touch a "dirty" object, like a desk, and with support from the therapist, refrain from washing. Gradually, they move on to more feared objects. Eventually the fears are markedly reduced, and in many cases they are eliminated. The behavior therapy also involved several techniques, including "thought stopping" (forcing people to stop the bad thoughts circling in their heads) and distraction (doing something else to distract oneself, instead of giving in to the bad thoughts or behaviors).

Changing behavior in a positive way helps brain function. Likewise, negative behavior can change the brain in a negative way. Another PET study looked at people with OCD during a time when they thought about their obsessive thoughts. Thinking the obsessive negative thoughts activated the basal ganglia and anterior cingulate gyrus, causing them to become more stuck on the thoughts that bothered them.

How you think and how you act influences brain function! Changing your behavior helps the brain work more efficiently and helps generations to come. Doing the right thing at home, at work, or everywhere else is in your brain's and soul's best interest.

To sum up this chapter: Before you say or do anything, ask yourself if your words or actions fit into the goals you have for your life. Do they fit your morals, your values, your beliefs, and how you want to live your life. "Do my words and actions fit the person I want to be." These words, spoken daily, will enhance the brain-soul connection.

Eleven

Healing Painful
Deep Soul Memories

To be wronged is nothing unless you continue to remember it.

— CONFUCIUS

THERE are powerful "memory-healing" tools available to any psychiatrist, psychologist, or layperson who pays attention to how people think and feel. Did you know that you have the power right now to quickly bring joy, sadness, or anger to someone else's soul? Through the years I have learned that I can make nearly anyone cry from deep soul pain, seethe with anger, or smile with delight in ten minutes or less, just by the questions I ask him.

I do not do this with patients, but if I wanted to I could make you cry by asking you to think about sad things in your life. I would ask you to think about the times in life you have failed, embarrassed yourself, sinned, or acted badly. I would ask you to think about the times that you have lost someone important to you. I might ask you to think about how you felt when you lost the beloved pet you had as a child. Thinking sad thoughts actually brings on feelings of melancholy, often with a flood of tears. Almost instantly, if I think about my grandfather's heart attack, the last two years of his life when he became depressed, his death, and funeral, I will start crying. Waves of sadness engulf me, and I hurt with every cell in my body. I miss him so much and hate how he suffered from a depression that I could have treated if I was just a few years more advanced in my medical training. I bet you have something like the memory of my grandfather haunting your soul.

If I'm feeling ill-tempered and want to make you feel angry, I'll ask you to think about the times you have been hurt, betrayed, or hassled by others. I'll ask you to think about the time that the neighbor's dog bit your child's face, a teacher graded you unfairly after you had worked hard in a class, a boss fired you for something that was not your fault, or a friend betrayed your trust. Anger is usually an easy emotion for people to find. There are so many things that can irritate or infuriate us. We can be upset by the actions of others, failed expectations of ourselves, and even at God for natural disasters. Focusing on these memories immediately brings back negative feelings. When I remember the time that a friend was brought to the emergency room after a suicide attempt and the doctor on call angrily told her how to really kill herself if she was interested, my whole body feels turned inside out. My muscles become tense. My hands feel cold and start to sweat. My breathing rate escalates and becomes shallower, and my heart starts to hurt and beat faster. I still cannot believe a professional could be so stupid. She later used the method he suggested to kill herself while locked in a confessional, likely praying for God's forgiveness. I hate what this person did, and my body remembers it.

If I'm in a good mood and want to make you smile (which is more typical for me), I'll ask you to think about the times you felt competent, confident, and connected. I'll ask you to think about the people you love who are good at loving you. I'll ask you to think about the times you felt joy in your life, and the times you were hugged, appreciated, and honored. I'll ask you to think about your successes, your pleasures, and the cat that gives you adoring looks, purrs in your lap, or greets you at the door. For most of us, unless we are depressed, there are so many memories that make us smile. I almost always smile when I think of playing with my kids on the beach in Hawaii when they were little. We were living in the islands at the time. I smile when I think of the first day that I met my wife. I smile when I think of the people I have helped through the years. And I smile when I think of the most amazing gift I ever received from one of my patients. During one appointment, a twelve-year-old patient came into my office with a small package. As I unwrapped it and saw what was in the gift box, I smiled as wide as I ever had smiled. In the package was a ceramic SPECT camera, an exact replica of the one in my office. Lying on the table of the camera was a penguin. Anyone who knows me knows I collect penguins. The gift was so thoughtful and personal that I truly felt loved and appreciated. The thought of it will always make me smile.

Directed Memories

We are a sum of our memories. Memories give us our personality, our reactions to emotional events, our remembered joys, sorrows, pleasures, and pain. Beautiful, sweet memories help us feel happy and stable. Painful memories are toxic to the soul. Memories, and the associated feelings we have about them, are stored in multiple centers in the brain. Even though memories are about past events, they remain quite alive in the present and effect all we are and all we do. All current experience is filtered through the brain's memory system. In many ways we are hostages of our past experiences unless we know how to properly manage memory and our emotions. You can learn how to direct and control your memories by choosing which memories your brain focuses on. You can direct your memories to stabilize and raise your mood, increase motivation, and improve your attitude toward life. "Directed memory" is one of the best emotional management techniques available to you.

Directed memory focuses your attention on the things in your life that help you to feel happy and stable. Make a list of the ten times you felt most competent in life (at school, work, or in your relationships with others), happy (in any area of life), or connected to others. Describe each of these memories in detail, using as many of the five senses as possible. What colors do you re-member? What smells were in the air? Was there music? Try to make the picture come alive. In a metaphorical sense you are go-ing through the library shelves of daily experience and looking for the right book.

If you have been involved in a long-term relationship with someone, recollecting the history of your happy times together will enhance the bond between you. Positive memory traces ac-tually encourage behavior that strengthens interpersonal bonds. By encouraging affirming thoughts in yourself—in other words, by recalling your partner's caress, how he or she was helpful to you this week, a look or gesture that was particularly touch-ing—it will tune you in to a positive feeling, which in turn will encourage you to act lovingly. It might remind you to call your wife during the day, or to remember what gift you could give your husband on his birthday that will make him especially happy, or help both of you be supportive when times are tough.

Whenever you feel sad, mad, or anxious, recall a positive memory in as much detail as possible. I have helped many people through the stresses of divorce. Often, someone going through divorce beats themselves and their ex-partner up emotionally. There can be wild mood swings. Anger and frustration are ex-tremely common emotions that accompany divorce. Many people think they could have done better and tend to recall the times they failed or acted badly. Try to balance the bad memories with the loving ones. Remember the times of love, giving, and tenderness. You are not all good or all bad—we all fall some-where in between. Make sure you have a balanced approach.

Once a patient told me she had trouble going into stores. She felt cold and clammy, anxious and irritated with herself for feel-ing so upset. I asked her to remember the last time she went to the store and felt well. I asked her to picture feeling well when she went into a store. Her task was to go to the store focused on when she did well rather than being overfocused on when she felt ill. She relayed to me many memories of times she went to the store feeling well. After a short time, she was able to go back to the store. Focus on failure and fear brings failure and fear. The memories you focus on matters. Focus on memories that help you feel healthy.

Disconnecting Painful Memory Bridges from the Past

Memories bridge the past and present in both positive and negative ways. When I smell praline candy my mind immediately flashes back to being five years old. I see myself standing on the stool in my grandparents' kitchen next to my grandfather, a master candy maker, who is wearing his apron and making praline candy. Although these memories are four decades old, I feel happy, loved, and hungry for pralines. There are, however, many toxic memory bridges disrupting lives that are unknown to most people. These phantom memories impair love and work, and lead to anxiety and emotional pain.

Here are a number of examples of painful, destructive memory bridges from my clinical practice and clues on how to uncover their origins:

- Quite often Betsy's seven-year-old son, Blair, refused to obey his mother. She repeated her daily requests—such as brush your teeth, get ready for bed, sit down and do your homework—many times to Blair and threatened him with severe consequences when he acted contrary. But Betsy rarely followed through with the consequences, and she and Blair were constantly locked into power struggles. When I uncovered this pattern during therapy with Betsy, I asked her to tell me about the last time they struggled. It was that very morning. Blair had refused to get out of bed and get ready for school, and he made everyone's day start late. *I asked Betsy what she felt during the morning's battle with Blair.* She said she felt angry and powerless. *I then asked her to go back in time to remember the first time she had those feelings: angry and powerless.* Almost immediately, she remembered yelling matches between her mother and father when she was a child. She was angry because she thought the neighbors could hear the fights and she felt powerless to do anything but hide in her room. *I then asked her if she could go back even further in time to remember a time when she felt angry and powerless.* She said she remembered a time when she was even younger, when her drunken father beat her up, leaving bruises on her back. She sobbed as she told me these stories. There was a lot of emotion and a lot of emotional bridging between Blair and her father that in the present prevented her from being firm with Blair. Every time she tried to be firm with Blair, her mind bridged back to her erratic father. She couldn't be firm without feeling like she was abusing him, so she did nothing but whine and nag, some of the worst things a mother could do to a child.

- Chuck and Liesel were married for only five months when they started having problems. It was the second marriage for both of them. Five to seven days a month Liesel was moody, edgy, and irritable. On several occasions she yelled at Chuck and stormed out of the house, vowing not to return. Chuck did not console her or go after her. He felt tied to his chair, physically frozen with fear. Later he would just chastise her for acting badly, saying he was sick of her behavior and wanted to leave. They came to see me after one of these bouts. When I uncovered the pattern between them, I realized that I needed to work with both of them. I ordered a SPECT scan on Liesel right before her next menstrual period, during the worst time of her cycle, and then ten days later, during the best time of her cycle. Right before her period she had an overactive anterior cingulate, which normalized during the good time of her cycle. I diagnosed Liesel with premenstrual syndrome (PMS) and prescribed Prozac, which has been very helpful for many women with this problem. *I asked Chuck what he felt dur-*

ing Liesel's tirades. He said he felt afraid and mad. *I then asked him to go back in time to remember the first time he felt afraid and mad.* He remembered the battles with his ex-wife. She had been very emotional, and they had had many dramatic fights during their fifteen-year marriage. He didn't want any part of a replay. *I then asked him if he could go back even further in time to remember a time when he felt afraid and mad.* After some prodding, he remembered a time when he was small, three or four years old, when his older brother tied him up and locked him in a closet. He stayed in the closet for three hours before his mother found him crying on the floor. He became teary-eyed as he told me the story. There was significant emotional bridging between Chuck and Liesel and Chuck's past. The emotional bridges prevented the couple from forming an intimate bond, and Chuck still carried memory scars from his first marriage and even earlier memory scars from the aggressive sibling play.

LIESEL'S **PMS SPECT** STUDY (UNDERSIDE ACTIVE VIEW)

Day 26, Worst Time of Cycle   *Day 5, Best Time of Cycle*

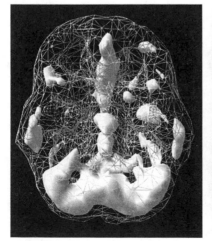 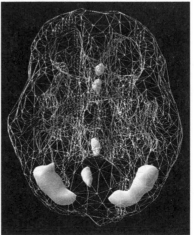

Increased anterior cingulate activity   *Normal anterior cingulate activity*

• Debbie, a thirty-two-year-old mother of twin girls, tried to kill a dog at the park. She had brought her eighteen-month-old twins to the park to play and relax. All of a sudden a playful golden retriever ran near the twins. Debbie was outraged. A foreign feeling of anger exploded inside her, and she chased the dog to kill it. When the dog ran away, Debbie sat on the ground and cried uncontrollably. When I saw Debbie a year later for problems with anxiety, she told me the story. *I asked Debbie what she felt when the dog ran toward her children.* She said she felt blind rage, unlike anything she had ever felt. *I then asked her to go back in time to remember the first time she had a feeling like that.* She sat in silence for about five minutes, until tears began to roll down her cheek. "I remember a time when I was eight years old and in third grade," she said. "I was walking home from school with my six-year-old brother. From nowhere, a vicious dog came at us barking and showing his teeth. I stood in front of my brother to protect him and kicked the dog in the face as hard as I could when he came at us. The dog howled and ran off a ways. I felt relieved until I saw the dog run toward me again. I was ready for him. At the last minute, the dog veered off from me and ran toward my brother and bit him on the leg. My brother screamed in pain. I beat the dog with my backpack and kicked him in the ribs. He ran off. My brother required forty stitches."

• After she told me this story, she said she hadn't thought about it in years but thinks now that she has always felt sadness, guilt, and rage. When the dog ran at her children, all of the rage from the past added to the present and overcame her. I then asked her if she could go back even further in time to remember a time when she felt rage. She couldn't remember anything else.

Each of these stories highlights how past memories can invade the present and influence behavior. Uncoupling painful past memories helps us live in the present free from unwanted unconscious influences. There are two methods I've found helpful for uncoupling past memories: disconnecting painful emotional bridges (DPEB) and EMDR (eye movement desensitization and reprocessing). DPEB is a rapid way of uncovering negative emotional memory bridges. EMDR has powerful brain-healing effects.

DPEB is a simple yet powerful tool for understanding behavior. It stems from a discipline called hypnoanalysis, which had its origins in the 1940s. I have seen this tool quickly work in clinical practice to help my patients understand and disconnect these emotional bridges. You can put it into practice yourself. One of the main ideas of hypnoanalysis is that negative behaviors are based on past memories that are either toxic or misinterpreted. Many practitioners believe it is best done in a hypnotic trance. I have found through the years that hypnosis is often unnecessary, although in complex cases it still may be very useful. This technique usually requires a five-step process. Here are the steps (it is often helpful to write the answers to each step).

Whenever you have a painful or disruptive memory or feeling, do the following things:

1. Write down the details of the last time you struggled with the painful or disruptive memory or feeling, or felt suffering.
2. Write down what you were feeling at the time. Describe the predominant feeling.
3. In your mind, imagine yourself on a train going backward through time. Go back to a time when you first had that feeling. Write down the incident or incidents in detail.
4. After you finish, see if you can go back even further to a time when you had those original feelings.

5. If you have a clear idea of the origins of the feelings, disconnect them by reprocessing them through an adult or parent mind-set, or reframe them in light of new information. Blow up the emotional bridge with the idea that what happened in the past belongs in the past and what happens now is what matters.

Let's go back through the examples listed above with this five-step method.

BETSY

Betsy felt ineffective as a parent and struggled with her son.

1. *Write (or tell) details of the last time you struggled, had the painful or disruptive memory or feeling, or felt suffering.* I asked Betsy to tell me about the last time they struggled. It was that very morning. Blair had refused to get out of bed and get ready for school, and he made everyone's day start late.
2. *Write down what you were feeling at the time. Describe the predominant feeling.* I asked Betsy what she felt during the morning's battle with Blair. She said she felt angry and powerless.
3. *In your mind, imagine yourself on a train going backward through time. Go back to a time when you first had that feeling. Write down the incident or incidents in detail.* I then asked Betsy to go back in time to remember the first time she had those feelings: angry and powerless. Almost immediately, she remembered yelling matches between her mother and father when she was a child. She was angry because she thought the neighbors could hear the fights, and she felt powerless to do anything but hide in her room.
4. *After you finish, see if you can go back even further to a time when you had those original feelings.* I then asked her

if she could go back even further in time to remember a time when she felt angry and powerless. She said she remembered a time when she was younger yet that her drunken father beat her up, leaving bruises on her back. She sobbed as she told me these stories. There was a lot of emotion, and a lot of emotional bridging between Blair and her father. The emotional bridges prevented her from being firm with Blair. Every time she tried to be firm with Blair, her mind bridged back to her erratic father. She couldn't be firm without feeling that she was abusing Blair, so she did nothing but whine and nag.

5. *Disconnect the emotional bridges through an adult or parent mind-set, or reframe them in light of new information. Blow up the emotional bridge with the idea that what happened in the past belongs in the past and what happens now is what matters.* It was critical for Betsy to blow up these emotional bridges. They were ruining her relationship with her son and likely ruining his life. Because of her lack of firmness he would never develop good prefrontal cortex function and Blair would always whine and cry to get his way. If she continued her ineffective parenting strategies based on painful childhood emotional memories, Blair would have problems with authority that would follow him into adult life. With this new information Betsy saw her adult self comforting and teaching the little girl within. She told the child that the childhood problems were a long time ago and she didn't have to let those feelings control her anymore. In fact, she told the inner child that those feelings were ruining her relationship with her son. A healthy mother, she said, is firm and kind. The emotional bridge was exposed and disconnected. From time to time the negative feelings would try to reattach themselves, but she quickly recognized them and put them out of her mind.

CHUCK

Chuck felt tied up in his relationship with his wife, Liesel, and had trouble dealing with her mood swings.

1. *Write (or tell) details of last time you struggled, had the painful or disruptive memory or feeling, or felt suffering.* On several occasions Liesel yelled at Chuck and stormed out of the house, vowing not to return. Chuck did not console her or go after her. He felt tied to his chair, frozen with fear, and couldn't move. Later he would just chastise her for acting badly, saying he was sick of her behavior and wanted to leave.

2. *Write down what you were feeling at the time. Describe the predominant feeling.* I asked Chuck what he felt during Liesel's tirades. He said he felt afraid and mad.

3. *In your mind, imagine yourself on a train going backward through time. Go back to a time when you first had that feeling. Write down the incident or incidents in detail.* I then asked Chuck to go back in time to the first time he felt afraid and mad. He remembered the battles with his ex-wife. She had been very emotional, and they had had many dramatic fights during their fifteen-year marriage. He didn't want any part of a replay.

4. *After you finish, see if you can go back even further to a time when you had those original feelings.* I then asked him if he could go back even further in time to remember a time when he felt afraid and mad. After some prodding, he remembered a time when he was small (three or four years old, he thought), when his older brother tied him up and locked him in a closet. He stayed in the closet for three hours before his mother found him, crying on the floor. He became teary-eyed as he told me the story.

5. *Disconnect the emotional bridges through an adult or parent mind-set, or reframe them in light of new information. Blow up the emotional bridge with the idea that what*

happened in the past belongs in the past and what happens now is what matters. A number of steps were important for Chuck to blow up these emotional bridges. Treating Liesel's PMS was helpful. She triggered him less. It was also important for Chuck to forgive and disconnect from his ex-wife's behavior. He realized that she too may have had an unrecognized brain problem. In addition, it was important for the adult Chuck to go back in his mind to the closet in his childhood, unlock the door, and let the fearful boy out and wipe away his tears (and maybe metaphorically sock the nasty older brother). Disconnecting the past memories frees Chuck to live in the present.

DEBBIE

Debbie went into a rage and tried to kill a dog who ran toward her twins.

1. *Write (or tell) details of last time you struggled, had the painful or disruptive memory or feeling, or felt suffering.* Debbie had brought her eighteen-month-old twins to the park to play and relax. All of a sudden a golden retriever ran at her twins and scared them. Debbie was outraged. A foreign feeling of anger exploded inside her, and she chased the dog to kill it. When the dog ran away, Debbie sat on the ground and cried uncontrollably.

2. *Write down what you were feeling at the time. Describe the predominant feeling.* I asked Debbie what she felt when the golden retriever ran at her twins. She said she felt blind rage, unlike anything she had ever felt.

3. *In your mind, imagine yourself on a train going backward through time. Go back to a time when you first had that feeling. Write down the incident or incidents in detail.* I asked Debbie to go back in time to remember the first time she had a feeling like that. She sat in silence for about five minutes, until tears began to roll down her cheek. "I re-

185

member a time when I was eight years old and in third grade," she said. "I was walking home from school with my six-year-old brother. From nowhere, a vicious dog came at us barking and showing his teeth. I stood in front of my brother to protect him and kicked the dog in the face as hard as I could when he came at us. The dog howled and ran off a ways. I felt relieved until I saw the dog run toward me again. I was ready for him. At the last minute the dog veered off from me and ran toward my brother and bit my him on the leg. My brother screamed in pain. I beat the dog with my backpack and kicked him in the ribs. He ran off. My brother required forty stitches." After she told me this story, she said she hadn't thought about it in years but thinks now that she has always felt sadness, guilt, and rage. When the dog ran at her twins, all of the rage from the past added to the present and overcame her.

4. *After you finish, see if you can go back even further to a time when you had those original feelings.* I then asked her if she could go back even further in time to remember a time when she felt rage. She couldn't remember anything else. Sometimes only one emotional event bridges to the present.

5. *Disconnect the emotional bridges through an adult or parent mind-set, or reframe them in light of new information. Blow up the emotional bridge with the idea that what happened in the past belongs in the past and what happens now is what matters.* Debbie went back to the dog incident when she was eight years old. Her adult self told the child that she did the best she could, and much better than most eight-year-old girls. She needed to feel proud of her intent and effort and leave the guilt behind. She was able to disconnect the emotional bridge as she realized the intensity of emotion was connected to the past and there were many wonderful dogs.

Here is one more example of how this technique can be helpful. Nate, fifteen, came to see me for panic attacks. He had several episodes a day when he felt like he was choking or drowning. His breathing became shallow, fast, and labored. His heart raced, he broke out into a sweat, and he felt as though he was dying. He hated these episodes. The fear of having them was so overwhelming that he stopped going to school. I went through the following steps with him during our second visit.

1. *Tell me about the last time that you had a panic attack.* Nate said it was the day before. He was eating dinner when all of a sudden he felt like he was starting to choke. He couldn't get air, his heart started to race, he was sweating, and he felt as though he was going to die.

2. *Tell me what you were feeling at the time. Describe the predominant feeling.* Nate said he felt as though he was going to die.

3. *In your mind, imagine yourself on a train going backward through time. Go back to a time when you first had that feeling.* I asked Nate to go back in time to remember the first time he felt he was going to die. He sat there for a minute and then started to choke. I thought he was having a panic attack in front of me. I asked him to breathe slowly and tell me what was going on. He slowed his breathing, wiped his brow, and began to tell me about a time when he was six years old. He was sitting at a lunch table at school and accidentally swallowed a plastic wrapper from a candy bar. He started to choke on the wrapper. Initially, no one saw him. He said he started to turn blue. He couldn't breathe and no one noticed. He thought he was going to die. After what seemed an eternity, a teacher saw him and performed the Heimlich maneuver on him, dislodging the wrapper. He had forgotten about the event.

4. *After he settled down and composed himself, I asked him to go back even further in his mind to see if there was an*

earlier time when he had the feeling he was going to die. To my utter amazement, he closed his eyes and said he remembered a time when he was very young. He was coming out of a very dark place into a place filled with bright lights, lights that felt hot. People were moving around. He felt fear. He couldn't breathe, and something awful covered his face. He felt as though he was going to die. Nate had just told me about a birth experience. When he opened his eyes, I asked him if he knew anything about his birth. He said no. No one had ever talked to him about it. I asked his mother to come into the room. I asked her about his birth experience. She told me how he was a meconium baby, a situation in which feces from a baby get into the amniotic fluid and pose a danger for the baby. He was born blue and had to be resuscitated by the doctor. His mother said she had never talked about it with Nate. She didn't want to worry him.

5. *Disconnect the emotional bridges through an adult or parent mind-set, or reframe them in light of new information. Blow up the emotional bridge with the idea that what happened in the past belongs in the past, and what happens now is what matters.* With Nate's mother in the room, I took Nate back to both of those times. First, in regard to the birth experience, I had the teenage Nate go back and explain to the baby what happened. The baby was in trouble for a short while, but the doctors helped clean him up so he could breathe normally. I then took Nate through the candy wrapper incident and had the teenage Nate tell six-year-old Nate that he is grateful to the teacher who helped him and that he is alive, well, and healthy (and he needs to stop eating candy wrappers).

Note: This is a very powerful tool. If this process brings up painful memories that do not go away in a short time, seek professional help from a licensed therapist to finish the process.

EMDR

Eye movement desensitization and reprocessing (EMDR) is another powerful tool used to disconnect emotionally disruptive memories from current life experiences. The focus of EMDR is the resolution of emotional distress arising from difficult childhood memories, or recovery from traumatic events, such as automobile accidents, assaults, natural disasters, and combat trauma. EMDR was developed by psychologist Francine Shapiro, beginning in 1987. While walking around a lake she noticed that a disturbing thought disappeared when her eyes spontaneously started to move back and forth from the lower left to the upper right visual fields. She tried it again with another anxiety-provoking thought and found that the anxious feeling went away. In the days that followed she tried the technique with friends, acquaintances, and interested students and found the technique helpful in relieving anxiety. She then went further to work with patients and developed a technique that is now used worldwide as a very effective treatment for patients with anxiety and post-traumatic stress disorder.

The mainstay of the EMDR technique involves having clients bring up emotionally troubling memories while their eyes follow a trained therapist's hand moving horizontally back and forth. Following a specific protocol, the clinician helps the client identify the images, negative beliefs, emotions, and body sensations associated with a targeted memory or event. Through the therapy positive statements and beliefs replace the negative ones. The believability of this new belief is rated while the client thinks of the disturbing event. After the client is prepared for EMDR, he or she is asked to bring to mind all the negative information identified with the problem. The client follows the fingers of the clinician horizontally back and forth to produce the voluntary eye movements. After each set of eye movements (several minutes in duration), the client is asked how he feels. The clinician supports the client as he processes the upsetting material, and directs the course of treatment. The goal of

EMDR treatment is the rapid processing of information about the negative experience and movement toward an adaptive resolution. This means a reduction in the client's distress, a shift in the client's negative belief to positive belief, and the possibility of more optimal behavior in relationships and at work.

EMDR is one of the most rapid and effective treatments I have ever personally seen as a psychiatrist. It is important that EMDR be done by a trained therapist. You can contact the national EMDR International Association at www.EMDRIA.org for a list of certified EMDR therapists. According to EMDRIA,

> No one knows for sure how EMDR works but through imaging techniques we are beginning to see its effects. What research has suggested so far is that when a person is upset, the brain cannot process information in its usual manner. The event that provoked the upsetting feelings becomes "frozen in time," and "stuck" in the information processing system (anterior cingulate gyrus). When a person remembers this event, he becomes flooded with the sights, sounds, smells, thoughts, and emotions of the original event as intense as when it actually occurred. Such upsetting memories may have a profoundly negative impact on the way a person sees the world and relates to other people. Present-day incidents and interactions re-stimulate the experience of this upsetting event. EMDR appears to produce a direct effect on the way the brain processes upsetting material. Researchers have suggested that the eye movements trigger a neurophysiological mechanism that activates an "accelerated information processing system." Accelerated information processing is a phrase used in EMDR to describe the rapid working through, "metabolizing," of upsetting experiences. Following successful EMDR treatment, the upsetting experiences are worked through to "adaptive resolution." The person receiving EMDR comes to understand that the event is in the past, realizes appropriately who or what was responsible for the event occurring, and

feels more certain about present-day safety and the capacity to make choices. What happened can still be remembered by the person, but with much less upset.

An analysis of fifty-nine studies of post-traumatic stress disorder (PTSD) treatments indicated that EMDR and behavior therapy were both effective for reducing the symptoms of PTSD. EMDR treatment time was shorter than for behavior therapy (five vs. fifteen hours). Other controlled studies have shown that EMDR is effective in treating phobias, in reducing stress in law enforcement employees, and helping reduce the distress experienced by traumatized children.

Under the guidance of psychologist Jennifer Lendl, an EMDR trainer, we have been doing EMDR at the Amen Clinic for the past five years. I have seen it be very helpful for anxiety reduction, PTSD, and performance enhancement. We have studied EMDR with brain SPECT imaging before, during, and after treatment. EMDR is a brain treatment. It changes brain function. We have seen that EMDR calms the focal overactive areas of the brain. In PTSD, for example, we see a *diamond pattern* on SPECT, which is excessive activity in the anterior cingulate gyrus (top point of the diamond), basal ganglia (two side points of the diamond), and limbic-thalamus (bottom point of the diamond). This pattern fit nicely into the symptomotology of PTSD. People who have been traumatized and develop PTSD symptoms (such as flashbacks, nightmares, worries, quick startle, anxiety, depression, and avoidance) are frequently overly concerned and worried (anterior cingulate traits—get stuck), anxious and hyperalert (basal ganglia), and filter everything through negativity (limbic-thalamus). EMDR calms all of these areas on SPECT. Here are three of our cases:

Leslie was twenty-three years old when she first came to see me. She had a history of two prior violent rapes (at ages fifteen and twenty-two), a physically abusive love relationship, and the death of her mother at age thirteen. Her symptoms were nightmares, depression, anxiety, and worry. A SPECT study conducted before her treatment showed the diamond pattern: overactivity in the anterior cingulate (problems shifting attention), basal ganglia (anxiety), and limbic areas (depression and negativity). After four psychotherapy sessions with EMDR, Leslie felt significantly better. When we repeated her SPECT study, there was marked calming of activity in all three areas.

PTSD SPECT STUDY (UNDERSIDE ACTIVE VIEW)

Before Treatment   *After EMDR*

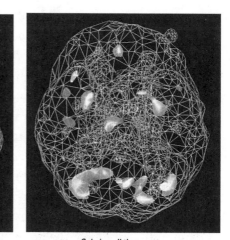

Increased anterior cingulate,   *Calming all three areas*
basal ganglia, and deep limbic activity

Katie, thirty-two, was involved in a traffic accident in which a truck veered across the center dividing line into her lane and she had to swerve off the road, landing in a ditch. For weeks she had problems sleeping, experienced constant anxiety, and couldn't drive. She cried a lot and often flashed back to the accident. She had no prior history of trauma. A SPECT study conducted before her treatment showed the diamond pattern: overactivity in the anterior cingulate, basal ganglia, and limbic areas. After three sessions with EMDR, Katie felt significantly better, slept better, was less anxious, and was able to drive. When we repeated her SPECT study, there was marked calming of activity in all three areas.

I also personally used EMDR to help myself through a very difficult time. In late 1996 I was invited to give the State-of-the-Art Lecture in Medicine to the Society of Developmental Pediatrics on brain SPECT imaging. The lecture generated a heated discussion. A pediatrician from the Bay Area stood up and criticized my work. He said people quoted me and my brain-imaging research as a justification for administering medication to ADD children. I said that we give glasses to children who can't see. If you can see physical brain problems on SPECT with people who have ADD, doesn't it make sense to treat it? Shortly after the meeting, someone anonymously (I suspected this pediatrician) reported me to the California Medical Board. In California, a physician who does anything outside the generally accepted standards of medicine in the community can have his license revoked. The law is meant to protect the public, but it can also stifle innovation. What I was doing with brain SPECT imaging was certainly different from what my colleagues were doing.

For a year I answered questions, gave the state medical board copies of research articles, hired an attorney, and appeared at interviews. Many times I felt like running away. I was dealing with a tremendous amount of anxiety. I tend to be a bit anxious as it is. I am thankful that the investigator for the medical board was an intelligent man who listened to the facts. The first board reviewer, a psychiatrist who had no experience with brain imaging, said that I was conducting my practice outside the standard of care. He said that there was never an indication for brain SPECT imaging. The investigator, who had done his homework, knew that the reviewer was wrong. He agreed to send my work to the departments of neurology and nuclear medicine at UCLA.

Several months later, the investigator read me a letter detailing the results of the UCLA investigation. They said I was doing good, innovative, and appropriate medicine. They hoped that I would continue the work and continue to publish the findings.

The investigation was over. In fact, today I am now an expert reviewer for the California Medical Board.

During the investigative process I felt anxious and tense, had trouble sleeping, developed nightmares for the first time in my life, and constantly suffered from an upset stomach. When I talked about the stress with Dr. Lendl, she suggested EMDR. "We're studying EMDR in others, it looks as though you need it too." she said.

A SPECT study conducted before EMDR showed a brain consistent with emotional trauma: overactivity in the anterior cingulate, basal ganglia, and limbic areas. This scan was different from my baseline scan a couple of years before.

The process of EMDR was fascinating. As Dr. Lendl moved her fingers, I felt like I was on a train watching all of the events related to the anxiety. I thought about the fear of failure, losing my license, being unable to further develop the brain science I loved, and being embarrassed in front of my family and friends. As Dr. Lendl kept moving her fingers, the anxiety lessened and I spontaneously began to replace the negative images with healthier ones. "You have a wonderful attorney to help you, what you are doing helps many people, even if you lose you will have helped many people, your family and friends will always love you whether you're a doctor or work in a grocery store, it will be okay, God will always be there for you." Four EMDR sessions eliminated the anxiety I felt. I slept better, and the upset stomach went away. My follow-up scan showed overall calming of my emotional brain.

Timeline

One more technique that I have found valuable in clinical practice to help people understand and heal memories is to have them develop their own personal autobiographies or timelines. In this technique you graph your life on paper. Start with your grandparents. Write what you know about each of them, where they came from, what their personalities were like, what they did for work, and what their joys, sorrows, and significant developmental events were in life. Do the same thing for your parents. It is often very instructive to learn where you came from. It holds the keys to many of life's misunderstandings. Do you know about your parents and grandparents? Do you know about their lives? If not, now is a great time to find out. Most people find this information so helpful in grounding their lives in a history.

After studying the prior two generations in your family, graph your own life. Take a horizontal piece of paper and write a number for each year of your life: 1, 2, 3, 4, 5 . . . 46, etc. Write something you remember or have been told about each year of your life. To be balanced, try writing something positive and negative or happy and sad about each year, if known. If you have no early recollection, ask your parents or older siblings to fill in some of the gaps. This technique will help give your life a context for understanding present joy and pain.

Psychotherapy Can Change the Brain

As we have seen with EMDR, psychotherapy, a software program, can change brain functioning. Imaging has also shown that psychotherapy can alter brain functioning in borderline personality disorder with mild depression. Finnish researchers used SPECT scans to show that the neurotransmitter serotonin was markedly decreased in the limbic and anterior cingulate area of a patient with this diagnosis, compared with healthy control subjects. After one year of weekly psychotherapy, the patient's serotonin levels returned to normal levels; she had received no medication. According to a lecture by Dr. Bernard Beitman of the University of Missouri at Columbia, psychotherapy reroutes signals from the sensory limbic brain that would ordinarily go directly to the amygdala up through the prefrontal cortex. The result is that patients learn to respond more consciously to external situations or stimuli instead of simply reacting in a habitual, nonadaptive manner. Dr. Beitman believes that functional neuroimaging has put psychiatry on the threshold of grasping the mechanisms of self-consciousness. Dr. Barton Blinder from the University of California at Irvine and many other brain science pioneers believe that successful psychotherapy, which leads a patient to fresh insights and new cognitive or behavioral patterns, has direct effects on the brain. Learning guides brain development and can produce major changes in brain "hardware." Dr. Blinder said that changes in insight, motivation, and behavior that result from successful psychotherapy are reflected in modifications of neural structures. Functional neuroimaging is giving psychiatrists the tools to objectively document these changes.

Twelve

Prayerful Brain Enhancement

WHEN I was a small child, my mother taught my six siblings and me to say the Rosary, which consists of five Our Fathers (the Lord's Prayer) and fifty Hail Marys (a special prayer to Mary, the mother of Jesus). We said the Rosary at home and in the car on the way home from our weekly visits to my grandparents. My mother also taught us to say grace at mealtimes and to say our prayers before bed. Prayer was comforting and helped me feel a sense of connection to my mother, because we were doing something important together, and to God, who must be listening if Mother thought it important. The sense of connection was and still is comforting. Little did I know then that prayer and meditation would be shown by scientists to have major health benefits.

Physicians Larry Dossey in his book *Healing Words* and Dale Matthews in *The Faith Factor*, as well as others, have written about the scientific evidence of the medical benefits of prayer and other meditative states. Some of these benefits are known to include reduced feelings of stress, lower cholesterol levels, improved sleep, reduced anxiety and depression, fewer headaches, more relaxed muscles, and longer life spans. People who pray or read the Bible every day are 40 percent less likely to suffer from hypertension than those who do not. According to a study at

San Francisco General Hospital, patients who were prayed for had a lowered risk of congestive heart failure, fewer cardiopulmonary arrests, and less pneumonia; used fewer antibiotics; and were less frequently intubated. A Duke University study of 577 men and women hospitalized for a variety of physical illnesses, published in 1998, showed that the more patients used positive coping strategies like seeking spiritual support from friends and religious leaders, having faith in God, and praying, the better their moods and the higher their quality of life. A 1996 survey of 269 family physicians found that 99 percent believed prayer, meditation, or other spiritual and religious practice can be helpful in medical treatment; more than half said they currently incorporate relaxation or meditation techniques into treatment of patients.

Some of the most powerful personal experiences I have had as a physician have been praying with my patients. I do not do it routinely, but I do pray out loud when I believe it will enhance the session or when my patients ask to have few minutes of shared prayer. I have found that it often sets the stage for both physical and emotional healing. We pray for wisdom, guidance, high skill levels, and healing, however it may come about—spiritual and medical, medicine, dietary, or lifestyle changes. During and after prayers, the sense of connection between the patient and myself seems to increase many times and remain high. I remember one man who came into my office fearful of seeing a psychiatrist. He had obsessive-compulsive disorder and problems with his temper. He did not want to be labeled as crazy, and he did not want God left out of the healing process. He asked if we could start the meeting with a prayer. The prayer settled him down and increased his trust in my willingness to be someone who respected his needs.

From my perspective as a psychiatrist and brain researcher, there are a number of reasons why prayer and meditative states help patients. Prayer and meditation teach us to focus and quiet our minds. They encourage mindful discipline. Children receive no formal training in attention, focus skill, or meditation. Attentional problems, such as attention deficit disorder, are a national epidemic. It seems to me that praying with children, as my mother did with me, occurs much less frequently than it did forty years ago. The brain, left untrained, is restless like the wind. Buddhists have long compared the untrained mind to a wild monkey leaping erratically from branch to branch. The mind needs guidance and training to be at its best. Done properly, daily prayer and meditation help focus and strengthen the brain's abilities. They encourage self-control through consistency and repetition. It is likely that daily prayer and/or meditation solidify new neural circuits. In addition, they can give us hope (now and hereafter). Certain prayers and meditations, such as the Lord's Prayer and the Prayer of Saint Francis, also give us clear moral guidelines.

Using brain SPECT, Andrew Newberg and colleagues at the University of Pennsylvania studied meditation. They chose to investigate the neurobiology of meditation, in part, because it is a spiritual state easily duplicated in the laboratory. They scanned nine Buddhist monks before and during prolonged meditation. The scan revealed distinctive changes in brain activity as the mind went into a meditative state. Specifically, activity decreased in the parts of the brain involved in generating a sense of three-dimensional orientation in space. Losing one's sense of physical place could account for the spiritual feeling of transcendence, beyond space and time. Another functional brain study of transcendental meditation (TM) showed calming in the anterior cingulate and basal ganglia, diminishing anxiety and worries and fostering relaxation. I have also scanned several religious leaders before and during deep prayer and meditation. The common theme of the scans is an overall enhancement of PFC activity because the brain is more focused, with decreased anterior cingulate, basal ganglia, and limbic activity. This evidence shows that the brain is calmer, less anxious, more relaxed, and more positive during the meditative state.

Prayer and meditation are essential to spirituality, enlightenment, and optimal brain function. The costs of an untrained, unfocused mind are myriad. Buddha said, "More than those who hate you, more than all of your enemies, an untrained mind does greater harm. More than your mother, more than your father, more than all of your family, a well-trained mind does greater good." Psychiatrist Roger Walsh of the University of California at Irvine wrote in his wonderful book, *Essential Spirituality:* "If our minds are out of control, our lives are out of control." Teaching prayer and meditation helps to rein in the mind to do good for our lives and souls. According to Dr. Walsh, prayer, meditation, and directed attention are very powerful tools.

> The mind has a remarkable quality to mirror and take on the qualities of whatever we attend to. If we listen to an angry person or watch a violent scene our minds start to boil with anger. If we focus on a loving person, our minds tend to fill with love. Once this is recognized, two things quickly become apparent: 1) If we could control attention, we could concentrate on specific people and memories to evoke desired qualities such as love and joy. 2) What we put in our minds is just as important as what we put in our mouths. Our mental diet affects our mental health . . . Wise attention . . . cultivates a healthy mind. What we concentrate on we become, and once we can control attention, we can concentrate on anything we wish.

The Bible and the teachings of the great religions provide many references on how to pray, meditate, quiet and focus our minds. I believe the important issue is learning how to direct your attention in a positive direction and sustain it for an ever-increasing period of time. Novices find that they have a limited attention span for meditation, but with practice anyone can improve their inner focus.

Here are some suggestions:

1. Repeat an important prayer over and over for several minutes. The Rosary is a good example. My favorite prayers for meditation are the Lord's Prayer, the Prayer of Saint Francis, and the Twenty-third Psalm. Write your own prayers or meditations or use a book that you like of prayers or scriptures compiled by others.

THE PRAYER OF SAINT FRANCIS OF ASSISI

Lord, make me an instrument of your peace,
Where there is hatred, let me sow love;
where there is injury, pardon;
where there is doubt, faith;
where there is despair, hope;
where there is darkness, light;
where there is sadness, joy;
O Divine Master, grant that I may not so much seek
to be consoled as to console;
to be understood as to understand;
to be loved as to love.
For it is in giving that we receive;
it is in pardoning that we are pardoned;
and it is in dying that we are born to eternal life.

2. Establish a routine. Pray or meditate at certain times each day. Before you get up in the morning, at lunch, after dinner, whatever works for you. Also, say grace before meals—establishing a ritual and an attitude of gratitude at mealtime can be very comforting for both children and adults. Pray at night before going to bed.
3. Focus on a word or phrase and repeat it over and over. Harvard professor Herbert Benson, in *Beyond the Relaxation Response,* showed the dramatic health benefits derived from meditating for short periods each day. He had patients simply focus on a single word, such as "one," and

repeat the word over and over. Focusing on the word brought patients into a meditative state.

4. Focus on the people, events, and things you are grateful for each day. Direct your mind to the good things in your life—to your health, your relationships, your joys, your interests, your abilities. If you are depressed, your mind will naturally turn to negative feelings, thoughts, and ideas. Training your mind to focus on gratitude will have a profound effect on your mood and health. According to Buddha, "We are what we think. All that we are arises from our thoughts. With our thoughts we make the world. It is good to control them, and to master them brings happiness. But how subtle they are. How elusive! The task is to quiet them, and by ruling them find happiness." People are as contagious as viruses.

5. Focus on a spot on the wall a little bit above your eye level. Do it for longer and longer periods of time. This is one of the ways hypnotic trances are induced. Hypnosis, in its purest form, is focused concentration. Initially you'll notice that as you focus on the spot, your eyes will naturally drift away. Gently keep bringing them back. Over time, you'll notice you can hold your gaze for longer and longer periods of time and that your body will go into a quick state of relaxation.

6. Focus on a spot on your body. I often tell my patients to focus on their chest and find a warm spot in that area. Most people can feel a warm spot when directed to do so. Then, with your eyes closed to decreased distractibility, allow the warm spot to get larger and larger, covering your whole chest; then go into your neck, abdomen, hips, legs, ankles, and feet. Many people like this exercise and find it very comforting.

7. Focus on warming your hands. The hands are a very sensitive part of the body. They have many nerve endings, compared to other areas. When you warm your hands, your

whole body feels relaxed. You warm your hands by dilating the capillaries in the skin. This mechanism sends a relaxing signal to the rest of your body, and you feel calm all over. I have found that by using sophisticated biofeedback equipment, people can learn to warm their own hands by as much as fifteen or twenty degrees, causing profound relaxation and concentration. When I do this meditative exercise, I think of holding a warm cup of hot chocolate, putting my hands near a blazing fire, holding a warm puppy, or touching the warm skin of someone I love.

8. Do progressive relaxation. In progressive relaxation you focus on your forehead, tense the muscles, and then relax them. Next, focus on your face, tense the muscles, and then relax them. Then, progressively working your way down your body, you tense and relax each muscle group from your neck, shoulders, arms, forearms, hands, fingers, chest, abdomen, upper legs, lower legs, ankles and feet and to your toes. Spend about fifteen seconds with each group, tensing and relaxing them two or three times. Likely, you'll notice that your whole body and mind will feel relaxed at the end of five to eight minutes.

Directed Breathing

Temper problems, anxiety, impulsivity, restlessness, insomnia, and lack of focus are very common problems when the brain and soul become disconnected. I have found that a very simple breathing technique helps to combat these problems. Like brain activity, breathing is also involved in everything you do. Breathing is essential to life and involved in many religious practices, such as deep spiritual meditation. The purpose of breathing is to get oxygen from the atmosphere into your lungs, where your blood supply picks it up and takes it to every cell in your body. Breathing also allows you to blow off waste products, such as carbon dioxide, to keep your internal environment healthy. Every cell in your body needs oxygen in order to function properly;

too much carbon dioxide causes feelings of disorientation and panic. Brain cells are particularly sensitive to oxygen, as they start to die within four minutes when they are deprived of oxygen. Slight changes in oxygen content in the brain can alter the way a person feels and behaves. When a person gets angry, breathing becomes more shallow and its rate increases significantly (see diagram, opposite page). This breathing pattern is inefficient and the oxygen content in the angry person's blood is lowered, while toxic carbon dioxide waste products increase. Subsequently, the oxygen/carbon dioxide balance is upset, causing irritability, impulsiveness, confusion, and bad decision-making.

Learning how to direct and control your breath has several immediate benefits. It calms the basal ganglia, which controls anxiety; helps the brain to run more efficiently; relaxes the muscles; warms the hands; and regulates the heart's rhythm. I teach my patients to become experts at breathing slowly, deeply, and from their bellies. In my office I have some very sophisticated biofeedback equipment that uses strain gauges to measure breathing activity. I place one gauge around a person's chest and a second one around their belly. The biofeedback equipment then measures the movement of the chest and belly as the person breathes in and out. Men especially breathe exclusively with their chest, an inefficient way to breathe. If you watch a baby or a puppy breathe, you notice that they breathe almost solely with their bellies. That is the most efficient way to breathe.

Expanding your belly when you inhale flattens the diaphragm, pulling the lungs downward and increasing the amount of air available to your lungs and body. Pulling your belly in when you exhale causes the diaphragm to push the air out of your lungs, allowing a more fully exhaled breath, which once again encourages deep breathing. I teach my patients to breathe with their bellies by watching their breathing pattern on the computer screen. Over twenty to thirty minutes, most people can learn how to change their breathing patterns, which relaxes them and gives them better control over how they feel and behave.

I've included several simple drawings to help you understand the anatomy of healthy and unhealthy breathing.

BREATHING ANATOMY

The diaphragm is a bell-shaped muscle that separates the chest cavity and abdomen. When most people breathe in, they never flatten the diaphragm, and thus with each breath they have less access to their own lung capacity and have to work harder. By moving your belly out (flattening the diaphragm) when you inhale, you flatten the diaphragm and significantly increase lung capacity and calm all body systems.

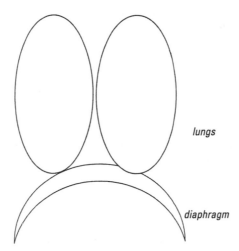

lungs

diaphragm

HEALTHY BREATHING ANATOMY DURING INHALATION (FLATTENING THE DIAPHRAGM AND EXPANDING LUNG CAPACITY)

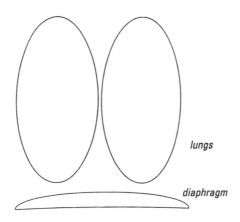

lungs

diaphragm

BREATHING DURING ANGER

The large waveform is a measurement of abdominal or belly breathing, obtained by a gauge attached around the belly; the smaller waveform is a measurement of chest breathing, obtained by a gauge attached around the upper chest. At rest, this person breathes mostly with his belly (a good pattern), but when he thinks about an angry situation, his breathing pattern deteriorates, markedly decreasing the oxygen to his brain (common to anger outbursts). No wonder people who have anger outbursts often seem irrational!

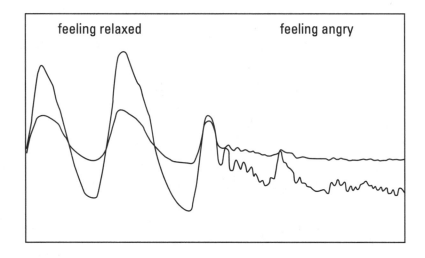

feeling relaxed   feeling angry

Few of you have access to sophisticated biofeedback equipment, so try the following exercise on your own. Lie on your back and place a small book on your belly. When you inhale, make the book go up; when you exhale, make the book go down. Shifting the energy of breathing lower in your body will help you feel more relaxed and in better control of yourself. You can use this breathing technique to gain greater focus and control over your temper. It is easy to learn, and it can also be applied to help with sleep and anxiety issues. Another breathing tip: Whenever you feel anxious, mad, or tense, take a deep breath, hold it for four to five seconds, and then slowly blow it out (this takes about six to eight seconds). Then take another deep breath, as deep as you can, hold it for four to five seconds, and again slowly blow it out. Do this about ten times and odds are that you will start to feel very relaxed, if not a little sleepy.

Here's an example of how helpful this technique can be. Twenty-two-year-old Bart came to see me for problems with anxiety and temper. During my first session with him I noticed that he talked fast and breathed in a shallow, quick manner. One of my recommendations was for Bart to do three sessions of breathing biofeedback. He was amazed at how easy this form of breathing was and how relaxed he could make himself in a short period of time. He noted that his level of anxiety improved, and he had better control of his temper.

I have used this technique myself for fifteen years, whenever I feel anxious, angry, or stressed, or have trouble falling asleep. It sounds so simple, but breathing is essential to life, and when we slow down and become more efficient at it, most things seem better. I have scanned myself on a number of occasions. My own SPECT scans reveal that my basal ganglia work overtime; indeed, my "hot" basal ganglia fit with my life. I tend to be anxious, want to please others, bite my fingernails when I'm tense or watching a close ball game, and have to fight off the "fortune-telling ANTs." When I breathe diaphragmatically and pray, my basal ganglia calm down, helping me feel less stressed and giving me greater peace within.

On the following page is the scan of one of my patients, Mary, who was deeply religious. She came to see me for problems with anxiety and a past history of physical abuse from her alcoholic father. In the first scan Mary is at rest. The instructions were for her to let her mind wander. The second scan was taken after she was taught diaphragmatic breathing and simple prayerful meditation; in Mary's case I asked her to repeat the Prayer of Saint Francis over and over. Note the overall calming of brain activity, especially in the emotional centers of the brain.

DIAPHRAGMATIC BREATHING AND PRAYER SPECT STUDY
(UNDERSIDE ACTIVE VIEW)

Resting State   *Meditative State*

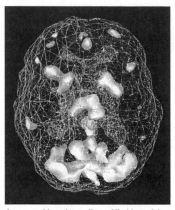 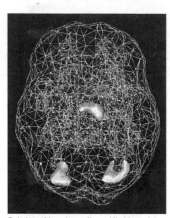

Increased basal ganglia and limbic activity   *Calming of basal ganglia and limbic activity*

Regular prayer and meditation enhance spiritual focus and also allow you time to calm your mind and body to focus on the most important issues of your existence.

Thirteen

Soul to Soul

Connectedness

The love of God, unutterable and perfect,
flows into a pure soul the way that light
rushes into a transparent object.
The more love that it finds, the more it gives
itself; so that, as we grow clear and open,
the more complete the joy of heaven is.
And the more souls who resonate together,
the greater the intensity of their love,
and mirror-like, each soul reflects the other.

— DANTE (1265–1321)

One way of dealing with other people is often "I-It," they are mere
things to us. But when we engage in true interaction, deep interaction, in
which we care and empathize, in which we open ourselves up to
the other person as a true individual, we enter the spiritual realm. This
is the "I-Thou" realm.

— MARTIN BUBER

SOCIAL connection and soulful connectedness are critical to human health. Having a healthy brain helps you get and keep connections with others. In his wonderful book *Love and Survival*, cardiologist Dean Ornish details the many benefits of having close relationships. Dr. Ornish cites numerous studies indicating that those who feel close, connected, loved, and supported have a lower incidence of depression, anxiety, suicide, heart disease, infections, hypertension, and even cancer. Likewise, those who participate in or draw strength from their religious beliefs also tend to be healthier overall. Love enhances brain function, and a healthy brain enhances our ability to love and be connected to others.

One of the most striking findings during my seven years as a military psychiatrist was that the incidence of suicides and suicide attempts among military service personnel and their dependents peaked in the months of January and July, according to military statistics. In a civilian population, suicide is highest in April. What was responsible for the discrepancy between the civilian and military populations? In the military, January and July are the months of military moves. When people move, they become disconnected from their social support network and are at greater risk for depression and suicide. I frequently treated military wives who became depressed for six months after a move. Their depression seemed to lift after they developed a new social network—friends, church organizations, social groups. The women who did not become depressed were much more skilled in getting involved and developing social support right away.

Having strong social support networks can also delay the brain's aging process. Maintaining relationships and participating in social activities have been associated with improved memory and intelligence in the elderly. Not at all coincidentally, social isolation is considered a risk factor for cognitive decline. In a study reported in the *Annals of Internal Medicine* in 1999, 2,812 community-dwelling persons sixty-five years of age or older were followed for up to twelve years. Social isolation at the beginning of the study, as measured by the absence of such things as having a spouse, maintaining contact with friends or relatives, and participating in group activities, was significantly associated with subsequent worsening of cognitive impairment, as measured by a questionnaire. Social isolation was also associated with increased illness and earlier death.

I believe that social bonding is one of the key principles behind the success of support groups like Alcoholics Anonymous. For years, clinicians have known that one of the best ways to help people with serious problems like alcoholism is to get them to connect with others who have the same problem. By seeing how others have learned from their experiences and gotten through tough times in positive ways, alcoholics can find the way out of their own plight. While gaining information about the disease is helpful, forming new relationships and connections with others may be the critical link in the chain of recovery.

The Christian group Teen Challenge is a powerful modern-day example of social support and healing. Assembly of God minister David Wilkerson started Teen Challenge on the streets of New York City, working with drug addicts. His story is detailed in the stirring book *The Cross and the Switchblade*. I became personally acquainted with Teen Challenge when I was stationed in Germany as a young army medic. The church I attended at the Ninety-seventh General Hospital Chapel in Frankfurt was involved in supporting the drug treatment group. One of my best friends and mentor, Thomas Muzzio, was a missionary to the group. I met many people who benefited from the program and later became counselors in it. Drug treatment nationwide has a very poor success rate, yet Teen Challenge had a very high success rate for people who completed the program. My personal belief was that drug addicts benefited from a belief in a higher power, developing meaning for their lives beyond themselves, and being connected to a body of believers.

I often think about Paul, the twenty-year-old son of a military first sergeant who was a hard-core heroin user. Estranged from his family and friends, Paul ended up living on the streets in Frankfurt. He prostituted himself to older men for money, often ate out of garbage cans, and had been in trouble with the police for petty theft to support his drug habit. One of the Teen Challenge missionaries witnessed and shared testimony about Jesus Christ as Lord and Savior with him on the street. Paul agreed to go to church with him. After the church service, Paul shared his drug problems with the missionary. The missionary told him about the Teen Challenge program. Paul, relieved to get food and a bed, agreed to visit it. Even though Paul had several relapses, three months later he was drug free for good, and a year later he worked at Teen Challenge as a drug counselor. The first time I heard him share his testimony in church, I developed goose bumps all over my body. There is more to healing than medication. Belief and social support can be remarkably powerful.

Social support is also critical for people fighting cancer, heart disease, and other serious illnesses. Stanford psychiatrist David Spiegel demonstrated the effectiveness of support groups for women with breast cancer. He and his colleagues compared two groups of women, both with metastatic breast cancer. Both groups received state-of-the-art medical treatment. The study group also received one ninety-minute support group a week for a year. As a group, those who participated in the support group had survival rates twice as high as those who didn't.

Enhancing emotional bonds between people enhances brain function. In one large study in which patients were treated for major depression, the National Institutes of Health compared three approaches: antidepressant medication, cognitive therapy (similar to ANT therapy, discussed earlier), and interpersonal psychotherapy (enhancing relationship skills). Researchers were surprised to find that each of the treatments was equally effective in treating depression; many people in the medical community think that the benefits of medication far outweigh the benefits of therapy. Not surprising was the fact that combining all three treatments had an even more powerful effect. So not only were pharmaceuticals and professional therapists helpful, but patients played a significant role in helping each other. How you get along with other people can either help or hurt your limbic system! The more you get along with those around you, the better you will feel.

The improvements patients with depression obtain from interpersonal psychotherapy (IPT) appear to go all the way to the brain, in research reported by Dr. Stephen D. Martin. Brain SPECT studies showed that the function of brain structures critical to mood regulation can return to normal after a short course of IPT. "We're starting to see some fascinating consistency in the data," said Dr. Martin of the University of Durham in Sunderland, England, at the annual meeting of the American Psychiatric Association in 1999. Researchers at the university's Cherry Knowle Hospital performed SPECT studies on twenty-seven adult patients with major depression. The investigators then randomly assigned fourteen of the patients to receive the antidepressant venlafaxine, while thirteen other patients began weekly one-hour IPT sessions. After six weeks of treatment, depression scores improved significantly in both groups. A second round of SPECT studies after treatment in both groups also showed significant improvement, especially in the area of the deep limbic system and anterior cingulate gyrus, indicating patients were less depressed and less overfocused on bad feelings. The imaging findings, according to Dr. Martin, support the notion that brain changes contribute significantly to both the development and resolution of major depression. "We may be looking at a pattern of holistic etiology in which both targeted psychotherapy and medication can influence neurophysiology," he said. Our day-to-day interactions with others enhance or hurt how the brain works. Being more connected to the people in your life helps to heal the brain. Love is as powerful as drugs and usually a lot more fun.

People Are Contagious

Who you spend time with matters. When you are with positive, supportive, and loving people, you feel happier and more content, and you live longer. This is not only intuitively true; research has demonstrated it again and again. For example, in a study at Case Western Reserve in Cleveland, Ohio, ten thousand men were asked, "Does your wife show you her love?" The detailed health histories of the men who answered yes, followed over ten years, showed fewer ulcers, less chest pain, and longer lives than whose who answered no.

When you spend time with negative or hostile people, you

tend to feel tense, anxious, upset, sick, and less intellectually alert. Being around people who make you feel stress causes your body to secrete excessive amounts of adrenaline, which make you feel anxious and tense, and put you on your guard. Increases in the stress hormone cortisol can disrupt neurons in the hippocampus, one of the main memory centers in the brain. Through the years I have had many people tell me that living with a person who suffered from schizophrenia, bipolar disorder, depression, panic disorder, attention deficit disorder, or borderline personality disorder has had a negative impact on their physical and emotional health. The chronic stress for family members associated with these illnesses when they are untreated or undertreated can be devastating. Mothers of untreated ADD children, for example, have a higher incidence of depression themselves and often complain that they are physically sick more often and cognitively less sharp than before they had the child.

In my experience, a hallmark of unhappy people is that they have a tendency to surround themselves with negative people—people who do not believe in them or their abilities, people who put them down, discourage them from their goals, and treat them as though they will never amount to anything. Surrounded by these types of people, sooner or later you get a clear message that you are no good. You might be asking yourself, "Now, who would spend time with people like that? Those people must have a hard time making friends, or have a need to punish themselves."

Before we look at this question, I want you to examine your own situation. Are you surrounded by people who believe in you, people who encourage you to feel good about yourself? Or do you spend time with people who are constantly putting you down and downplaying your ideas? Who are the five people you spend the most time with? Are they positive or negative? Positive, I hope. But why do some people surround themselves with negative people? Isn't it a bit odd? Actually, it's easy to understand. People who grow up in negative environments often grow up to be negative. It is what they are used to and, in a strange sort of way, it is what they are comfortable with, what their brain knows. A wise Indian shaman once told me, "People do not seek happiness, they seek familiarity." If an insecure parent continually belittles his child to make himself feel better, the child grows up believing that he is no good and that he is not worthy of being around people who make him feel good. In addition, if something traumatic like divorce or death happens in a family when the child is young, the child often erroneously believes he was at fault and carries around tremendous guilt for a long time. Some children who witnessed parents struggle through a difficult marriage get the message programmed into their brains that relationships are inherently problematic and get caught in incompatible relationships.

Adults, as well as children, can be beaten down after years of living through a difficult marriage or being in an abusive job situation. Many people will stay in a job they hate, for example, because their boss leads them to believe that no one else would hire them and they are lucky to have that job. Just as in an abusive marriage, these employees have their self-esteem beaten down to the point where they believe that they cannot go beyond their abusive environment.

Past relationships have a real impact on present ones. If your past relationships were filled with negativity, chances are the present relationships will be the same unless you make a conscious effort to overcome the past. It takes effort to overcome difficult foundational relationships, but I see people doing it daily. Changing the people you spend your time with may be an important step in changing your chances for success. A positive environment is growth enhancing, a negative one chokes and suffocates growth. Here are several exercises to enhance social support and connections.

Inventory Your Interactions

In order to change your interactions with those around you, you must first get an idea of who you spend the most time with and what those relationships are like. List the five people with whom you spend the most time. Then answer the following questions about each of those relationships.

1.
2.
3.
4.
5.

How much time do you spend with each?

In what context or situations do you come together?

Do you look forward to being with that person?

How do you feel prior to seeing him?

How does she treat you when you're with her?

Is he critical or supportive?

Does she make overtly hostile remarks, or does she abuse you in a more subtle way?

How do you treat him?

How do you feel when you're with her?

Are you able to hear what she has to say without being defensive?

How do you feel when you're away from him?

After you answer these questions, rate how you feel about each of the relationships on a 1 to 10 scale, with one being a very negative relationship and ten being an uplifting and supportive relationship.

Change the Negative Interactions

We all teach others how to interact with and respond to us. If, by our actions, we teach them that they must respect us or we'll have nothing to do with them, they either treat us with respect or they leave us alone. If we teach them that we'll accept their negative comments or verbal or physical abuse, they may abuse us. Be clear and consistent about the bottom line. Quite often, low self-esteem gets in the way of good boundary setting, and some of us accept the abuse because somehow we think we deserve it. Well, let me tell you—you don't deserve it!

Once relational patterns are established, they can be changed. Follow these six steps to changing your negative interactions with others:

1. Recognize and be clear about what, specifically, each of does to contribute to the negative interaction. Specify incidents, dates, etc.

2. Take responsibility for what you do to add to the negative situation—and change it.

3. Tell people they are important to you (if they weren't, you wouldn't be bothering with them), and that some of the things they do cause you to feel hurt or put down. Be specific: "When you cut me down in front of other people, it really hurts my feelings."

4. Ask them to change. First, tell them how upset their behavior makes you feel, and then ask them to change it. (Often, this is all it takes.)

5. If asking doesn't change the behavior, make it uncomfortable for them to treat you that way, i.e., "If you do that again I'll return your anger with fire—I won't allow you to treat me like that in front of others!" Make it clear which behaviors you'll accept and which you won't. Be ready to back up words with action.

6. If that still doesn't work, raise the heat further. In order for change to take place, the person must feel uncomfortable, sometimes very uncomfortable. Often this may mean threatening to terminate the relationship unless a person is willing to get help. Negative relationships usually take

more out of you physically and emotionally than they are worth.

Before you get out of negative relationships, you need more information: Can you change your interactions? Can the other person change his? If others are teachable, you need to teach them how to treat you. Whether you recognize it or not, you've been doing that all along. If you find yourself unable to teach others to treat you with respect, odds are it's because you believe you don't deserve respect. If that's the case, you may need professional assistance to help you work on your own self-worth.

Decrease the Time You Spend with Those Who Put You Down

If the negative people in your environment are unwilling or unable to change, decrease the amount of time you spend with them. Remember, if your environment is negative, so are you. Obviously, you may not be able to totally eliminate your interactions with some of these people, such as parents or close relatives. But you don't have to spend as much time with them. The time is better spent with those who uplift or encourage you.

Here are some actions to take:

- Call them only half as much as usual, or wait for them to call you.
- If they start in on you, find a way to get off the phone.
- Spend your coffee breaks with new people.
- If you need to communicate with them, write them a letter.
- Keep a schedule of things to do, so that when they ask you out you don't say yes out of boredom.

At the same time, you need to establish new, positive relationships. When you meet someone who adds good things to your life, take care of the relationship. Call, be kind, be interested. Ideas on ways to meet new, more positive people:

- Go to five different congregations in five weeks—see in which one the people make you feel most comfortable.
- Join a support group.
- Go to lunch with someone new, someone you may never have thought you'd like to have lunch with—expand your horizons.
- Take a fun class at your local community college or through the adult education program, even if you already have a degree.
- Start a hobby you've never tried before, one that includes other people—sailing, hiking, table tennis, square dancing, volleyball or any team sport, photography, volunteering for a local service agency—the possibilities are endless.

Keys to Effective Relationships

I teach my patients the following eleven relational principles to help maintain social connections and keep their deep limbic systems healthy:

1. Take responsibility for keeping your relationships strong. Don't be the one who blames your partner or your friends for the problems in the relationship. Take responsibility for the relationship and look for what you can do to improve it. You'll feel empowered, and the relationship is likely to improve almost immediately. Taking responsibility does not mean blaming yourself for all of the problems. It starts with the question, "What can I do today to make our relationship better?" Blaming others for relationship problems is easy, almost natural, but very destructive.

2. Never take the relationship for granted. In order for relationships to be special, they need constant nurturing. Relationships suffer when they get put low on the priority

list of time and attention. Take time every day to let the people in your lives know you love them. You need love like you need air and nutrition. Focus energy on your relationships to help them stay satisfying.

3. Protect your relationships. A surefire way to doom a relationship is to discount, belittle, or degrade the other person. Build the other person up. Notice what you like about the people in your life a lot more than what you do not like. You shape the behavior of others by how you treat them.

4. Assume the best. Whenever there is a question of motivation or intention, assume the best about the other person. Motivation is complex and often hard to understand. Assuming the worst about someone most often causes isolation, cynicism, and loneliness. Even if you occasionally err in your judgment, overall you will have much more support in your life to deal with the disappointments. Some people tell me that they are pessimistic and distrusting; that way, they are never disappointed. I tell them that even though it is true there is less chance of being disappointed, they will likely die sooner than others who have a more positive attitude toward others.

5. Keep relationships fresh. When relationships become stale or boring, they become vulnerable to erosion. Stay away from the "same old thing" by looking for new and different ways to add life to your relationships. The brain accommodates to routine. When you do the same thing over and over, the brain actually uses less energy (it already knows how to handle routine) and becomes sluggish or looks for more interesting pursuits. To keep relationships and the brain young and healthy, come up with new and different ways of doing things with those you love.

6. Notice the good. It's very easy to notice what you do not like about a relationship. That's almost our nature. It takes real effort to notice what you like. When you spend

more time noticing the positive aspects of the relationship, you're more likely to see an increase in positive behavior.

7. Communicate clearly. I'm convinced most of the fights people have stem from some form of miscommunication. Take time to really listen and clarify what other people say to you. Don't react to what you think someone means; ask them what they mean and then formulate a response.

8. Maintain and protect trust. So many relationships fall apart after there has been a major violation of trust, such as a sexual affair or another form of dishonesty. Often hurts in the present, even minor ones, remind us of major traumas in the past and we blow them way out of proportion. Once a violation of trust has occurred, try to understand why it happened.

9. Deal with difficult issues. Whenever you give in to another person to avoid a fight, you give away a little of your power. If you do this over time, you give away a lot of power and begin to resent the relationship. Avoiding conflict in the short run often has devastating long-term effects. In a firm but kind way, stick up for what you know is right. It will help keep the relationship balanced.

10. Time. In our busy lives, time is often the first thing to suffer in our important relationships. Relationships require real time in order to function. Many couples who both work and have children often find themselves growing further apart because they have no time together. When they do get time together, they often realize how much they really do like each other. Make your special relationships a "time investment," and it will pay dividends for years to come.

11. Touch is necessary for humans. The limbic brain is involved not only in emotional bonding but in physical bonding as well. Physical connection is also a critical ele-

ment in the parent-infant bonding process and for the developing brain. The caressing, kissing, sweet words, and eye contact from the mother and father give the baby the pleasure, love, trust, and security it needs to develop healthy deep limbic pathways. Without love and affection, the baby does not develop appropriate deep limbic connectedness and thus never learns to trust or connect. He feels lonely and insecure, and grows irritable and unresponsive. Touch is critical to life itself. In a barbaric thirteenth-century experiment, German Emperor Frederick II wanted to know what language and words children would speak if they were raised without hearing any words at all. He took a number of infants from their homes and put them with people who fed them but who had strict instructions not to touch, cuddle, or talk to them. The babies never spoke a word. They all died before they could speak. Even though the language experiment was a failure, there was an important discovery. Touch is essential to life. Salimbene, historian of the time, wrote of the experiment in 1248, "They could not live without petting." This powerful finding has been rediscovered over and over, most recently in the early 1990s in Romania, where thousands of orphaned, "warehoused" infants went without touch for up to years at a time. Many of these children developed serious behavioral problems like social aloofness, aggressive behavior, and learning problems. I have performed a number of SPECT studies on such children, so I have seen firsthand that the absence of human connection causes decreased activity in all areas of the brain.

When Untreated Brain Problems Interfere with Relationships

Underlying neurobiological problems can truly sabotage relationships. Let's take a look at how each brain system can interfere with relationships.

- Depression can cause a person to feel distant, disinterested in sex, irritable, unfocused, tired, and negative.
- Anxiety causes sufferers to feel tense, uptight, physically ill, and dependent and to avoid conflict. Partners often misinterpret the anxiety or physical symptoms as complaining or whining and do not take the level of suffering seriously.
- Obsessive tendencies, as we have seen, cause rigid thinking styles, oppositional or argumentative behavior, holding on to grudges, and chronic stress in relationships.
- Prefrontal cortex issues, such as ADD, often sabotage relationships because of the sufferer's impulsive, restless, and distractible behavior.
- Temporal-lobe problems may be associated with frequent rage attacks, anger outbursts, mood swings, hearing things wrong, and low frustration tolerance.

While helping your partner get help, try to:

- Empathize with the other person and try to see the world through their eyes of frustration and failure.
- Go to at least some appointments with the doctor together. When I treat adults with brain problems, I prefer to see both partners together, at least some of the time, to gather another perspective on the treatment progress. I'm often amazed at the different perspective I get from a person's partner.
- Get all the information you can. Both partners need clear education on the brain problem, its genetic roots, how it impacts couples, and its treatment.
- After the initial diagnosis, take a step back from the chronic turmoil that may have been present in the relationship. Look at your relationship from a new perspective and, if need be, try to start over.
- Set up regular times for talking and checking in.

- Set clear goals for each area of your life together and review them on a regular basis. Evaluate whether your behavior is getting you what you want. For example, I want a kind, caring, loving, and supportive relationship with my wife, but sometimes her behavior upsets me. I can impulsively respond in an angry way or I can choose to respond in a loving, helpful way, which more closely matches my goals with hers. As we saw in Chapter 9, when you know what you want, you are much more able to make it happen.
- Set clear individual goals and share them with each other. Then look for ways to help the other person reach his or her own personal goals.
- Avoid stereotyped roles of "caretaker" and "sick one."
- Talk out issues concerning sex, money, and child rearing in a kind and caring manner.
- Frequently check in with each other during social gatherings, to see the comfort level of each partner.
- Get away alone together on a regular basis.
- Work together parenting children. Children with brain problems put a tremendous strain on relationships. This is magnified even further when one of the parents has a brain problems as well. See yourselves as partners, not adversaries.
- Praise each other ten times more than you criticize!
- Get rid of the smelly bucket of fish (hurts from the past) that you carry around. Many couples hold on to old hurts and use them to torture each other months to years later. These smelly fish are destructive and stink up a relationship. Clean them out of your life.

Here are other issues to consider when brain problems interfere with relationships:

- Get help early. Once you recognize the possibility that a brain problem is present, seek help. Often education is all that is needed to get people into treatment. Start by using the questionnaire in Chapter 8 to get an idea of which brain system or systems may be involved. My clinic has literally thousands of real-life stories of people who read one of my books, recognized their spouse, lover, parent, or child in a particular story, and sought help. We have saved many relationships just by optimizing brain function.

- When one person in a family has trouble, it is more likely that another family member may have difficulties as well, so we often suggest screening. Screen family members for brain problems because many brain problems have genetic underpinnings. Trying to effectively treat a family when one or more members have an untreated brain problem is inviting frustration and failure. Parents with untreated ADD may have trouble following through on medication schedules for their children or with the parent-training suggestions given as part of therapy. An undiagnosed sibling often sabotages her brother's or sister's improvement by her own conflict-seeking behavior.

- Get rid of guilt. Guilt is an issue for many in a family where one or more members have a brain problem. Resentment, bad feelings, and anger are common among family members, yet these feelings make parents, spouses, or siblings doubly uncomfortable because they are not "supposed" to have bad feelings toward people they love who are sick, and they end up burdened by feelings of guilt. We teach family members that these resentments are normal, given the difficulties in the family. Explaining the biological nature of brain problems to family members often helps them understand the turmoil and have more compassion toward the person, while alleviating any guilt they might feel.

- Split families: Divorce is more common in families where there are brain problems. This may be due to many factors, such as the increased turmoil caused by the children or the interpersonal problems of the adults. Parents often blame each other for the problems and begin to pull apart. For parents who work outside of the home, it is difficult to be at a job all day long and then come home to a house filled with tension. On the other hand, the stay-at-home parent hardly wants to be in a battle zone all day and then have a spouse come home who doesn't want to hear about all the problems of the day. After a while, people get burned out and they may look elsewhere for some satisfaction in their lives. This dynamic may make them more vulnerable to becoming workaholics or having extramarital affairs.

Gain Access to Your Own Good Brain

The internal problems associated with brain problems can ruin lives and relationships. It is essential to seek help when necessary. It is also critical for people not to be too proud to get help. Too many people feel they are somehow inferior if they seek help. I often tell my patients that in my experience it is the successful people who seek help when they need it. Successful business people hire the best possible outside consultants when they are faced with a problem that they cannot solve or when they need extra help. Unsuccessful people tend to deny they have problems, bury their heads, and blame others for their problems. If your attitude, behavior, thoughts, or feelings are sabotaging your chances for success in relationships, get help. Don't feel ashamed, feel as though you're being good to yourself.

In thinking about getting help, it is important to put these brain system problems in perspective. First off, I have patients get rid of the concept of "normal versus not normal." "What is normal anyway?" I ask. I tell my patients that "normal" is the setting on a dryer, or that Normal is a city in Illinois. Actually, I spoke in Normal, Illinois, at a major university several years ago. I got to meet Normal people, shop at the Normal grocery store, and see the Normal police department and fire department. I even met Normal women. They were a very nice group, but really not much different from those folks in California. The Normal people seemed to have all of the problems I mention in this book. I also tell my patients about a study published in 1994, sponsored by the National Institutes of Health, in which researchers reported that 49 percent of the U.S. population suffer from a psychiatric illness at some point in their lives. Anxiety, substance abuse, and depression were the three most common illnesses. At first, I thought this statistic was too high. Then I made a list of twenty people I knew from my social and church circles. Eleven were taking medication or in therapy. Half of us at some point in our lives will have problems. The same study reported that 29 percent of the population will have two separate, distinct psychiatric diagnoses and 17 percent of us will have three different psychiatric diagnoses. In my experience, very few people are completely without these problems. In fact, in doing research, one of the most difficult challenges is finding a "normal control group."

Most of us have traits of one or more brain system misfires. Sometimes the problems associated with each section are subclinical, which means they don't get much in your way, and sometimes the problems are severe enough that they significantly interfere with the day-to-day functioning of your life. When they interfere, it is time to get help.

One of the most persuasive statements I give patients about seeking help is that I am often able to help them have *more access* to their own good brain. When their brain does not work efficiently, they are not efficient. When their brain works right, they can work right. I will often show them a number of brain SPECT studies to demonstrate the difference in the scans on and off medication or targeted psychotherapy. As you can imagine after looking at the images in this book, when you see an underactive brain versus one that is healthy—you want the one that is healthy.

What to Do When a Loved One Is in Denial About Needing Help

Unfortunately, the stigma associated with "psychiatric illness" prevents many people from getting help. People do not want to be seen as crazy, stupid, or defective and do not seek help until they (or their loved one) can no longer tolerate the pain. Men are especially affected by denial. Many teenagers also resist getting help even when faced with obvious problems. They worry about labels and do not want yet another adult judging their behavior.

Here are several suggestions to help people who are unaware or unwilling to get the help they need:

1. Try the straightforward approach first (but with a new brain twist). Clearly tell the person what behaviors concern you. Tell him the problems may be due to underlying brain patterns that can be tuned up. Tell him help may be available—not to cure a defect but rather to optimize how his brain functions. Tell him you know he is trying to do his best, but his behavior, thoughts, or feelings may be getting in the way of his success (at work, in relationships, or within himself). Emphasize access, not defect.

2. Give the person information. Books, videos, and articles on the subjects you are concerned about can be of tremendous help. Many people come to see me because they read a book of mine, saw a video I produced, or read an article I wrote. Good information can be very persuasive, especially if it presented in a positive, life-enhancing way.

3. When a person remains resistant to help, even after you have been straightforward and given her good information—plant seeds. Plant ideas about getting help and then water them regularly. Drop in an idea, article, or other information about the topic from time to time. If you talk too much about getting help, people become resentful and won't get help to spite you. Be careful not to go overboard.

4. Protect your relationship with the other person. People are more receptive to people they trust than to people who nag and belittle them. I know that for myself, I do not let anyone tell me something bad about myself unless I trust

the other person. Work on gaining the person's trust over the long run. It will make her more receptive to your suggestions. Do not make getting help the only thing that you talk about. Make sure you are interested in her whole life, not just her potential medical appointments.

5. Give the person new hope. Many people with these problems have tried to get help and it did not work or it even made them worse. Educate him on new brain technology that helps professionals be more focused and more effective in treatment efforts.

6. There comes a time when you have to say enough is enough. If, over time, the other person refuses to get help, and his or her behavior has a negative impact on your life, you may have to separate yourself. Staying in a toxic relationship is harmful to your health, and it often enables the other person to remain sick. Threatening to leave is not the first approach I would take, but after time it may be the best approach.

7. Realize that you cannot force a person into treatment unless she is dangerous to herself, dangerous to others, or unable to care for herself. You can only do what you can do. Fortunately, today there is a lot more we can do than even ten years ago.

Social connections are necessary for a healthy brain, and a healthy brain makes positive social connections more likely. Connectedness is the essence of our humanity. Strive to be closer to someone today, and make it a top priority in your life.

Fourteen

Mind Medication and the Soul

**Does Medication Make You Someone
Different or the Person You Really Are?**

IN recent years, psychiatric medications have become an intimate part of American culture. They are mentioned in songs,
movies, stock reports, and everyday conversations. Prozac, Zoloft,
Paxil, and Ritalin have graced the covers of *Time, Newsweek,
U.S. News & World Report,* the *Wall Street Journal,* the *New
York Times,* the *Los Angeles Times,* and magazines and news-
papers across the country. These medications have been major
topics on nearly every television news show, newsmagazine, and
talk show. There have been national debates over the issue of
medicating children for ADD. Physicians have argued over
whether or not Prozac is dangerous, overprescribed, or a wonder drug. Many religious leaders argue that society is taking the
easy way out by prescribing medications for conditions that relate to nothing more than having sin in your life. Medication is
a national topic, an issue that cuts to the soul of our society and
to us as individuals.

In my mind, the answer to the moral issue of medication is
clear and simple. When there is an underlying brain problem
that interferes with a person's life, such as ADD, depression,

bipolar disorder, obsessive-compulsive disorder, schizophrenia, or panic disorder, it is neglectful or downright abusive to withhold medication. Would you think of not giving glasses to a child who could not see clearly? Would you think of not giving a diabetic insulin at the risk of his life? Would you withhold chemotherapy from a child who has leukemia? Of course you wouldn't. That would be abusive and inhumane. Then why are we arguing about giving medication to children, teens, or adults with brain problems? Despite the overwhelming evidence, many lay and professional people still do not perceive the brain as an organ that can have problems just like your heart, lungs, thyroid gland, kidneys, or gut. To me, it is stunning that there is still the great divorce between the brain and the body. Even though the issue is clear—we should give medications when they are appropriate—it is not simple or without risks.

Positive Soul Aspects of Medication

When medication is properly prescribed, it can literally save lives, marriages, jobs, relationships between parents and children, and even a person's relationship with God. It can prevent murder, affairs, stealing, drug abuse, and high-risk sexual behavior. When, through medication, you can help someone's brain work right, he or she is more likely to work right and be dramatically more effective in life. Here are several examples:

SARI

Sari, a forty-two-year-old homemaker, had regularly threatened to divorce her husband. Each time she threatened to leave, it was within the ten days of her menstrual period. The year I first saw Sari, she had actually left her husband on three separate occasions and had taken her six-year-old daughter, Jenny, with her each time. These separations were very hard on Jenny, who developed separation anxiety problems. Jenny had refused to go to school, which is why her parents brought her to see me. I learned about the cyclic nature of Sari's separation behavior.

When I first met Sari, it was several days after a difficult month. Her menstrual period had started several days before, and things had significantly settled down. She felt remorseful for putting Jenny through the turmoil. She said that she had had menstrual mood problems for many years. As part of a research study on PMS, I decided to perform two brain SPECT studies on her. The first one was done four days before the onset of her next period—during the roughest time in her cycle—and the second one was done eleven days later—during the best time of her cycle.

In Sari's premenstrual brain study, before the onset of her period, her anterior cingulate gyrus (the brain's gear shifter) was significantly overactive, as were her basal ganglia and limbic areas. These abnormalities lead to trouble shifting attention, being rigid and controlling, and overfocusing on negative or anxious feelings. There was a dramatic change in her second scan taken eleven days later, a full week after the onset of her period. The anterior cingulate gyrus and limbic system was normal, and

SARI's PMS SPECT STUDY (UNDERSIDE ACTIVE VIEW)

Day 27, Worst Time of Cycle   *Day 4, Best Time of Cycle*

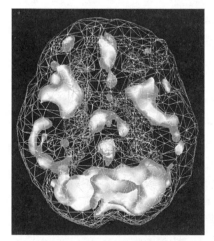 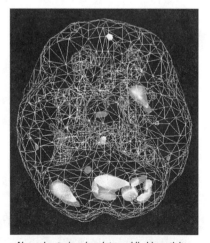

Increased anterior cingulate, basal ganglia, and limbic activity   *Normal anterior cingulate and limbic activity and mildly increased basal ganglia activity*

there was only mild increased activity in the basal ganglia. I often use serotonergic medications like Zoloft to help the symptoms associated with anterior cingulate gyrus, basal ganglia, and limbic hyperactivity seen in PMS. On Zoloft, her moods were more even and she got along better with her husband, and Jenny's anxiety began to settle down. Briefly, we tried taking her off the Zoloft after a year, but the cyclic mood changes returned. Her husband called me within a month to beg me to put her back on it. Is Sari really who she is when her hormones go awry and her irritability disrupts the lives of everyone in her family? Or is she really who she is when the Zoloft helps to calm the anterior cingulate gyrus and she has better control over her moods and behaviors? I would opt for the second answer.

SAMUEL

When I first met Samuel, age ten, I thought he was the nastiest, most negative and oppositional child that I had ever met. He argued with everything that his mother asked him to do. He constantly teased his younger sister. He was failing at school. He had no friends. When his mother brought him to see me, he would never talk directly to me. He was rude, and he frequently embarrassed his mother by his negative behavior. Another child psychiatrist had diagnosed him with ADD and put him on Ritalin, which made him worse. He was also tried on several other stimulant medications, but they also aggravated his condition. My initial diagnosis was oppositional defiant disorder, which I tried to counter with psychotherapy. The therapy didn't work because Samuel was totally uncooperative. I had his parents take my parent-training class, which didn't seem to make much difference. After several months I ordered a brain SPECT study, which showed dramatic increased activity in his anterior cingulate gyrus, causing him to be stuck in these negative patterns of behavior. I started him on Prozac. Three weeks later Samuel was a completely different child. When he saw me come into the waiting room, he stood up, smiled at me, and said, "Hi,

Dr. Amen, it's nice to see you again." He had never been polite or cordial to me before. After the medication, he was more compliant and more helpful with his sister, and he did better in school. He has been on Prozac for three years. He tells me that it helps him feel better and have more control over his own moods and behavior. He doesn't feel that the medication controls him; rather, it allows him to control himself. He told me, "I always wanted to be polite, but my brain didn't let me."

SAMUEL'S SPECT STUDY (TOP DOWN ACTIVE VIEW)

Before Treatment   After Treatment

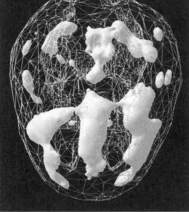 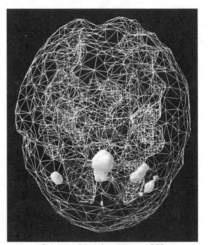

Marked hyperfrontality, increased anterior   Calming of the cingulate and PFC
cingulate and lateral prefrontal cortex activity

RED

Red, a forty-five-year-old married accountant, came to see after a serious suicide attempt. He was going through a marital separation because he had terrible problems with his temper. In addition, he held grudges, got stuck into loops of negative thinking patterns, had obsessive thoughts, and was moody and irritable. He described himself as the king of anger. His estranged wife reported episodes in which Red would become so upset about something that he would lose control and break furniture or put holes in the walls at home. Red had a childhood history of a head injury. As part of his evaluation, a brain SPECT study was done, which showed decreased activity in his left temporal lobe and marked increased uptake in his anterior cingulate gyrus. I started him on Depakote (to stabilize his left temporal lobe) and Anafranil (which has been used in patients with obsessive thinking). Over the first three months of treatment, I adjusted the doses of medication. Red, his separated wife, and his three children noted a marked positive response. He was less irritable, markedly less aggressive, more flexible, and happier. He reported that he was more effective in interpersonal relationships, especially with his children. He and his wife reconciled. Of note: When we first saw him in our office he was angry, negative, demanding, and very difficult to treat. After his medication treatment, he was a joy to be around. He was thoughtful, grateful to feel better, enjoyable to be around, and able to work with the people who wanted to help him. After three years of continued improvement, a follow-up brain SPECT study revealed a marked normalization of Red's brain activity.

TERRY

Terry, twenty-three, was brought to see me by her parents. Her mother had read one of my books and was desperate for help. Terry experienced her first depression the year she left home for college, followed by four suicide attempts in the past two years. She couldn't stop crying. She had fits of anger for little reason. She reported low energy, constant anxiety, and unrelenting suicidal thoughts. She had been hospitalized on a number of occasions but took medication only for very short periods of time. Terry believed it had the power to change her personality or cause side effects, so she always stopped it before it had a chance to work. After my initial session with Terry, I knew something was the matter with her brain. Her SPECT study showed marked decreased left temporal lobe and prefrontal cortex activity, accompanied by increased limbic activity. Seeing her own brain scan convinced Terry for the first time that her problem was medical and would be most effectively treated with medication to balance the neurochemicals in her brain. After two months of faithful adherence to her individualized program, she felt more even and happier, and the suicidal thoughts were gone.

Effective medication for a troubled brain gives a person more access to her spiritual resources, indeed her own essence, strength of will, good judgment, and focus. Medication isn't magic, and it doesn't make someone better; it balances the brain so people can use the tools they have to make better choices and decisions. As we have seen throughout the real-life stories in this book, every improvement, large and small, in the health of the brain strengthens our physical and psychological selves.

Negative Soul Aspects of Medication

As helpful as medication can be, its benefits may come at a price. One has to weigh the pros and cons of medication, be thoughtful about its use, and work with someone who is highly skilled in psychopharmacology. Unfortunately, the vast majority of physicians prescribing psychotropic medications are primary-care physicians who have little or no training in psychiatry. Here are several examples of antidepressant drug therapy that did more harm than good.

JUAN

Juan, a twenty-eight-year-old construction worker, began taking Prozac thirteen years ago, when it first came on the market. A very proud man who had lost his job around the same time that his girlfriend broke up with him, he went to see his family physician for depression. He complained of being sad, worried, angry, and easily frustrated, compounded by his fiery temper. Prozac had been so helpful for a number of the family physician's patients, and so he prescribed it for Juan. But over the next several days Juan's depression deepened. His temper increased in frequency, he wasn't sleeping, and he was filled with even more negative thoughts than before starting the medication. When Juan told the family physician about his suicidal thoughts, he quickly got him off Prozac and sent him to see me. Besides the mood problems, Juan also had periods of déjà vu and complained of seeing "shadows," which I knew meant he was experiencing temporal-lobe symptoms. This was before my SPECT work, so I ordered an EEG, which showed slowing in his left temporal lobe. I started him on the mood-stabilizing anticonvulsant carbamazepine to stabilize the functioning in his temporal lobe, which seemed to help him right away. It wasn't until we began the brain-imaging work three years later that we started to understand that many patients with temporal-lobe problems become worse on medications like Prozac. Juan, and many others who got worse on Prozac-like medications, had a problem in his left temporal lobe. It had been injured in a car accident several years before the onset of his symptoms.

JOSHUA

Seven-year-old Joshua had trouble with his behavior ever since he was two years old. He was an angry, irritable, negative, and moody little boy. His mother saw a show on television about the power of St. John's wort, an herb with antidepressant effects. The show's host said that St. John's wort helps people become more positive, hopeful, and cooperative, so she put Joshua on the herb. Within the next week, Joshua had become even more aggressive at home and at school. During one tantrum he had threatened to kill his mother. He woke up frightened every night because he had dreams of decomposing bodies. Three weeks later his mother stopped the St. John's wort and the intense erratic behavior seemed to subside. The mother then brought him to me for consultation. By that time, I had already been doing a study on people who got worse on St. John's wort. Almost all of them had temporal-lobe problems. Unsurprisingly, Joshua's scan showed marked decreased activity in the left temporal lobe. I started him on Depakote, which completely changed his personality to someone who was calmer, more in control of himself, less anxious, and less impulsive.

After listening to a number of stories such as Joshua's, I came to realize that St. John's wort is a good mild antidepressant when it is prescribed properly, but in the wrong patients it can make things much worse. One of my worries about herbal treatments like St. John's wort is that anyone can buy these substances over-the-counter at every pharmacy and health food store. Self-medicating with St. John's wort can be a lethal mistake, since the herb can exacerbate or worsen temporal-lobe symptoms and cause a vulnerable person to commit a terrible act.

LIZZY

Eleven-year-old Lizzy's pediatrician prescribed the antidepressant Zoloft for depression and oppositional behavior. Within three days, her condition dramatically worsened. She wasn't sleeping, she had three-hour tantrums, and she cut her wrists. Lizzy seemed to settle down after the doctor took her off Zoloft. A few weeks later, he tried her on the antidepressant Luvox. Within twenty-four hours she started to have the same negative reaction. This time she broke out a window at home and threatened her mother with the broken glass, at which point she was hospitalized. A SPECT study showed overall increased activity across the whole surface of her brain, a finding we have seen consistent with manic-depressive disorder, which sometimes gets triggered by antidepressants. She did much better on the mood-stabilizing medication Neurontin.

Side Effects

Another soulful issue with psychotropic medications is side effects. I have seen that side effects can play a major positive and negative role in the lives of people. For example, many antidepressant medications have sexual side effects, such as delayed orgasm, decreased interest, or decreased feeling. For many men, the side effect of delayed orgasm or decreased feeling can be very helpful, especially with premature ejaculation problems. The medications may allow a man to last longer sexually and subsequently feel more competent as a lover and more capable of satisfying his partner. The increased sexual ability helps the man and his partner to connect at a deep soul level. They are able to connect intimately with their bodies, where before there was distance and insecurity. On the other hand, delayed orgasm in a woman (and less often in a man) can cause great frustration for her and her partner. She may try and try to have an orgasm during intercourse and end up feeling dry, sore, and frustrated, which subsequently may lead her to avoid her partner's sexual advances. The memories of pain and frustration in the sexual situation may pervade other aspects of their lives together.

The decreased sexual interest that accompanies many of these medications may be helpful or hurtful. When a marital partner who previously was sexually interested in his or her spouse suddenly stops having interest, that can cause many negative or insecure feelings, such as "You don't love me." "You're having an affair." "I'm not attractive to you." Marital disconnection can lead to affairs. On the other hand, decreased sexual interest may actually make more people compatible. If one partner has a much higher libido than the other person, it may help to balance the couple's sexuality. My friend Dwayne McCallon, M.D., who is medical director of the Buena Vista Correctional Facility in Buena Vista, Colorado, started giving pedophiles the anti-obsessive antidepressant Zoloft to decrease their repetitive, obsessive sexual thoughts about children. He said that it has been very effective in helping many of the inmates.

"Will I Be Someone Different?"

Frequently, patients tell me that they do not want to take medication because they do not want to be someone different. They want to be who they are in their natural state. They fear that medication will change their personality or even their very essence. I tell my patients that the right medication optimizes their brain and they can be more truly themselves because they have access to their own good brain function. To make my point, I often use a computer analogy. You may have a fast, wonderful computer, but if it doesn't have enough random-access memory (RAM), it will not work fast and may be prone to locking up or shutting it-self down. A computer needs all of the hardware and software working together. I also use a car engine analogy. You may have a wonderful Corvette, but if the engine is not tuned properly it is likely to backfire, use too much gas, stall in the middle of inter-sections, or break down on the highway. Getting the brain to work right, in whatever way possible, is good for the soul. Opti-mizing the brain will give you full use or access to your own in-tellectual, emotional, and spiritual abilities.

Medication Decisions

Consider medication when your thoughts, feelings, or behaviors significantly interfere with your ability to function at your po-tential, whether at home, in relationships, at work, school, or on the job. I'm not suggesting that medication is the first thing you consider. It is important to use all of the ways available to you for healing, but it should be on the list. Here are some examples of when to consider medication:

- Your temper causes you to be estranged from the people you love.
- Your inability to stay focused causes you to perform at a mediocre level at school when you have a much higher po-tential.
- Your level of negativity makes you chronically sad and makes it hard for other to be around you.
- Your lack of energy causes you to stop playing with your children.

- Your level of disorganization prevents you from completing tasks.
- Your compulsive cleaning leaves no time for the people in your life.
- Your memory problems interfere with your job performance.
- Your lack of motivation keeps you from looking for a job or finding a career.
- Your level of anxiety causes you to drink too much alcohol. Or
- Your feelings of hopelessness cause you to give up pursuing your dreams.

Have a clear goal in mind for the medication, such as increased focus, better mood stability, improved energy, less anxiety or agitation, or increased empathy. Clears goals allow you to track the effectiveness of the medication to see if it is doing what you hope over the long run. Here are some examples of clear medication goals:

- Increase attention span and learning.
- Decrease distractibility.
- Decrease restlessness or hyperactivity.
- Decrease impulsiveness and increase thoughtfulness.
- Decrease irritability.
- Decrease obsessive thoughts or compulsive behaviors.
- Improve mood.
- Improve motivation.
- Improve temper control.
- Overall, improve functioning at school, at work, at home, in relationships, and within yourself.

Understand the natural resistance to medication. Many people fear taking medication, commonly because they worry about losing control. Effective medication actually gives a person more control over his thoughts and behaviors. I once had a discussion with a fourteen-year-old young man with a serious temper problem. He had just been suspended from school for hitting another teenager who had made fun of him. On his scan he had clear left temporal lobe problems, which he probably inherited. He had some very violent people in his extended family. He refused to take medication because he didn't want to lose control and he didn't want the medication or his parents controlling him. As I sat with him in front of the SPECT computer monitor and showed him his brain, I said, "The medication won't cause you to lose control. It will, in fact, help you gain greater control over yourself. Enhancing your temporal-lobe activity, it helps give you the maximum amount of control. If you still want to hit someone, you'll be able to, but you will do it more on your terms rather than on an impulse or whim. Odds are you'll rethink the need to be aggressive."

Some people worry that medication masks or sugarcoats underlying psychological problems. They would rather get to the root of the problem than use medication as a Band-Aid solution. This may be a valid concern for some people, but not for others. Without a functional brain-imaging test like SPECT, it's hard to know. My experience is that when there is an underlying brain problem, medication does not mask it—it treats it. It goes directly to the brain and helps correct the underlying physiology responsible for the problem.

There are other occasions when medication blunts feelings and prevents healing. Traumatic events from the past may need a psychological treatment for trauma to uncover and eliminate the anxiety related to a past rape, incest, or child abuse. Without dealing with the underlying issues, medication will never be fully effective. I once treated a woman who came to our clinic with symptoms of depression and anxiety. She had tried medication with her family physician, but it did not help her. As I hunted for further solutions, I learned that she had a multiple personality disorder that stemmed from being repeatedly sexually abused by a neighbor of the family. He had threatened to kill her dog if she told anyone. She needed intensive psychotherapy and medication to heal.

I have another patient who came to see me for depression. She was in a terrible marriage. She was being emotionally and periodically physically abused by her severely narcissistic husband. She didn't want to leave her husband for the standard reasons, including money, shame of failure, children, and security. But even four marital counselors didn't help to make things better. I told her she could take antidepressants to help with her depression, but they would mask the problem—her failed relationship with her husband. She needed to deal with the problem. She decided to see a lawyer and start divorce proceedings, instead of taking medication. Surprisingly, filing for divorce jolted her husband into positive action. He came to me for an evaluation, got a scan in which we found very poor activity in his prefrontal cortex (the part of his brain involved in empathy, learning from mistakes, and impulse control), and took medication that helped him be much more positive, empathic, and more like the husband my patient felt she had married. Eventually they reconciled and did very well together.

Throughout this book, I have tried to give a balanced perspective on healing the soul's brain that includes both medication and nonmedication approaches. Balance is critical. Too often psychiatry is accused of too easily reaching for a pill. Others use medications too late in the healing process. As we have seen, biological, psychological, social, and spiritual factors influence brain function and healing best occurs when all aspects are explored.

Psychotropic medications are not good or bad. It is really the attitude we take toward them and their proper use. They can literally save someone's life and enhance the soul, or if used improperly, they can steal a life and rob someone of his soul. As a society we need to take a balanced approach to medication and be excited about the possibilities for healing and careful about potential side effects.

It is my belief that psychotropic medications are best prescribed by a psychiatrist who specializes in the use of medication. Because of our managed-care environment, primary-care physicians are being forced more and more to prescribe these medications. That may be good for simple problems, but it is often a mistake for more complicated ones. If I have chest pain, I'm going to see a cardiologist. I want the best care possible from the most experienced professional I can find. Once you find an experienced physician, make sure to strive for good communication. Learn as much about the medication as possible, including the benefits and side effects. If the medication does not work the way you hope, be persistent. Sometimes it takes several tries to get the best results.

Fifteen

Forgiveness, a New Look

Wise people seek solutions. The ignorant only cast blame.
—TAO TE CHING

It is better to pardon. Not forget, but forgive.
—THE DALAI LAMA

Blessed are the merciful, for they shall obtain mercy.
—MATTHEW 5:7

FORGIVENESS is a divine act. All of the world's major religions talk about God's willingness to forgive our failings. Forgiveness is also a human action. We are told that God forgives our failings so that in turn we can forgive others. Many people feel the most human, the most connected to others and God when they can forgive a failing of another and move beyond the pain. Forgiveness is not just requested in the Bible, it is strongly encouraged. In the Gospel according to Matthew, Jesus says, "For if you forgive men when they sin against you, your heavenly Father will also forgive you. But if you do not forgive men their sins, your Father will not forgive your sins." In a sense, every time we forgive someone we reflect on the image of God in us.

For me personally, one of the most powerful outcomes of brain-imaging research has been a new and deeper understanding of people. Forgiveness is easier as I look at the people whose behavior has hurt me in a new way. The brain work adds an additional piece of information that helps the pain. Some of the memories still hurt, but they are not as painful when I feel them through the lens of understanding the brain.

One of the most painful experiences in my own life occurred when Jeff, an employee of the Amen Clinic, became paranoid and nearly destroyed our offices. He got into the clinic late one night and tore up furniture, broke the windows in the reception area, smashed cabinets, and threw files around the office. The next morning I was sitting in church at my daughter's eighth-grade award ceremony. I received a 911 call on my pager. I ignored it. My daughter was about to receive a Presidential Scholar Award, and nothing was going to rob me of the moment. The 911 pages kept coming and coming. My wife gave me one of those disapproving looks that said *"You must be kidding, not now."* After Breanne received the award, I went outside and called the office. My office manager Shelley answered the phone. She was very upset, which was not at all like her. Usually she is the epitome of composure. She told me what happened, and we both knew who it was. Jeff had been acting more irritable over the past week. We had planned to talk to him later that day. My heart started to race when she said that he had left notes saying that he was going to come back and kill members of the staff. I called the police, and later that day Jeff was arrested and then committed to a local psychiatric hospital. I hated what happened. I hated how Jeff had scared my office staff. I hated the fact that an employee, who had been an integral part of our clinic, was himself suffering with a mental illness.

As part of a research project, we had scanned Jeff the year before. He had a brain pattern that was consistent with manic-depressive illness. When I told him the results of his scan, he admitted to me that he had had several prior psychotic episodes. He said that his erratic behavior caused him to get divorced, and he could no longer see his son. I told him to get help. I said that I would pay for the bills that his medical insurance didn't cover. I gave him the name of a very good local psychiatrist. He went a couple of times but then didn't follow through and stopped taking his medication.

Jeff called the office from the hospital several times, threatening the staff and leaving me demeaning and vulgar voice messages. I had to file a restraining order against him. I felt so sad because I knew that the behavior was not really Jeff. After he calmed down and the medication leveled him out, he sent Shelley and me a deeply felt letter apologizing for his behavior. He said that this erratic behavior had ruined many good opportunities in his life, and he would dedicate himself to getting it treated. Even though Jeff knew he couldn't come back to work at the clinic, we were able to remain in communication. I knew that his behavior was not a representation of his soul; it was the brain illness that drove him mad. Seeing his brain allowed me to put his behavior in a context of understanding and forgiveness. Other employers might have pressed charges against him, never talked to him again, or sued him for the damaged he caused.

I have seen how brain-imaging work has helped many people understand and learn to forgive the difficult behavior of others. It also helps them move beyond past hurts. They are able to see aberrant behavior in a completely different (and I think more accurate) light. Here are some examples from my own patients.

JOY

Joy, fifty-two, first heard me lecture at a support-group meeting in the Bay Area. I was talking about my brain-imaging work as it related to violence and suicide. After the lecture, Joy came up to me with tears streaming down her face. She told me that six of her family members had committed suicide: her paternal grandfather and grandmother, her father, her paternal uncle, and two of her brothers. She came to the meeting that night because her son had just attempted suicide and was in a nearby psychiatric hospital. She was so angry at him that she could barely bring herself to see him at the hospital. Knowing the family history and how much her father's and brothers' suicides had hurt her, she wondered how he could do that to her. They had talked about the family history of suicide on a number of occasions. He promised her that he would never kill himself. Through the lecture she discovered that families often have a genetic predisposition to depression, temporal-lobe problems, and violence (suicide is violence turned inward). These brain problems cause people to act in erratic and self-injurious ways. She said that the brain images helped her see her family's behavior in a different light, in the light of understanding. She felt the beginning of forgiveness in her heart for the people who had committed suicide, and she would work hard to get her son help without feeling angry with him. Several months later she told me that the insight she gained from the lecture gave her a completely different attitude toward people with mental illnesses and those who did terrible things.

VALERIE

Through the years I have treated many patients who have suffered from severe child abuse. The emotional chains of shame, guilt, and hatred for the abusers bind many of these people in knots, keeping them distant from others. On numerous occasions I have seen how understanding the brain helps to bring healing to the painful memories as they are filtered through the light of understanding. People are more able emotionally to move beyond the chains of the abusive behavior when they understand that the abuser was in large measure acting out of a damaged or dysfunctional brain.

Late one morning, Valerie, twenty-eight, tried to kill herself. She went into the garage, locked the doors, took four sleeping pills, and turned on the car engine. She was found by accident when a friend came over to ask her to lunch. Her friend knew that she was despondent of late and was trying to get her out of the house. The friend, hearing the engine on in the locked garage, called the police. When the police came, they broke the side garage door and pulled her from the car. Unconscious, she was rushed to the hospital. As the psychiatrist on call, I saw Valerie the next day, when she regained consciousness. Physically she was okay, mentally she was angry about being pulled back from the dead. She was mad at herself for not being more thorough with the suicide. She told me that she had been planning her death for months. She could no longer live with her memories.

Over the next few weeks in the hospital she told me about the demons that had haunted her since childhood. Her mother, a beautiful but uneducated woman, was a prostitute. She also had a drinking problem. Frequently she would leave young Valerie alone at night. On many occasions her mother's callers would sexually assault Valerie. Her mother didn't seem to notice. This went on for years. Finally, at the age of fourteen, Valerie ran away from home. Her mother had the police pick her up, and Valerie spent time in juvenile hall. She then went to a loving foster home for several years. At the age of seventeen, Valerie returned home. Her mother had stopped drinking and working as a prostitute. She had a regular job in a doctor's office and was attending AA meetings. Valerie felt happy to be back home. She and her mother started to bond for the first time since she was a little girl. But several months later, late at night, an old customer of her mother's showed up at the front door drunk, wanting sex. When the mother turned him away, the man pulled out a gun and shot her mother in her stomach. Valerie was in the shower when she heard the shots. Wet, she threw on her robe and ran to her mother. A few minutes later, her mother died in Valerie's arms. Valerie became very despondent. She was sent back to her foster home until she turned eighteen. She married shortly after her eighteenth birthday but picked a man who hurt her. She had many other relationships, but they never seemed to work for long. The only joy in Valerie's life was that she was a medical assistant who loved her work. But finally, her despair got to the point where she felt that she had no reasons left to live.

For weeks I listened to the nightmares of her past and the hopeless feelings she had about the future. After a few weeks, I asked her to balance each painful memory with a happy one. When she was directed to think about happy memories, she found that there were many. Her mother would read to her, play with her during the day, and take her to the park. When her mother wasn't drinking, she seemed to be a good listener. Her foster parents loved her very much and still kept in touch with her. I taught Valerie how to chose which memories to focus on. Her suicidal feelings subsided. She promised me that she wouldn't try to kill herself again and I discharged her from the hospital. I saw her as an outpatient twice a week in my office.

In the hospital we hadn't talked much about my brain-imaging work. When she came to my clinic, she saw SPECT images everywhere. She became very curious about them. She wanted to see the brain of an alcoholic. She wanted to see the brain of a murderer. She wanted to see the brain of someone who tried to kill herself. She wanted a scan. As you can imagine, I was not at a loss in talking about the brain's role in behavior. Her scan was very healthy, except for an area of decreased activity in her left temporal lobe, often responsible for dark or violent thoughts. The new understanding helped her work toward understanding and forgiving her mother's neglect and alcoholic behavior. She also started to let go of the hatred she had for her mother's murderer. I treated Valerie's left temporal lobe with neurofeedback, which she enjoyed. Valerie decided to go back to school to become a counselor. Understanding, forgiveness, and healing go together.

SUSIE

When Susie was seven years old, her mother and father separated. Tony, Susie's father, had been using cocaine and had lost his third job within a year. He was also controlling and abusive at home. When his wife, Tanya, told him to leave or she would call the police, he told her that he would kill her before he saw her with another man. The next year was a nightmare. Tony stalked Tanya and Susie: He followed them in the car, watched Susie at day care, and called and left threatening messages on the phone at home. He was obsessed with them. Tanya had filed a restraining order against him, which he violated on many occasions, but the police seemed indifferent. Things escalated. Without Tanya's knowledge, Tony was actually sleeping in the backyard behind a shed. He continued to use drugs, didn't go to work, and became more and more paranoid, more and more threatening. Then, in January 1995, he stabbed Tanya to death in the early morning hours. Tony then took Susie on a long drive. Later in the day, he started to sober up and realized what he had done. He called Tanya's mother, Betty, crying and telling her what he had done and where she could pick up Susie. The police arrested him three days later.

Betty was a friend of my sister who called me right away and asked me to see Susie. "She is going to need lots of help," my sister said. Betty told me about the awful crime. She said how conflicted she felt. Tony was not evil, he was sick, but how could she deal with the grief of her dead daughter. Initially there were many battles to fight: legal custody of Susie, dealing with the upcoming arraignment of Tony, expressing her outrage at the police for not heeding all of the times Tony broke restraining orders without consequences, and helping a seven-year-old deal with the loss of her mother.

Over the next five years, I saw Susie and Betty on a regular basis. I went through the murder and custody trials with them and Tony's visitation rights. It seemed that there was repeated and endless trauma for Susie and everyone else involved. Susie had nightmares and anxiety attacks. She loved her father and didn't understand why he did such a terrible thing. She was confused about her feelings. When Susie turned eleven, she started to ask me why her father killed her mother. We talked about drug abuse, obsession, fear of losing your family, and brain problems. We talked about how Susie could hate what her father did but still love him. The drugs made his brain misfire, and he acted badly. He wasn't bad; what he did was bad. The understanding of the connection between the brain and behavior helped both Susie and Betty move toward resolving the tremendous conflict they felt.

Couples and Forgiveness

I have a patient who has an illness called alexythymia, which is the inability to express emotion. His marital therapist referred him to me because his wife was constantly angry at him. Her complaint was that he could never express his feelings for her. She got angry as a way to get a reaction out of him. It never worked, and their marriage was spiraling downward. I ordered a SPECT study on him. It showed severe damage to his left prefrontal cortex, the part of the brain involved in emotionally expressive language. He had suffered several concussions playing football in high school. When his wife understood that he had a brain problem, she became more relaxed and understanding, and was able to forgive the hurts from the past. She had erroneously attributed his emotional lack of expression to a lack of caring, to willful misconduct.

Forgiveness Is Also Good for Your Soul and Your Brain

Holding on to anger and hurts from the past is detrimental to your body and soul. Over time, it sucks the life out of your spirit and does actual physical damage to your brain. Anger and resentment cause an increased production of the body's stress hormone, cortisol. In the short run, cortisol makes you feel sped up, tense, and overwhelmed. In the long run, heightened cortisol levels impair the immune system, making you more likely to become ill, and damage cells in the memory centers of the brain. New brain research has demonstrated that excess cortisol levels impair cognitive ability. Learning how to forgive and let go of the negative feelings you harbor has a healing effect on your overall well-being.

Forgiveness, a New Look

So where do we go from here? Can we translate this new understanding of the brain and the soul into tangible action. We have many choices. We can maintain the status quo, holding on to seventeenth-century French philosopher René Descartes's separation of the brain and the soul. Or we can take a new look by applying our new knowledge of the brain's involvement with everything from forethought to relationships while still holding people accountable for their actions. We need to evaluate and optimize the brains of people who suffer. We need to look for new answers when the old ones don't work. Here are some of my thoughts on where we should be going.

1. EVALUATE PEOPLE WHO DO BAD THINGS

We would save money and lives if every violent criminal had a neuropsychiatric evaluation and brain scan. Ninety-five percent of the criminals I have scanned had brains that didn't work right. Yet there is hope, because many of these brains can be optimized. Our system should mandate evaluations and encourage treatment.

A wonderful new model for evaluating criminal behavior comes from the superior court of Judge David Admire in Redmond, Washington. Judge Admire adopted two children who have been diagnosed with ADD and learning disabilities. They struggled in school and had problems with impulse control, attention span, and organization. He noticed that many of the criminals in his courtroom struggled with the same problems. He wondered if there was a connection. He teamed up with the Learning Disability Association of Washington and developed a screening tool for people going through the judicial system in his county. Everyone who is convicted of a crime goes through a screening process for ADD and learning disabilities. If a person's screen is positive for these problems, the court orders him to attend a fourteen-week life skills course to learn about his problems and develop better skills in managing his life. In the eight years that the program has been operating, the recidivism rate in the county has dropped from 69 percent to 29 percent. The savings already have amounted to millions of dollars.

Another exciting new model comes from Buena Vista Prison in Colorado. Pediatrician Dwayne McCallon has started a program for inmates with ADD, learning problems, and other psychiatric disorders. He screens the inmates for these problems and treats them with both medication and psychotherapy. He has noticed a significant decrease in violent episodes in the prison, and the inmates' time is shorter because of improved behavior in prison.

2. RETHINK PAST HURTS

The past hurts you have experienced may have occurred for different reasons other than you initially assumed. So often in my clinic I have patients tell me that they have to rethink the pain of their past in the light of new information. Forgiveness is much easier. They may have been angry at a parent, an ex-spouse, a child, a boss, or a friend. I have a patient, Kate, who was physically abused by an alcoholic father. She carried much resentment in her soul. Shortly after I started seeing her, she asked her father to come to the clinic for an evaluation. To her surprise, he agreed. He told her that he knew that he had hurt her in the past and that he was very sorry. He didn't understand why he acted that way. During his intake he told me about a time when he was twenty years old and was knocked unconscious for three hours, as a result of a car accident. I ordered a brain scan as part of his evaluation. It showed an area of marked decreased activity in his left temporal lobe, a finding often associated with head injuries and temper problems. With the father's permission, I showed the images to Kate. At the end of the session, she said that she felt a burden was lifted from her soul. "I had always thought that I was a bad girl and that was why daddy drank and why he beat me. Now I can see that it was his brain that didn't work right," she said.

3. FORGIVE YOURSELF

As it is important to forgive others, especially with this new brain information, it is even more important to be able to forgive yourself. Too often self-loathing occupies a person's brain and robs the soul of any joy that he or she may experience. Understanding the brain can be a first step in healing the pain of the past.

Through the years I have sat in front of our brain-imaging computer with thousands of patients, going over their brain scans. The biggest fear that many patients have had was that their scans would be normal and that their suffering or difficult behavior was the result of a weak will or a weak character. More often than not, I show them brain patterns that have been interfering with their lives. After people receive the information, many are grateful and hopeful of improvement. Others feel cheated. They think, "If only I knew about these problems twenty years ago, my life would be so much better." I encourage these people to take a balanced approach to the scan findings. I tell them to be hopeful for improvement, maintain good communication with their doctor, and forgive their past failings—there is more to them than they originally thought.

4. KEEP AN OPEN MIND

The brain-imaging work has taught me that things are not always as they seem. Someone who appears evil may, in fact, be suffering from a severe brain problem. Someone who is constantly negative to you may, in fact, be depressed. Someone who doesn't show up to work on time may have a severe organizational problem because his prefrontal cortex is underactive. Someone who flips you off on the freeway probably has an overactive cingulate gyrus and is better left to go his own way. Unfortunately, I have come across many physicians whose minds are completely closed to these connections between brain illness and aggression. A psychologist in Washington heard about my work and referred many patients to my clinic. When I was asked to speak in her community, I readily agreed. At my talk one of the child psychiatrists in town got up and criticized my work. He said it was too speculative and too new, and besides, he didn't need to look at the brain. He could tell what was wrong with people just by talking to them. I had been through this so many times before. I took a deep breath and slowly told the audience about the published research my clinic and others have done. I also said that it was time to look at the brain. We have the technology in place, and if my child was having problems, I would want to look at his brain before I gave him a diagnosis that might follow him for the rest of his life. I then asked the child psychiatrist how he would feel if he took his car into the shop for problems and the mechanic decided to change the fuel pump without ever popping the hood or turning on the car's engine, if he just decided on the solution to the problem by the symptoms that the doctor told him about the car. The child psychiatrist didn't respond. He said he was not going to engage me in verbal games. I responded that it's time we look at the brain with an open mind. It was obvious his mind was closed.

5. BE CAREFUL WHEN JUDGING OTHERS

The Lord sees not as a man sees, for man looks on the outward appearance, but the Lord looks on the heart (and in the brain).

— 1 SAMUEL 16:7 (PARENTHESES MINE)

Since I have been able to look inside the living human brain, my opinion on judging others has dramatically changed. I used to believe in the death penalty—I had sort of an-eye-for-an-eye mentality. The year after I started the brain-imaging work, I wondered how we could put anyone to death when they behaved out of a brain that didn't work right. It seemed inhumane and lacked the current understanding we have of the brain. I have a better understanding why Matthew quotes Jesus as saying, "Judge not, that you may not be judged. For with the judgment you make you shall be judged." A person's behavior is complex. God has it figured out, and judgment is best left to His realm. Of course, this doesn't mean we should let criminals roam the street. We have a responsibility to protect society. We should just approach judgment cautiously.

Award-winning British science journalist Rita Carter, in her book *Mapping the Mind,* eloquently addresses the issue of judgment and new brain science. She writes: "It seems unlikely to me that we will continue to punish people for misconduct when the crossed wires that spark their behavior become as clear to see as a broken bone. Rather, I hope (and expect) we will use our knowledge of the brain to develop treatments for sick brains that will be infinitely more effective than the long-winded, hit-and-miss psychological therapies we use today. Restraint could then be used only when such treatment fails, or for those who would rather lose liberty than their old habits."

6. BE HUMBLE

Above all, be humble. What we know about the brain and the soul is still in its infancy. What we know a hundred years from now will be dramatically different from our current knowledge. Humility is necessary in any endeavor to understand the truth. We need to be more inquisitive, more compassionate, more tolerant, and more vigilant at seeking new solutions to old questions.

EVEN though the brain is the hardware of the soul, it is not everything. We cannot fully excuse difficult behavior based on brain problems. Some people have criticized my work because I have testified about brain dysfunction for murderers, armed robbers, drug addicts, and rapists. In a number of cases my testimony has been instrumental in keeping people from the gas chamber. The critics say that I am advocating high-technology excuses for bad behavior. I am quick to remind them that no one goes home because they have a bad brain. They might not be executed, but they are not excused. In judgment we must consider

257

the brain. At this point in time, I believe science can say that the brain is very important to moment-by-moment behavior, and it must be considered in judging people. However, there are many other factors that must be considered. For example, why do many people with brain problems never do anything criminal or heinous? I often wonder what the difference is; maybe it's their upbringing, their devotion to God, or their belief in good. We must understand the other factors involved in difficult behavior.

References and Suggested Further Reading

Amen, Daniel. *Change Your Brain, Change Your Life*. New York: Random House, 1999.

Amen, Daniel. *Healing ADD. The Breakthrough Program That Allows You to See and Heal the Six Types of Attention Deficit Disorder*. New York: Putnam, 2001.

Ashbrook, James. *The Humanizing Brain: Where Religion and Neuroscience Meet*. Cleveland: Pilgrims Press, 1997.

Benson, Herbert. *Beyond the Relaxation Response: How to Harness the Healing Power of Your Personal Beliefs*. New York: Berkley, 1994.

Benson, Herbert. *Timeless Healing: The Power and Biology of Belief*. New York: Scribner, 1996.

Carter, Rita. *Mapping the Mind*. Berkeley: University of California Press, 2000.

Cornett, Carlton. *The Soul of Psychotherapy: Recapturing the Spiritual Dimension in the Therapeutic Encounter*. New York: Simon and Schuster, 1998.

Damasio, Antonio. *Descartes' Error: Emotion, Reason, and the Human Brain*. New York: Avon, 1995.

Damasio, Antonio. *The Feeling of What Happens: Body and Emotion in the Making of Consciousness*. New York: Harvest Books, 2000.

Dossey, Larry. *Healing Words: The Power of Prayer and the Practice of Medicine*. New York: Harper Mass Market, 1997.

Dossey, Larry. *Prayer Is Good Medicine: How to Reap the Healing Benefits of Prayer*. New York: HarperCollins, 1997.

Dossey, Larry. *Recovering the Soul: A Scientific and Spiritual Approach*. New York: Bantam Doubleday Dell, 1989.

Dossey, Larry. *Reinventing Medicine: Beyond Mind-Body to a New Era of Healing*. New York: HarperCollins, 1999.

Hallowell, Edward. *Connect: 12 Vital Ties That Open Your Heart, Lengthen Your Life, and Deepen Your Soul*. New York: Pocket Books, 2001.

Koenig, Harold. *The Healing Power of Faith: Science Explores Medicine's Last Great Frontier*. New York: Simon and Schuster, 1999.

Kolb, Bryan. *Fundamentals of Human Neuropsychology*. New York: W. H. Freeman, 1995.

LeDoux, Joseph. *The Emotional Brain: The Mysterious Underpinnings of Emotional Life*. New York: Touchstone, 1998.

Matthews, Dale. *The Faith Factor: Proof of the Healing Power of Prayer*. New York: Penguin, 1999.

Mesulam, M.-Marsel, ed. *Principles of Behavioral and Cognitive Neurology*. New York: Oxford University Press, 2000.

Miller, Bruce, and Jeffrey Cummings, eds. *The Human Frontal Lobes*. New York: Guilford Press, 1998.

Nelson, John. *Healing the Split: Integrating Spirit into Our Understanding of the Mentally Ill*. Albany: State University of New York Press, 1994.

Newberg, Andrew, and Eugene Aquili. *The Mystical Mind: Probing the Biology of Religious Experience*. Minneapolis: Fortress Press, 1999.

Newberg, Andrew, and Eugene Aquili. *Why God Won't Go Away: Brain Science and the Biology of Belief*. New York: Ballantine Books, 2001.

Ornstein, Robert. *The Right Mind: Making Sense of the Hemispheres*. New York: Harvest Books, 1998.

Pinker, Steven. *How the Mind Works.* New York: Norton, 1999.

Radin, Dean. *The Conscious Universe: The Scientific Truth of Psychic Phenomena.* New York: HarperCollins, 1997.

Ratey, John. *Neuropsychiatry of Personality Disorders.* Oxford, U.K.: Blackwell, 1994.

Ratey, John. *Shadow Syndromes.* New York: Bantam Doubleday Dell, 1998.

Ratey, John. *User's Guide to the Brain: Perception, Attention, and the Four Theaters of the Brain.* New York: Pantheon, 2001.

Robbins, Jim. *A Symphony in the Brain: The Evolution of the New Brain Wave Biofeedback.* Boston: Atlantic Monthly Press, 2000.

Roberts, A. C., ed. *The Prefrontal Cortex: Executive and Cognitive Functions.* New York: Oxford University Press, 1998.

Schiffer, Fredric. *Of Two Minds: The Revolutionary Science of Dual-Brain Psychology.* New York: Free Press, 1998.

Scott, John, Sr. *Hypnoanalysis for Individual and Marital Psychotherapy.* New York: Gardner Press, 1993.

Shapiro, Francine. *EMDR: The Breakthrough Therapy for Overcoming Anxiety, Stress, and Trauma.* New York: Basic Books, 1998.

Shorto, Russell. *Saints and Madmen: How Pioneering Psychiatrists Are Creating a New Science of the Soul.* New York: Henry Holt, 2000.

Worthing, Mark. *God, Creation, and Contemporary Physics (Theology and the Sciences).* Minneapolis: Fortress Press, 1995.

Clinic and Web Site Information

The Amen Clinics

The Amen Clinics were established in 1989 by Daniel G. Amen, M.D. They specialize in innovative diagnosis and treatment planning for a wide variety of behavioral, learning, and emotional problems of children, teenagers, and adults. The clinics have an international reputation for evaluating brain-behavior problems, such as attention deficit disorder, depression, anxiety, school failure, brain trauma, obsessive-compulsive disorders, aggressiveness, cognitive decline, and brain toxicity from drugs or alcohol. Brain SPECT imaging is performed at the clinics. The Amen Clinics have the world's largest database of brain scans for behavioral problems. Over the last twelve years, they have performed over twelve thousand brain SPECT studies.

The clinics welcome referrals from physicians, psychologists, social workers, marriage and family therapists, drug and alcohol counselors, and individual clients.

The Amen Clinic Newport Beach
4019 Westerly Place, Suite 100
Newport Beach, CA 92660
(949) 266-3700

The Amen Clinic Fairfield
350 Chadbourne Road
Farifield, CA 94585
(707) 429-7181

Web site: www.amenclinic.com

Brainplace.com

Brainplace.com is an educational interactive brain web site geared toward mental health and medical professionals, educators, students, and the general public. It contains a wealth of information to help you learn about the brain. The site contains over three hundred color brain SPECT images, hundreds of scientific abstracts on brain SPECT imaging for psychiatry, a brain puzzle, and much, much more.

View over three hundred astonishing color 3-D brain SPECT images on the following topics:

Aggression
Attention Deficit Disorder, including the six subtypes
Dementia and Cognitive Decline
Drug Abuse
PMS
Anxiety Disorders
Brain Trauma
Depression
Obsessive-Compulsive Disorder
Stroke
Seizures

Index

neurons, 19
Neurotonin, 81, 147, 238
neurotransmitters, 19, 47, 145, 146
  see also dopamine; serotonin
Newberg, Andrew, 29, 199
norepinephrine, 144, 145
Norpramine, 144
nortriptyline, 144
nuclear medicine, 10, 21–23
nutritional interventions, 137–41,
  143–45

obsessive-compulsive disorder
  (OCD), 6, 10, 16, 23, 109, 138,
  223, 231
  anterior cingulate gyrus in, 50, 54
  basal ganglia in, 50, 54
  behavior modification for, 171
  prefrontal cortex in, 37
  spirituality and, 27–28
occipital cortex, 15, 24
occipital lobes, 19, 20
  injuries to, 79
One-Page Miracle for the Soul
  (OPMS), 150, 153–56
oppositional behavior, 54, 120, 138,
  233
Ornish, Dean, 93, 209

Pamelor, 144
panic disorder, 3–5, 38, 54, 119,
  146, 214, 231
  medications for, 142
  negative predictions and, 162, 163
  painful emotional bridges and,
  187–88
paranoia, 72, 92, 123, 246, 251
parasympathetic nervous system, 67
parietal lobes, 19, 20, 122, 125
  injuries to, 79
paroxetine, 139
past hurts, healing, 173–96, 249–50,
  254
Past Remembering (Robinson), 75
Paul, Saint, 29, 62, 64, 156, 170
Paxil, 139, 147, 230
pedophilia, 11
Pentecostal churches, 112
permissiveness, 96–97
perseverance, lack of, 40
Persinger, Michael, 64
personality disorders, 97–103

personalization, 166, 168
phobias, 191
physical connection, 221–22
Pinocchio (movie), 31
political leaders, 124–26
Pollyanna (movie), 161–62
pornography, addiction to, 105, 106
positron-emission tomography
  (PET), 21, 171
post-traumatic stress disorder
  (PTSD), 191
Poussaint, Alvin, 57
prayer, 197–208
prefrontal cortex (PCF), 15, 31–44,
  140, 223, 235, 243
  character development and,
  88–94, 97
  deep limbic system and, 67–68
  focus on eternal values to
  enhance, 148–56
  healthy traits of, 37–41
  injuries to, 76, 79, 81, 89–90,
  107, 252
  leadership and, 115–18, 125
  during meditation, 199
  morality and, 86–88
  personality disorders and, 99,
  101, 102
  religion and, 108, 111–12
  strategies to optimize, 135–38
  unhealthy traits of, 41–43
premenstrual syndrome (PMS), 16,
  138, 143, 178, 179, 185,
  231–33
progressive relaxation, 203
Protestants, 9
Prozac, 139, 144, 147, 171, 178,
  230, 233–34, 236–37
psychoanalysis, 13
psychotherapy, 13, 195–96, 227, 233
  interpersonal, 212–13
  medication and, 242–43
  for personality disorders, 98
psychotic symptoms, 143
psychotropic medications, see medications

quantitative EEG studies (QEEG),
  20–21

racism, 7, 56–57, 120
Raine, Adrian, 86, 99